A FELLOWSHIP OF DISCONTENT

A Fellowship of Discontent

Hans J. Hillerbrand

HARPER & ROW, PUBLISHERS

NEW YORK
EVANSTON
AND LONDON

FIRST EDITION

LIBRARY OF CONGRESS CATALOG CARD NUMBER: 67–11509

B-R

To my colleagues
on the faculty of the
Divinity School of Duke University

—not to suggest that the title of this volume describes them, but in gratitude for several years of association and in the conviction that it is the academic theologian who is entrusted with the responsibility of interpreting the Christian faith in freedom and also, when necessary, in discontent

Contents

Preface

The simple intent of the five essays collected in this volume is to throw some light on several figures "on the fringe" of Christendom whose stories, like those of all dissenters, are often neglected in favor of more dramatic—and perhaps more important—happenings. I have sought to stress the biographical facet, not because the thought of these men was insignificant (as their stories unfold the opposite will become obvious), but because there seemed to be some virtue in simply telling how certain men in the history of the Christian church lived and died.

The exigencies of publishing have made it necessary to reduce the notes to a bare minimum and at several places to lump a number of citations together. I trust that this made neither for an obscure nor for an unscholarly documentation.

Professor G. F. Nuttall has graciously read parts of the manuscript and offered helpful suggestions. It is a privilege to acknowledge my appreciation. It is an equal privilege to acknowledge my debt to Mrs. Alfreda Kaplan of Durham, N. C., who typed the drafts of this manuscript and offered invaluable stylistic suggestions. In part, at least, the book is also hers.

HANS J. HILLERBRAND

September 1966

By Way of Introduction:

Of Reformers, Schismatics, Heretics, Apostates, Sectarians, and Radicals

Devoting this volume to the stories of Thomas Müntzer, Sebastian Franck, George Fox, Thomas Chubb, and David Friedrich Strauss may prompt some to detect a charming sense of historical disproportion—and scholarly naïveté—on the part of the author. Several are admittedly obscure characters, and all of them were, at best, supporting actors in the great drama of church history. The author accordingly labors under a twofold handicap—he must argue the appropriateness both of his subject matter and of his particular subjects, and, moreover, find some generalizing words that will help to reduce a chaotic phenomenon to manageable proportions. The essays hope to do the former; these introductory comments as well as the epilogue, in turn, hope to offer some tentative suggestions concerning the latter.

We can begin quite simply. The eventful and dramatic history of the Christian church—for Goethe a hodgepodge of *Irrtum und Gewalt*—tells the story not only of an impressive (or at least what once was considered impressive) procession of august institutions, principles, and men, but also of those who, at various times and for a variety of reasons, have deviated from this larger Christian community. As the lengthy title of this introduction conveys, a special nomenclature has been coined to describe this phenomenon. Christian history is not a homogenized phenomenon, but is characterized by intriguing diversity, and one need only glance at the list of 88 heresies in Augustine's *De haeresibus* to realize this. There is what might be called a fellowship of discontent, which extends, with exceedingly fluid lines, from the first century to our own. Simeon

Stylites, Pelagius, Francis of Assisi, Jan Hus, Martin Luther, Søren Kierkegaard are but a few names, picked at random. There are many more. An element of confusion—or complexity—therefore characterizes the history of the Christian church, which, empirically speaking, was never one, but always many. No theological definition can fully overcome the embarrassment resulting from the fact that the deviators, though at times only a party of one, have always insisted that they, too, were Christians, possessing the authentic interpretation of the biblical faith. Claim thus stands against claim, argument against argument. In the end, alas, no one can easily assert that his interpretation of the faith is the authentic one. A painful necessity compels the observer to reflect that few beliefs have been held "always and everywhere and by all."

The details of such parting of the ways between the institution and the individual, even as the measure of eventual *rapprochement* between the two, have varied widely. Some of the "outsiders"—certain monastic figures—succeeded in reaching an *entente cordiale* with the larger body after all, satisfied that the disagreement was only over incidentals; others deviated on substantial issues and broke radically with the larger church. Some created thereby a new tradition—at times by intent, at others by chance—from which in due time and season the exodus of another discontent soul would take place, thus repeating, with stereotypical regularity, the original development. Others walked their way alone; some died peacefully in bed, some rather violently—though, to be sure, never unwillingly—at the stake.

In the narratives of the history of the Christian church, these "outsiders" are often little more than footnotes. Clio, even when clad in ecclesiastical garb, prefers to smile on those who have been successful—and it seems to be the professional hazard of most "outsiders" to end in failure, at least as far as the larger Christian community is concerned. At times, however, a bold stroke of a writer has transferred these footnotes into the text. None other than Sebastian Franck did this. In his *Chronicle* he left little doubt that in his eyes the despised heretics were really the heroes of the faith. Most martyrologies—such as Foxe's *Acts and Monuments* or Arnold's *Unpartheyische Kirchen- und Ketzerchronik*—conveyed the same sentiment. Arnold introduced the term "impartial" to denote how history should be written, but we must not scrutinize his use of the term too closely, since impartiality for him meant mainly the revision of the standard perspective. But this is obviously a value judgment, based on theological penchant. So is, of course, the customary attitude which ignores or even denounces the "outsider." Since most people are part of the institution, a simple arithmetical reflection will tell us why the "outsider's" view of the "outsider" lacks in popularity.

Be that as it may, to allow these "outsiders" to fall into oblivion would surely impoverish Christian history. The stories of five of them —Protestant figures—are presented here, two from the sixteenth, one from the seventeenth, one from the eighteenth, and one from the nineteenth century. Each of the five illustrates a particular aspect of what might be called "radical religiosity," and thus their selection is not altogether arbitrary. Still, others could have been selected and they would have illuminated different aspects of the radical mentality. All the same, these other radicals would have told the same tale of spiritual discontent and of parting of the ways.

These five men probably show, at first glance, an intriguing incompatibility, and seem to have in common only that they were different —different from the larger Christian community, but also, as a matter of fact, from one another: the latter point is as important as the former. Thomas Müntzer and Sebastian Franck, the two sixteenth-century figures, had they ever met would have refused to have anything to do with one another. And here they are, side by side! Müntzer was a zealot, an aggressive fellow reminiscent of an Old Testament prophet consumed by zeal for the Lord. Franck, quite the contrary, was a prudent and circumspect soul who strove to make haste slowly and became a *cause célèbre* by default rather than by intent. George Fox, the seventeenth-century Englishman, combined characteristics of both his predecessors, yet the result was something new—exuberant yet gentle, flamboyant yet simple; Fox seems to have accomplished the rather remarkable feat of combining irreconcilable opposites. Thomas Chubb, of *docta ignorantia,* was neither wise, nor learned, nor spiritual—and yet he, too, is part of the narrative. David Friedrich Strauss, finally, appears as a somewhat painful prototype of the nineteenth-century German bourgeois. Some, willing to accept Müntzer, Franck, Fox, and Chubb, might question the wisdom of Strauss's inclusion—and with good reason. In contrast to the other four men, his genuine religious concern was meager. He was a scholar first, and a "radical" second; as a matter of fact, he was the latter only because he was the former. But he also claimed—at least for a good part of his life—to be a Christian and to possess the proper understanding of the Christian faith. If we honor his claim —as indeed we should—his place as a *bona fide* "radical" seems firm enough. Moreover, Strauss serves as good illustration for the ever present possibility that the "outsider" might throw out the baby with the bath—turn his back completely on the Christian faith. It is risky business to part company with the larger community, and Strauss shows this succinctly.

The main thesis of these essays is that these five men shared a common temper, even though they differed radically—if this term be admissible—in specifics from one another. Our intent is to expound such unity in diversity—and to argue, moreover, that both unity and diversity are good to know.

The term "radical" is a catch-all for a number of "questionable" phenomena that hover at the fringe of established Christendom. Its very breadth makes it difficult, and perhaps impossible, to obtain a definition. The term "radical" as used here, even as the term "reformer," will never convey more than a mood or a temper; the other terms will be more precise and to the point. Thus the heretic deviates from acknowledged dogma; the sectarian is concerned about the sociological expression of his faith; the schismatic separates himself from the church. The essays will not designate in each instance the peculiar character of the radical's religiosity—if they were heretics, or sectarians, or what have you. Actually, it is not easy to discern where Thomas Müntzer or David Friedrich Strauss erred in doctrine—though, of course, they did; certainly it is not what leaps to the mind when one considers their life and work. Likewise, Sebastian Franck's desire for a new religious community is enigmatic. We shall look for something more basic than specific deviation in doctrine or socialization in Müntzer, Franck, Fox, Chubb, and Strauss. We would see these five men as radicals, who differed with their larger Christian community, and who were proud of it. History is about chaps, the British say. Perhaps we can say that these essays are about religious chaps, excessively religious ones, who lived their religiosity divorced from the larger Christian community. They were no ordinary fellows, that is certain. But since they are part of the Christian heritage, our attention will mean justice to them and—perhaps—new insights for us.

Audiatur et altera pars—Let the other side, too, be heard.

A FELLOWSHIP OF DISCONTENT

1. The Impatient Revolutionary: *Thomas Müntzer*

> Tell me, you miserable bag of worms, who made you a ruler of the people whom God has purchased with his precious blood?
> —THOMAS MÜNTZER, Letter to the Count of Mansfeld

An Ambiguous Reputation

After Dr. Martin Luther had preached for several years and had taught the Gospel purely and clearly, the devil also sowed his seed and brought forth false and pernicious preachers through whom the Gospel was once more perverted and suppressed and much blood was shed. . . .

Satan took possession of one whose name was Thomas Müntzer. He was well taught in the Holy Scriptures, but did not remain on their path. Satan fooled him and led him away from the Scriptures so that he no longer preached the Gospel how men shall be saved. From a false understanding of the Holy Scriptures he deceitfully derived the false and seditious doctrine that all authorities should be killed and all goods henceforth should be in common. There should be no ruler and no king.

This Müntzer preached vehemently to the people, denouncing and scolding the rulers. They suppressed, burdened, exploited and treated meanly the poor in order to keep their own unprofitable pomp and luxury. They lived sumptuously to the detriment of the poor, whereas Christian love demanded that no one should be above his brother—since everyone was free. There should be community of goods.[1]

Thus began, with interesting allusion to biblical style, the melodramatic account of the life of Thomas Müntzer written by a hostile observer in 1525, the year of Müntzer's death. Though many other accounts followed in subsequent decades and centuries, they were but variations of the same theme. Thomas Müntzer is one of those poor figures in the history of the Christian church whose fate has been to have a singularly "bad press." This is due, in part, to the fact that he founded no church and gathered no followers. Those who wrote about him really wrote against him. In this none other than Martin Luther set the precedent. He called Müntzer the "arch-devil of Allstedt" and "satanic murder prophet"—a repayment in kind for some equally uncomplimentary epithets which Müntzer earlier had hurled against him. In May, 1525, the Wittenberg reformer published his *Terrible Story and Judgment of God over Thomas Müntzer,* in which he cited Deuteronomy 18:22 in support of the contention that "this murderous prophet used God's name to speak as the devil." Such a historically simplified, though theologically satisfying, view of Müntzer was normative for almost four centuries.

Of late there has been a more positive appreciation. Indeed, the distinct change in the assessment of Müntzer since the early part of this century constitutes one of the fascinating developments of contemporary Reformation scholarship. Theologians discovered that Müntzer had some creative theological insights after all and decided that he was, next to Luther, "the most independent and most creative and therefore also the most influential thinker in the age of the Reformation," as the German scholar Heinrich Böhmer observed a generation ago.[2] The most exuberant praise has come, however, not from the ranks of ecclesiastic historians—but from Marxist apologetes who took Müntzer's statement, that among Christians all things should be held in common, to mean that he was a social revolutionary, indeed, a Communist. A characteristic formulation of such Marxist perspective was provided almost a century ago by Friedrich Engels in his famous study on *The Peasant War in Germany*. Engels claimed that "just as Müntzer's religious philosophy approached atheism, so his political program approached Communism; even on the eve of the February Revolution, more than one present-day Communist-sect lacked as comprehensive a theoretical arsenal as was Müntzer's in the sixteenth century." In Marxist-oriented scholarship Müntzer, at long last, has come into his own as the real hero of the Reformation—indeed of German history. Thus the East German writer Karl Kleinschmidt not only asserts that Müntzer was "unquestionably one of the most learned men of his time" (a contention also made by Heinrich Böhmer), but also eulogizes that "behind the iron wall of its defending sons the united effort of workers, peasants, and citizens creates countless factories, mines, foundries, machine-lending-stations and production-co-operatives, schools, and universities, in which the dreams and visions of Thomas Müntzer are made contemporary and present. They carry the name of the one who once was the iron wall of the oppressed; they carry the name of the soldier and prophet of the coming great unity and independence of Germany: Thomas Müntzer."[3]

Viewing this maze of diverging assessments which have made Müntzer everything from a fantastic fanatic or theocentric theologian to a rebellious revolutionary, one is inclined to despair of the possibility of disentangling the web of fact and fiction and thereby arriving at an accurate sketch of this man's life and work. The temptation to write history in the subjunctive is, in the case of Thomas Müntzer, especially pronounced. The following pages seek to sketch a picture that remains faithful to the available sources. There are many gaps in the documentation of Müntzer's life, and this makes it necessary to fill in such details as seem most likely to harmonize with the available sources. Perhaps scholars have been too exuberant in supplying the detail and have taken Müntzer's enigmatic involvement in the Peasants' Rebellion in 1525 as the clue for his entire life.

Stormy Beginnings

Though other dates have been suggested, Thomas Müntzer was born in 1488, probably on December 20 or 21, as it was customary to baptize the newborn in the name of the patron saint of the day of birth. The birthplace was Stolberg in the Harz Mountains in central Germany, not far, by the way, from Eisleben, where Martin Luther was born. Little is known about Müntzer's background, but it seems probable that he came from a relatively well-to-do home. He attended school at Stolberg and at Quedlinburg, and in the fall of 1506 matriculated at the University of Leipzig. Later he studied at Frankfurt and possibly at Mainz. Whether he undertook a regular course of study we do not know, though there is some evidence that he received a Master of Arts degree as well as a Bachelor in Bible. Nonetheless, there seems to have been a certain restlessness in his wanderings from place to place, a trait that was characteristic of him until his death. Not that he was no serious student. Like many another brilliant youth, he was bored with the pedestrian monotony of prescribed academic studies. He read whatever he could lay his hands on: Plato, Augustine, Jerome, the proceedings of the councils of Basel and Constance—and the Bible, which he read in the original Hebrew and Greek. His financial resources seemingly allowed him to buy what he wanted. He was a "bibliomaniac"—unable to see a book without buying it. Once he ordered seventy-five books at one time, and on another occasion he purchased several copies of the same work and then proved tardy in regard to the payment.

Somewhere along the line Müntzer decided on an ecclesiastical career, for he was ordained to the priesthood. His activities of the next several years are unknown, but by 1516 he was provost of a convent of nuns at Frohse near Halle and in the following year probably a teacher at Braunschweig. A letter dating from his sojourn at Braunschweig asked for his opinion on the legitimacy of indulgences, an interesting bit of evidence for the recognition of his theological learning. About this time he received a small benefice from the city council of Halberstadt. His only obligation was to read Mass once or twice a year, and yet his economic situation was improved considerably. In 1518 he stayed briefly at Wittenberg, from where he moved on to Leipzig to become proofreader at a printer's shop. Thus he was present at the famous Leipzig disputation between Luther and Eck in 1519.[4] In his *Highly-Provoked Defense* of 1524, Müntzer charged Luther: "You were doing all right at Leipzig, held a bouquet of carnations in your hand while departing through the city gate and you drank good wine with Melchior Lother"—a statement which suggests a firsthand acquaintance with the event.[5]

For a year or so Müntzer was confessor to Bernardine nuns in the cloister of Beutnitz near Weissenfels. Then, in 1520, he moved to Zwickau, invited by the City Council and armed with a recommendation from Luther. Zwickau, situated near the border between Saxony and the kingdom of Bohemia, "the pearl in his land" as the Saxon Elector Frederick the Wise called it, had undergone important social changes in the closing decades of the fifteenth century. Originally noted for its beer brewing and weaving, Zwickau had seen the rise to prominence of the small silver-mining entrepreneurs. The town had become prosperous, though prosperity was limited to a few families. The old artisan families, on the other hand, once well-to-do and influential in the affairs of the city, found themselves increasingly reduced to poverty and insignificance. Silver mining debased the currency and raised prices, while wages remained the same. During the indulgences controversy this social unrest was supplemented by religious tensions not unlike those found elsewhere at that time. There was the customary anticlericalism, and Luther's proclamation found surprisingly quick response in the city. On the Zwickau City Council sat influential supporters of the Wittenberg professor, such as Hermann Mühlpfort, to whom Luther dedicated his treatise on *The Freedom of a Christian Man* of 1520. Johann Wildenhauer, called Egranus, was the leading minister of the town and he, too, was favorably disposed to the new teaching. Müntzer came to Zwickau as Egranus' temporary successor.

At the very outset of Müntzer's activity there was trouble. The first time Müntzer ascended the pulpit, on May 15, 1520, he poured out his indignation upon the rich mendicant monks. Instead of being concerned about the faith of the dying, they were concerned, he charged, about their riches. With their prayers they devoured the houses of the widows. They were the perverters of the church. A second sermon contained the same biting attacks.[6] The Franciscans retorted with attacks of their own, and appealed to the Bishop of Naumburg. The City Council in turn wrote to Duke John of Saxony, asking him to keep the mendicant monks from obstructing the preachers of the Word of God. Müntzer sought help from Luther, whom he called "the example and light of the friends of God." As far as Müntzer was concerned, the issue was serious: "I do not pursue my own work, but God's," Müntzer wrote in a letter, which was replete with Lutheran ideas—an indication that he was under the sway of Luther's proclamation and was concerned to propound the new evangel. Prophetically, Müntzer closed by saying that "even more difficult struggles are awaiting me. I am confident that God will rule in them all through your counsels and those of all Christians." Müntzer, only meaning to be a follower of Luther, was hardly a rabble rouser. A sermon of September 8, 1520, the day traditionally observed as the birthday of the Virgin, conveyed a warm spirituality. Müntzer asserted here that "the Virgin Mary is mediator between God and man," yet pointed out that only the birth and work of Christ bestow any significance to Mary.[7]

When Egranus returned to his pulpit in October, 1520, Müntzer had to yield the eminent post in the city to his colleague. Egranus was an Erasmian at heart, Müntzer a dedicated disciple of Luther. Thus conflict between the two men was unavoidable. Needless to say, both men had their supporters—those of Egranus called Müntzer a rebel and revolutionary, and those of Müntzer accused Egranus of striving for the favors of beautiful women "whom you entice that they comfort you with wine. You want to sit with the big shots."[8] A priest who had called Müntzer a rogue was bombarded with stones and manure, and wound up in a ditch. Müntzer announced boldly that the same fate awaited those of like mind.

About this time Müntzer made the acquaintance of Nikolaus Storch, a simple weaver, but well versed in Scripture. Storch radicalized Luther's stress on personal religion by insisting that God speaks to man as he did in the days of the Bible, namely, by way of direct and immediate revelation. God's spirit is all-important and even the Bible must be understood "spiritually." We know far too little about Storch, and Müntzer's contacts with him at this time, to make more than cautious observations. But Storch's notions, perhaps the inevitable consequence of Luther's teaching, were subsequently re-echoed by Müntzer. It is not easy to trace the measure of influence exerted upon Müntzer at this time. In the long run, however, this was surely the most momentous encounter Thomas Müntzer ever had.

The continuing tensions prompted the Zwickau City Council in February, 1521, to ask Egranus and Müntzer to resolve their differences. Egranus, no doubt, would have been willing to do this—but not Müntzer. Thereupon the irenic Egranus decided to move elsewhere rather than continue the conflict. Before leaving, he sent Müntzer a sarcastic letter which stated that he would patiently suffer being called a devil by Müntzer, and denounced Müntzer's use of German: "I feel that your spirit despises all art and learning." Egranus' departure must have told the Zwickau city fathers which way the wind was blowing, and a meeting of the Council on April 16 was to decide on Müntzer's future—but the day before, Thomas Müntzer left Zwickau and journeyed southward to Bohemia. The direction of his travel was no accident. Luther's support of Jan Hus at the Leipzig Disputation had caused Müntzer to interest himself in the records of the Council of Constance. He had undoubtedly become sympathetic with the Hussite tradition. One suspects that the proximity of Zwickau to Bohemia had brought Müntzer already into contact with Hussites. Sensing the kinship between the Hussite tradition and Luther's proclamation, he ventured southward to rally the Bohemians around the new evangelical proclamation.

He wrote a friend that he "was going to travel throughout all the world for the sake of the Word," took care of his last will and testament, and asked another friend, Markus Thomae, to accompany him to Bohemia quickly, "for the matter cannot be delayed." In June of 1521, the two men were at Prague. Müntzer called himself a messenger—an "emulus"—of Luther and propagated theological theses which he had largely borrowed from Melanchthon.[9] He stayed for the remainder of the year, and perhaps even longer.

Surely this Bohemian interlude was theologically fruitful for Müntzer. Direct evidence is lacking, but for a creative and eager mind such as Müntzer's the contact with Hussite thought must have been stimulating. Amadeo Molnar's suggestion that Müntzer became acquainted with the ideas of Brother Lucas' treatise *Scriptural consideration why the admission to the sacraments entails certain responsi-*

bilities is not only imaginative but also quite possible. The Hussite tradition placed considerable stress on the fruits of the spirit. Thus Brother Lucas, the outstanding theologian of the Hussites at the time, asserted that while "no works create the righteousness of God," it still remains that "once the righteousness of faith is attained, it does not subsist without works." Of course, Luther said virtually the same, but one feels that Müntzer encountered the postulate of the demands of the new life in Christ, the obligations placed on the believer upon embracing the Christian faith, in his contact with the Bohemian Hussites.[10]

At Prague, Müntzer preached publicly and on November 1, 1521, posted a *Manifesto*, the first extensive document of his thought.[11] "I, Thomas Müntzer from Stolberg, confess before the entire church and the entire world, wherever this letter may be seen . . . that more eagerly than any other man I know, I sought to be instructed in the high, invincible Christian faith." Thus began Müntzer's flaming attack against the Catholic church that "the Scribes have turned into a harlot." Boldly Müntzer called for renewal and reform.

Clearly the *Manifesto* was one more reforming pronouncement. Müntzer attacked the Romanists, the Pope, and the priests—and his burden was the reform of the church. "God will do marvelous things with his elect, particularly in this country. For here the new church will begin; this people is going to be the mirror of the entire world." At a few points, one can perhaps detect a slight shift of emphasis, compared with the Lutheran position, as, for example, when Müntzer writes that God will separate "in our time the wheat from the tares" —though this statement can certainly be interpreted in the sense of a distinction between the Catholic and the new evangelical church.

One notes also in Müntzer's *Manifesto* a strong emphasis on the "spirit"—referred to as the living voice of God, the inner Christ, God's Word, the gospel of Christ, the Scriptures, or even the Law. Thus Müntzer wrote that he wanted to worship not "a silent, but a speaking God," and observed "according to St. Paul the hearts of men are the paper or parchment on which God writes with his finger his immovable will and eternal wisdom." Again, one must be careful not to overstate the theological uniqueness of Müntzer's position at that time. The problem of the relationship between Spirit and Letter was a pertinent one for all reformers and was far from being satisfactorily resolved in those early years of the Reformation. Similar statements from the pen of Martin Luther can be easily cited.[12]

The *Manifesto* closed with a stark word of warning: "If you will not do this [i.e., accept the new understanding of the gospel], God will let you be smitten by the Turks within a year. Truly I know that my words are true. For them I will suffer as Jeremiah suffered. . . . Given at Prague in the 1521st year on the day of All Saints." Apparently the people of Prague were not impressed by Müntzer's pronouncement, for he remained a voice in the wilderness and the dramatic embracing of the new faith did not take place. Soon thereafter he left Prague, whether voluntarily or involuntarily we cannot tell, and began once more his restless wandering. Probably in December of 1521 he had received an invitation to become a teacher of Latin at a cloister near Erfurt with a remuneration of thirty guilders and a "secure life," but whether he accepted this invitation we do not know. In March, 1522, he wrote to Melanchthon, calling him an "organ of Christ" and criticizing him for ignorance of the "living Word." He indicated in this letter a familiarity with Luther's program of reform made after his return to Wittenberg. A cursory bit of evidence from late in 1522 suggests a contact with Andreas Bodenstein of Carlstadt, then still an eminent member of the theological faculty at Wittenberg, but increasingly impatient with the slow and haphazard progress of ecclesiastical reform. How the two discontent spirits established contact is as difficult to ascertain as their respective theological propensities at that time. That both were dissatisfied with Luther's program of reform seems evident.

Afterward, Müntzer preached at Halle, perhaps even spent the winter there, but then his trace is lost.[13] In a letter of March, 1523, he mentioned that he received only two guilders during the winter from the "domina"—perhaps the prioress of a monastery—and at the same time lamented the "misery of his expulsion."

The Reformer

In the spring of 1523, Müntzer began to play a more clearly discernible role in the drama of the Reformation. At Easter of that year he was appointed preacher at Allstedt, a small town not quite twenty miles south of Luther's birthplace, Eisleben. How he got there we do not know.[14] Here, following the precedent increasingly set by the reformers, he married a former nun.[15]

Müntzer's appointment at Allstedt must be taken as an expression of willingness on the part of the city fathers to undertake ecclesiastical reform. Müntzer had influential supporters in the city, and began to inaugurate various ecclesiastical changes. At Allstedt, even as at other centers of reform, Catholic practices continued despite the new evangelical insights. It was one thing to proclaim the new doctrines from the pulpit; it was quite another to make the necessary changes demanded by this proclamation. Müntzer promptly set to work. Above all, he was persuaded that the traditional order for divine services needed to be altered. It was in Latin, which the people could not understand and, moreover, was replete with what was spitefully called "Roman perversion." So Müntzer wrote several church orders to make ecclesiastical practice conform with theological theory. In 1523 he wrote his *German Church Order,* the following year the *German Evangelical Mass* and the *Order and Structure of the German Office*. The *German Church Order* was the first order for divine service in the German vernacular produced by the Reformation. This is noteworthy. Müntzer antedated Luther's liturgical effort and may well have directed Luther's attention to this question.[16] Perhaps his work is even superior—the burden of proof would be tedious—to Luther's effort. To be sure, the *German Church Order* followed the Catholic paradigm rather closely, and was, in the main, a translation from Latin into German. Müntzer wanted to make sure that the people could understand the service. Thus he rejected the use of Latin. Luther was more broadminded on this point—or more traditional-minded—and saw nothing wrong in principle with the continued use of Latin. Müntzer shared Luther's sentiment that outer form was unimportant, provided the people could understand and the theological perversion had been removed. "Every man may add or subtract what has been set by men and not by God," he wrote. He made some changes, perhaps even dramatic ones: he enlarged drastically the role of the congregation in the service—thus the words of the institution were spoken by the entire congregation and the Scripture lessons became much longer.

A letter from Müntzer to Luther during the summer of 1523 affords an interesting insight into the relationship between the two reformers. The tone is friendly and moderate. Müntzer acknowledged that "from the beginning I have known for a certainty that you did not pursue your cause, but that of all men," denied the responsibility for the disturbances at Zwickau, and affirmed the validity of dreams and visions, though carefully pointing out that there must be the support of the "testimony of Scripture." Otherwise the letter abounds in rather eccentric mystical notions—as for example, "No mortal can know if doctrine or Christ is false or true, unless his will conforms to the crucified one, unless he first suffers the moving and rising of the waters which everywhere overcome the spirit of the elect." In some measure the problem was one of language, but Luther, who had no use for anything eccentric, was little impressed, and remarked that

Müntzer "spoke with absurd and strange words and speeches, removed from Scripture so that you must consider him mad or drunk."[17]

Toward the end of 1523 Müntzer's theological maturation reached its apex. The tangible result came early in 1524 with the publication of two treatises, *On Phony Faith* and *Protestation or Declaration.* Here Müntzer's difference with Luther found concrete expression. Müntzer attacked the "faked faith of Christendom" in fourteen propositions, to which he appended an open letter to "his dear brother Hans Zeiss, castellan at Allstedt," adding some further points to his exposition. The foe was Martin Luther, and to those who knew the lay of the land, it was clear whom Müntzer had in mind when he remarked that they "had not agreed regarding ceremonies" or when he exclaimed that "he who does not have the bitter Christ will eat himself to death from honey," or when he commented that "the apostles attained faith only with difficulty. None of them thus wanted to burst in like our mad, lusting pigs."[18] Two ideas dominated the two treatises: the inadequacy of the understanding of the Christian faith as it was proclaimed by the old and new church alike, and the seriousness of the Christian commitment. Müntzer emphatically insisted on the need of Christians to become Christlike. The Christian must experience the bitter Christ and take up the cross. The "Scribes," on the other hand, do not know "the fear of the Lord" and fail to walk the path of suffering. Grace is not "cheap" but "costly"; while rejecting the Catholic notion of merit, Müntzer asserted that the believer's conformity with Christ is one that leads through suffering, death, and resurrection: the believer must experience what Christ experienced. Müntzer echoed a mystic notion here—which can be found in Luther—and suggested the ways in which it could be related to the *sola gratia* theology of Luther.

The *Protestation* set forth the concrete illustration for the general case against the old and new church. The practice of infant baptism was the practical outgrowth of an inadequate understanding of the Christian faith. "True baptism has not been understood," Müntzer wrote, and added "the entrance into Christianity has become an animal-like monkey-business." He challenged the "Scribes" to cite a single Scripture passage to show that a child was baptized by Christ or his disciples. The practice of the early church was the proper one: "Thus in the days of the apostles only adults were accepted, after a lengthy period of instruction and were called Catechumenos." This means that baptism is not a sacrament; it is only a symbol—a symbol for the "God-wrought motions of our spirit."

The first enemy of importance—and for Müntzer the incarnation of evil—was Count Ernst of Mansfeld, in whose territory Allstedt was situated. The Count thought that the people should not attend Müntzer's "heretical services and sermons" and ordered accordingly. Müntzer promptly challenged the Count to appear in Allstedt and prove that his teaching was heretical. Otherwise, he would consider the Count a "rogue, evil fellow, Turk and heathen, and prove this truly from Scripture." Afterward, Müntzer must have had second thoughts on the matter, for he wrote the Count admitting that he called him a "heretical rogue and robber," but pointing out politely that the Count had prohibited the people from attending his services. Ernst, in turn, wrote a sulky letter to the Saxon Elector in which he claimed that this prohibition had been issued in line with the Imperial Mandate of May, 1521; he had never kept anybody from hearing the Word of God.

The Elector demanded an explanation of the whole matter from the Allstedt City Council, and—as an afterthought—also wanted to know who had installed Müntzer as minister in the first place.[19] Müntzer's reply, of October 4, offered a metaphysical explanation. "After Almighty God made me a serious preacher I am accustomed also to blow the loud, movable trumpet that it might sound with the eagerness of God's knowledge and not spare one man on earth." More concretely, Muntzer observed that he had engaged in the name-calling because the Count had obstructed the free access to the proclamation of the Word of God, and he had no right to do so. In Müntzer's letter, incidentally, occurred the famous phrase "the sword will be taken from the rulers and given to the jealous people resulting in the fall of the godless." To see this as the first open declaration of Müntzer's radical political plans would have surely surprised even Müntzer.[20] The comment was hardly more than an expression of Müntzer's understanding of God's work in history, namely, that the godless will not prevail against the godly because God would not allow this. God would give the rule to his people. The antagonism, suggested by Müntzer here, was not between the ruler and the people, but between the godly and the ungodly. As one reads this touchy sentence, it becomes obvious that Müntzer, in beseeching Frederick as "highborn and gracious Elector" who is "to look graciously upon this letter," wants to persuade the Elector of God's purpose in history. Elector Frederick presumably had little inclination to become deeply involved in a sophisticated theological debate and insisted bluntly that Müntzer promise the Allstedt City Council that he would desist henceforth from vehement attacks.[21]

At any rate, Müntzer was neither arrested nor even reprimanded.

He continued his efforts and, according to contemporary reports, thousands came to Allstedt in 1524 to hear his sermons.[22] Though this may well be another instance of a rather casual use of figures on the part of sixteenth-century chroniclers, Müntzer's popularity seems to be sufficiently documented. By that time Müntzer had arrived at a sociological expression of his insistence on serious Christianity. He founded a *Bund*—a league or covenant—whose true nature continues to baffle scholarship. It has been called everything from a "conspiratorial secret society" to the prototype of the Anabaptist concept of the church.[23] It probably was neither, but simply a sectarian gathering of those who wanted to be serious Christians. Admittedly biased reporters, from whom we have the only authentic comments, stated that those who joined the *Bund* pledged that they would "stand by God and his Holy Gospel." Müntzer seemingly expressed a "sectarian" impulse, though interestingly embedded within the larger setting of the congregation. He did not strive for a complete separation, but sought to combine the small conventicle of serious believers and the larger throng of nominal Christians.

In March, 1524, occurred a disturbance near Allstedt in which Müntzer—who in July, 1523, had written "his dear brethren at Stolberg to avoid improper uproar"—was not involved, but clearly incriminated. A chapel near Allstedt contained a miraculous image of the Virgin, a popular pilgrimage shrine, where replicas of healed limbs and reproductions of houses saved from fire, hail, or storm were exhibited. In March a throng of incensed adherents of the New Faith burned down the chapel. Müntzer had used vehement language against the chapel and the pilgrimages and had spoken of the "house of the devil" and of idolatry, but probably he had nothing to do with the actual burning. The nuns who cared for the chapel appealed to Duke John of Saxony, who demanded an explanation from the Allstedt authorities. The city fathers, surely under Müntzer's influence, stalled at first, but were finally ordered to appear at the ducal residence at Weimar. Here they were told to take care of the matter within two weeks. Nothing happened. Duke John categorically demanded a satisfactory settlement, whereupon the City Council responded with an evasive statement, probably written by Müntzer, which pledged proper obedience to the ruler, blamed the nuns, and insisted that the devil had been worshiped in the chapel. The enemies of the gospel would "wish to eliminate us if they only had a chance."[24] Elector Frederick was not satisfied with such response and Duke John, whom he consulted, demanded in May that the culprits be apprehended within two weeks and punished. Some time later the

Allstedt city fathers informed the Duke that their investigations had not yet yielded any results and asked for additional time.[25] A compelling reason may have slowed down the investigations—at least a letter of Castellan Zeiss mentioned that in recent memory most public officials in Allstedt had died a violent death—"which I, according to the will of God or God's call, must also expect. No chicken or rooster will then cry for me."

In June the City Council wrote that the destruction of the chapel was an act pleasing in God's sight. Idolatry and blasphemy had long ruled there and "the poor people ignorantly worshiped the devil." The Duke was admonished not to defend the godless. Should he demand that they continue the false worship, they would not obey—"as little as we will be subject to the Turk." Duke John forwarded the letter to his brother Frederick, who sternly told the city fathers not to tolerate similar acts in the future. His theological point was simple: "If your teaching and instruction are from God, that which you mean to suppress and destroy by force, will decay by the grace, power and merit of God even without human hand, force, and suppression."[26] Early in July, Müntzer was told to print only those books in Allstedt which had been approved, since otherwise the imperial mandate concerning the publication of books would be violated.

Thomas Müntzer obviously had become a nuisance, and Duke John decided to go to Allstedt and see for himself. Together with his son John Frederick, he went to the city, and in mid-July Müntzer had the opportunity to preach before the two rulers. Müntzer's text for the occasion came from the second chapter of Daniel, that unforgettable passage in which the prophet interpreted the writing on the wall for King Nebuchadnezzar. That Müntzer should use this passage is telling; he meant to talk about what was foremost in his mind—not about justification or the church, Scripture or the sacraments, but about God's work in history. One must not see this sermon as another expression of Müntzer's quest for a radical overthrow of the social order. The two rulers were addressed most politely; Müntzer called his guests "cherished fathers" and "esteemed princes" of Saxony, yet he challenged them to take their place in the realization of God's purpose in the world. The opposition to Luther, "Brother Fattened Swine and Brother Soft Life," was explicit, as was the call to the rulers to "step boldly on the cornerstone as Saint Peter did." Müntzer's own place in all this was obvious: "A new Daniel must arise," he said, and added, "and interpret your vision." The parallel was clear: "Nebuchadnezzar made the holy Daniel an officer in order that he might execute good, righteous decisions." To make sure that his illustrious guests did not miss the point—after all, the day was hot, the sermon long, and its argumentation at times incoherent—Müntzer pointed out that the divine law taught that "the godless rulers should be killed, especially the priests and monks who revile the gospel as heresy for us and who wish to be considered at the same time as the best Christians."[27]

There is no evidence that the princes were impressed by Müntzer's pronouncement, if indeed they understood it. At any rate, no dramatic suppression followed, an indication that Müntzer's sermon could be taken as an exegetical exercise about God's work in history rather than Müntzer's own involvement. Later Müntzer promised not to publish any tracts without having submitted them to a censor.[28] He would "say and write what is incontestable and what can be answered before all generations, despite the Scribes who obviously deny the Spirit of Christ." He would also, as he told the rulers, "faithfully let you read all my books." There is some question whether Müntzer's deed followed his word—at least there is no evidence that the subsequent publication of the Daniel sermon was ever approved by the Saxon authorities—but, of course, the sermon had been delivered before he made the promise. In August, Müntzer did submit a manuscript for approval—only to go ahead and publish a different version.

At this juncture Martin Luther intervened. Familiar with Müntzer's two treatises of early 1524 as well as with the developments in Allstedt, and perhaps even with the Daniel sermon, Luther took up the pen and wrote his *Letter to the Princes of Saxony Concerning the Rebellious Spirit.*[29] Satan himself had established a nest in Allstedt, Luther asserted, though he conspicuously avoided mentioning Müntzer by name. Luther bypassed the theological points at stake and confined his comments to the relationship between preaching and public order. As far as mere "preaching" was concerned, everyone should be allowed "courageously and freely to preach whenever they can and whatever they want to." There must be divisions and the Word of God must struggle and fight. "If their spirit is pure they will not be afraid and will prevail. If ours is right we will also not be afraid. Let the spirits meet one another and contend together." On the other hand, if civil disobedience is advocated under the disguise of the proclamation of the Word, if "they want to break and hit with the fist," then the rulers must intervene. Luther's treatise constituted ample proof that by August, 1524, Müntzer's activities at Allstedt were widely viewed with concern and associated with civil insurrection. The facts do not fully corroborate this view, for the turbulence at Allstedt was not greater than that at Wittenberg in 1521 or at

Zürich in 1523. Yet this perspective was to have serious repercussions for Müntzer.

Late in July a local ruler forbade his subjects to go to Allstedt. At that time, Müntzer wrote two indignant letters in which he recapitulated his understanding of the place of a godly government and argued that "if the rulers act not only against the faith, but also against natural law, they must be strangled like dogs." The second letter repeated the same somewhat uncomplimentary exhortations, but made it clear that he did not have a general insurrection in mind —after all, he had affirmed "in all his sermons that there are pious servants of God at the Court." He was thinking only of certain godless rulers!

A third letter, written a few days later, continued the same argument, and added extensive biblical support for the position. Müntzer asserted the necessity of a new *Bund* among the truly elect. "A proper covenant must be established so that the common man and the pious ruler unite for the sake of the Gospel." Rather typically, Müntzer did not say that the people would rise against the godless rulers, but that the pious people and rulers should unite for "the sake of the Gospel." A report on this sermon by one of the Allstedt officials used somewhat different language: The "preacher" had asserted that he would oppose all tyrants who set themselves against the gospel and he had admonished the people to band themselves together and set force against force.[30] Duke John responded promptly. Müntzer and four Allstedt officials were ordered to appear at Weimar on August 1 for interrogation.[31] On that day Müntzer was informed of the two charges against him. He had entered into a secret conspiracy and had also publicly denounced the rulers. Müntzer admitted the existence of the *Bund*, but maintained that "they might properly make such a permissible covenant so that they might hear the Gospel in unhindered fashion." When several statements from one of his sermons were read to him in which he supposedly had denounced the rulers, Müntzer replied that "he had never spoken such or similar words."

The representatives of Allstedt, simple men that they were, claimed that they had heard, seen, and said nothing. They had not heard of any attack on the part of Müntzer against the Elector. To be sure, the "preacher" had spoken vehemently at times and had exhorted them to form a *Bund* against the godless, but this was only for the defense of the gospel and there could be nothing wrong in this. The Saxon authorities condescendingly called the city fathers "poor and simple people," and told them that the rulers did not hinder the proclamation of the gospel. Therefore no need for a special *Bund* existed. The city fathers were sternly reprimanded, warned to be obedient to governmental authority, and then dismissed. Müntzer was interrogated a second time, ordered to dissolve his *Bund*, and told that, after consultation between Duke John and Elector Frederick, he would be informed of their decision. In the meantime he was to return to Allstedt. We do not know how Müntzer took his investigation. One year later, a frankly partisan pamphlet appeared in Wittenberg with the title *A Profitable Dialogue or Conversation Between a Müntzerite Enthusiast and an Evangelical Pious Peasant.*[32] In this tract the peasant claimed to have been present at the Weimar Castle on the day of the interrogation: "I stood in the courtyard, closing a carriage. When Müntzer left the building, after talking with the rulers and the counselors, I heard the Castellan ask him how it went. But Müntzer's face had turned yellow, like that of a dying man's, and he said to the Castellan: 'Why, how should it go? I will have to proceed to another territory.' He was greatly despaired."[33] We cannot tell whether this supposed eyewitness saw what he reported or reported what he saw. Yet one can well understand Müntzer's dejection. He must have been shocked at the realization that the Saxon authorities were cool toward the gospel—his first awareness that the rulers were not supporting his cause and thus were by definition the godless ones he had been talking about. Yet, the interrogation ended without any explicit condemnation. Müntzer left a manuscript at Weimar for examination in accordance with his earlier promise, an indication, perhaps, that nothing dramatic had happened.

And so Müntzer returned to Allstedt. According to the "peasant" of the *Profitable Dialogue,* who also claimed to have been an eyewitness of the affairs at Allstedt, Müntzer was ridiculed and insulted upon his return. On August 3 he was cited to appear before the City Council and was informed of the dissolution of the *Bund* and the closing of his printing shop. Müntzer furiously shouted that "if the rulers tie my hands and do not allow me to write what has to be written against Luther, then I will do against them what I can."[34] He quickly offered a conciliatory interpretation of his statement and seemingly convinced those present that he had not really meant what he had said. Afterward the City Council requested the Elector to continue Müntzer's printing press and also asked for a public disputation so that Müntzer might defend himself against Luther. Otherwise, the report stated, there might be bloodshed. Müntzer added a note of his own. Omitting the salutation proper for men of high standing, and calling himself "a serious servant of God," he asked not to be kept from preaching to "poor Christendom." He appealed for a free hearing, though "not in a corner, but before all the nations of men who in faith suffered invincible temptation and found their despair of the heart."

By this time Müntzer must have realized that his situation at Allstedt was impossible. "When I returned from the interrogation at Weimar, I planned to proclaim the serious Word of God. Then came the counselors and wanted to put me into the hands of the greatest enemies of the Gospel. When I found that out, I could not stay, but shook off their dust from my shoes, for I saw with my own eyes that they cared more for their oaths and duties than the Word of God."[35]

Exodus from Allstedt

Duke John was informed of Müntzer's exodus from Allstedt in these words: "In the night of the Sunday after Sixti [the 7th of August] the Preacher Thomas Müntzer, together with a goldsmith from Nordhausen, climbed secretly over the city walls and departed without bidding leave."[36] The day after his departure Müntzer informed the Allstedt City Council that he "had business to transact in the country and would therefore ask you cordially not to be annoyed or suspicious." A few days later followed a different communication which denounced the counselors who had been with him at the Weimar interrogation as "arch-Judases" and scolded the city for its unwillingness to adhere to the true gospel.[37] On August 15, Müntzer wrote once more, conceding that his "business" had taken him somewhat farther and that he had no intention of returning to Allstedt. He asked to be relieved of his ministerial responsibilities, wrote for his books, and requested support for his wife, who had stayed at Allstedt, probably wondering as much as the City Council about the whereabouts of her husband. Early in September, Müntzer instructed his servant to get the remainder of his belongings, including a little pig, from Allstedt.

Müntzer directed his steps to Mühlhausen, a free city of five thousand inhabitants, situated about forty-five miles southwest of Allstedt. Though the population had declined somewhat during the preceding half-century, it was still one of the larger towns of Germany—twice the size of Leipzig. The ecclesiastical situation in the city was typical of an uncertain and fluctuating time. In 1523 the City Council had affirmed the imperial edict suppressing Lutheran preaching, but early in the same year Heinrich Pfeiffer, a former monk, had returned to his native city full of enthusiasm for the new evangelical proclamation. His first public pronouncement came on a Sunday in February, after the conclusion of a religious procession, while beer was loudly offered by a vendor to the seemingly exhausted worshipers. Pfeiffer jumped upon a rock and shouted, "Listen and I will tell you about another beer."[38] He then began to preach Luther's evangel, denounced priests and monks, and announced that he would preach more of the same the following day. He must have made an impression, for soon thereafter a delegation requested the City Council to appoint Pfeiffer minister in Mühlhausen. Though the Council promptly declined this, Pfeiffer continued to preach in the city. When the City Council sought to have his sermonic activities curtailed, Pfeiffer made a dramatic appearance in a pulpit, asking all those who desired to stand by the gospel to raise their hands. The response was overwhelming and the Council, cognizant of the popular sentiment, was forced to tread softly. In July a meeting of disgruntled citizens drew up a constitution of fifty-four articles which included a revision of the administrative set-up of the city as well as certain religious changes. The Council at first stalled, and then declined to accept these articles. Matters got out of hand and toward the end of August Pfeiffer was expelled—only to return before the year had passed.

Müntzer had met Pfeiffer somewhere along the line, and Mühlhausen was thus a convenient choice for the homeless Müntzer. Luther, who tried to keep an eye on things, had warned the Mühlhausen city fathers of Müntzer's arrival. "It is rumored that one Thomas Müntzer is about to come to your town," he had written, and called Müntzer a "false spirit and prophet walking in sheep's clothes but in reality a daring wolf."[39] When Müntzer arrived the Council wrote to the Saxon authorities to inquire about him, but apparently dropped the matter there.

Müntzer stayed for about a month in this socially and politically troubled city, and his role is somewhat enigmatic.[40] At the end of September both he and Pfeiffer were expelled, whereupon the two men proceeded southward to Nürnberg.[41] Müntzer had, upon his flight from Allstedt, contacted the bookseller and subsequent Anabaptist Hans Hut and given him the manuscript of his commentary on the first chapter of Luke, with a view to having it printed at Nürnberg.[42] The preface of the *Explicit Revelation* indicated that Müntzer meant to write a series of tracts on the entire Gospel of Luke, an intention which the turbulent course of events prevented him from realizing.[43] Müntzer discussed two problems—the true understanding of faith and of God's work in history. The first concern was, at all odds, the dominant one. Müntzer sought to "bare the faked faith of the faithless world" and do so by presenting the nature of true faith. Faith must wrestle with unbelief, must cling to what natural man considers impossible. Zacharias and Mary were for Müntzer dramatic illustrations for such faith. Zacharias knew his wife to be old and barren and Mary knew no man—yet both had faith. The Lutheran scribes, Müntzer asserted, lack such "experienced faith" and merely point to the Scriptures, exhorting people simply to believe. But this is erroneous, for the direct testimony of God-wrought faith must precede everything else. Scripture will only serve as the confirmation or authentication. What man has personally experienced will be authenticated in Scripture.[44]

Müntzer doubtless presented here some incisive formulations. Luther had shown him that religion was, above all, personal—to be personally appropriated, believed, lived, and died in.[45] But he overlooked—whether by intent or by default is difficult to establish—that Martin Luther held virtually the same definition of faith, which was categorically contrary to experience, hope, or reality. To be sure, Luther never put the premium on suffering, as did Müntzer, nor did he posit the priority of the Spirit over the Letter, as was Müntzer's characteristic. But the basic notions were the same. If the church, as Luther had asserted, did not convey the truth of the Christian faith, and if moreover the common man was practically removed from that consultation of Scripture to which Luther directed him, and indeed true religiosity was personal, vital, exuberant faith, then Müntzer's solution to the problem of religious authority—that God must personally speak his truth to each believer—is certainly a significant one and Protestant Spiritualism has subsequently echoed Müntzer's theme.

Müntzer's faith meant self-denial. "Brother Soft-Life," as he called Luther, "wishes to have faith, yet wants to keep his power and riches." But such is not possible. "We will serve God, without fear of men, in holiness and righteousness, that is an undeceivable, experienced faith."[46] The *yes* to God is the *no* to the world—to the old church and to the new, which both suppress the true faith for the sake of worldly gain. The true believer must repudiate also to the high and mighty—"God rejects such bigshots as Herod and Caiaphas," Müntzer said, and must reprimand the poor—the people "must be reprimanded severely for their improper lusts for they brazenly waste their time without permanent inclination to a serious understanding of faith."

This was the tract which Hans Hut was supposed to see through to publication. When Müntzer reached Nürnberg, to inquire about the state of affairs, he had another manuscript in his pocket, the *Truly Occasioned Defense Against the Spirit-less and Soft-living Flesh at Wittenberg,*[47] his acid and vehement reply to Luther's *Letter Concerning the Rebellious Spirit*. Luther had dedicated his pamphlet to the Saxon rulers and used the customary salutation: "To the eminent and highborn rulers and lords, my gracious lords." Müntzer dedicated his work to "the eminent, first born ruler and almighty Lord Jesus Christ, . . . my most gracious Lord," presumably to make everyone aware of the difference between Luther's worldly and his own spiritual allegiance.[48] The tract was a string of furious explosions of personal animosity against Luther, whom he labels "the pope of the Lutheran Scripture perverters," "Dr. Liar," the "archheathen," the "shameless monk," the "proud, blown-up, sly dragon," the "chaste Babylonian woman," the "asinine, spiritless, soft-living flesh of Wittenberg which I would like to smell roasted or cooked in its own juice." Müntzer was as creative in coining abusive epithets as he was in writing theology. But beyond such warfare of words was a more serious purpose. Müntzer recounted the happenings at Allstedt and, above all, reiterated his position concerning the "false faith" of Wittenberg and the importance of the law for the believer.

One need not read far in this last tract from Müntzer's pen to sense that here was the voice of a discouraged and dejected man. The sparkle and exuberance of the Daniel sermon have disappeared; the language has become more biting, more severe, more radical. One also senses that Müntzer was despairing at the course of events. The emphasis of the Daniel sermon had been "spiritual." Müntzer had argued that the truly elect is the person who is open to the direct leading of the Spirit. Now a legalistic orientation became prominent. The Law had become important. Müntzer presupposed, no doubt, the proper recognition of the importance of the Spirit. His concern was to argue the centrality of the "law"—the demands placed upon man by God.

The *Truly Occasioned Defense,* far from being a revolutionary treatise, was the outcry of a man who had heard God's command and had pledged himself to its realization. "If you call this insurrection," Müntzer wrote in the tract, with the kind of semantic sophistication that would become a Scholastic, "then I am, of course, an insurrectionist." He was concerned about the fulfillment of the divine commandment. The particular structure of the social order was a distinctly secondary concern—his *Bund* was to unite rulers and common people against all godless, and not the people against the godless ruler. To be sure, the happenings at Allstedt and his dealings with the Saxon authorities had increasingly confirmed to Müntzer that these authorities, because they suppressed the gospel, were godless. His understanding of God's rule in history demanded that the godless —ruler or common man—could not persist, especially not in these last days. Quickly the suspicious eyes of the Nürnberg authorities fell upon both Pfeiffer and Müntzer. Andreas Osiander, one of the ministers in the city, found, much to his consternation, that Müntzer wanted "to make us into Jews." But before the theological point could be argued, Pfeiffer was expelled. Müntzer, who was also under scrutiny, was to be given back his Bible; his other books were to be further examined. How long Müntzer stayed in Nürnberg is difficult to surmise. According to his own recollection, "many people in Nürnberg asked me to preach, but I answered that I had not come for this purpose, but rather to see my writings into print." To clear himself from the accusation that haunted him like an evil spirit, Müntzer added, "I could have played a smart game with those of Nürnberg, if I had desired to incite rebellion as the deceitful world accuses me."

On the day of Pfeiffer's expulsion the Nürnberg City Council asked one of the ministers to assess Müntzer's *Explicit Revelation* and four days later the tract was prohibited.[49] The printer received a reprimand from the City Council, but this did not keep him on the straight and narrow path—for two years later, after publishing an explosive tract which prophesied the forthcoming advent of the Kingdom of the Spirit, he was hanged.

Despite such a handicap, Müntzer found a printer for his second tract. But no sooner had it been printed than the City Council confiscated it—quite thoroughly, as a matter of fact, for only one copy survives.[50] By that time Müntzer had already left the city. He traveled southward to Basel, perhaps directed to that city and its eminent minister, Johann Oecolampadius, by Hans Denck, the young schoolmaster of St. Sebald, whom Müntzer had met at Nürnberg. Oecolampadius reported later that he had welcomed Müntzer according to the biblical exhortation of Matthew 25:35 and had dined with him the following day.[51] They conversed about Müntzer's controversy with Luther, about infant baptism, and governmental authority. Müntzer claimed subsequently that Oecolampadius encouraged him "to preach to the people." If this is an accurate recollection—and, of course, we cannot tell—it would constitute another bit of indirect evidence for Müntzer's relatively "harmless" character. Oecolampadius would hardly have encouraged him, had their conversation revealed revolutionary zeal on the part of Müntzer. Accordingly, Müntzer preached in the Klettgau and the Hegau near Basel on "how one should rule according to the Gospel."

The Peasants' Unrest

Here Thomas Müntzer came into contact with the simmering unrest of the peasants. Much has been written about this unrest which afterward erupted into insurrection. Regional peculiarities, varying goals and programs make it difficult to offer adequate generalizations. What took place in 1524 was the outgrowth of long-standing discontent primarily social in character. The peasants felt that their established place in society was usurped by others. Thus the demands of the peasants were largely for the restoration of the traditional rights and privileges. Luther's proclamation no doubt added oil to the fire—unwittingly, to be sure, but discernibly all the same.

The Klettgau was one of the centers of unrest, but the scarce evidence suggests that Müntzer's presence made little if any difference.[52] Early in 1525 Müntzer was back in Mühlhausen, and by February the town was viewed with the same suspicion as had been Allstedt a year earlier.[53] According to the *Chronicle* of Mühlhausen, Müntzer "preached and had a large following. Whenever somebody questioned him in the streets, he had his book ready, sat down and taught publicly."[54] In March the City Council was deposed and a new "eternal council" was put into office. The new Council ordered the Mass to be said in German. The property of the churches was to be sold. Though Müntzer probably played an insignificant role in this, even according to the hostile Mühlhausen *Chronicle* just cited, he surely found the development welcome. A godless government had been overthrown, and a godly one placed in its stead. The proclamation of the gospel was no longer hindered.

In the meantime the restlessness of the peasants slowly reached a fever-pitch. In April the *Twelve Articles,* a south German peasant manifesto, was passed from hand to hand in Thuringia.[55] By the end of the month the countryside in central Germany was in turmoil. In Langensalza, some ten miles from Mühlhausen, unrest broke loose on April 25. The City Council was forced to agree to a doubling of its membership and was confronted with a list of grievances. When word of this happening reached Mühlhausen, several hundred men decided, under Pfeiffer's leadership, to go to Langensalza to support the cause. But by the time they arrived, things had calmed down and moderation had won the day. The "helpers" were refused entrance into the city, but were given a keg of beer and told to go home.

Müntzer's involvement in the course of events is more than enigmatic. Despite the fact that he has long been seen as the instigator of the uprising, there is virtually no concrete evidence supporting this contention.[56] Müntzer seems to have played the role he had always cherished—as a preacher of God's Law. The peasants' uprising would have taken place without Müntzer, who was naïvely "otherworldly" and showed little regard for economic matters. His language was at times evasive, but when he talked about the "poor" he meant the "poor" in spirit, the "people" were the elect, and the "rulers" were the godless. "The artisans' sweat tastes sweet to them, but such sweetness will turn into bitter gall. No hesitation or deception will help. Truth must come forth. No faked acceptance of the Gospel will help. The people are happy, they have to eat and desire to do so as Amos and Matthew write."

Müntzer's role can be best understood when we recall his dualism between the elect and the godless. Müntzer was persuaded that he was one of the elect and his foes were the enemies of the gospel. His bouts with the authorities prompted him to label the rulers as godless. The uprising of the peasants, with its religious rationale and directed against the rulers, must have appeared to him as a concern akin to his own. The irony was not so much that Müntzer incited the peasants to open insurrection, but rather that he fell under the sway of the peasants' proclamation and identified their cause with his own. In this he was partly right, partly mistaken. After the debacle was over and he had, aided by torture, reflected on the turbulent action of the spring of 1525, he wrote to the people of Mühlhausen that "it is highly necessary that you do not suffer defeat as did those of Frankenhausen, which undoubtedly had its reason in the fact that everyone sought his own profit more than the righteousness of Christianity." In retrospect, Müntzer was persuaded that the peasants had deceived him, since they had been concerned about material gain rather than the gospel.

Early in May the peasants gathered near Frankenhausen. They asked Mühlhausen for two hundred men—to which Müntzer replied that not only such a small group but indeed all would come. Müntzer accompanied this band, probably—we do not know—as chaplain. Zeiss, who surely was no biased partisan of Müntzer, watched Müntzer all along and remarked that "contrary to what is said—Müntzer is not a leader or master of this band. He is nothing but the preacher of those of Mühlhausen . . . they pay no particular attention to him, even though he tries to be important with his writings."[57]

On May 12 the Mühlhausen contingent joined the peasants at

Frankenhausen. That day Müntzer wrote to his old enemy Count Ernst of Mansfeld. He signed the letter "Thomas Müntzer with the Sword of Gideon," and admonished the Count "that for the sake of the name of the living God you desist from your tyrannical raging lest you continue to incite God's wrath over you. You have begun to torture the poor Christians. You have labeled the holy Christian faith a roguery. You have dared to suppress the Christians. Tell me, you miserable bag of worms, who made you a ruler of the people whom God has purchased with his precious blood?" Another Count of Mansfeld also received a letter full of scriptural allusions and the offer "if you recognize, according to Daniel 7, how God has given authority to the common people and appear before us to give an account of your faith, we shall treat you graciously and consider you a brother." Müntzer had clearly identified the cause of the peasants with that of God—and thereby with his own. From then on he was more than an innocent bystander; he was an active participant.

By that time three weeks had passed since the first insurrection in central Germany. The rulers were consolidating their forces and, despite Müntzer's verbosity, the situation of the peasants became increasingly precarious. The peasants must have become aware of this, for on May 13 Müntzer wrote a letter to "our dearest brethren, the congregation at Erfurt" for help "in manpower and armory, so that we may fulfill what God himself has spoken in Ezekiel 39:25: 'I will redeem you from them who command you in tyranny.' " Müntzer's propensity found poignant expression in this letter—God's elect are called upon to aid God in the fulfillment of his eternal purpose.

On May 14 Landgrave Philipp of Hesse appeared with 1,400 horsemen outside Frankenhausen and established his camp half a mile from the city.[58] The next morning the peasants moved north of the city onto the slope of the Kyffhäuser mountain where, with a dense forest behind them, they felt themselves to be in an unassailable position. Perhaps this helped them to regain their confidence, for they sent a bold note to the Landgrave: "We confess Jesus Christ. We are not here to inflict something on somebody (John 2) but to maintain divine justice. Thus we are not here to shed blood. If this is also your wish, we do not want to harm you." The Landgrave's response gave no indication that he was impressed. Since they had "variously blasphemed our redeemer Jesus Christ with words, fire, and other denunciations of God," the rulers had gathered, as those to whom God had given the sword, to punish them. If, however, they would turn over "the false prophet Thomas Müntzer" the Landgrave would let mercy rule.

We do not know what happened in the camp of the peasants upon the receipt of this response and many a question must thus go begging for an answer. Possibly the peasants were so sure of themselves that they saw no reason to hand over their spiritual guide. Perhaps they did not understand that they could have saved their own necks by sacrificing Müntzer's. There is also the possibility that Müntzer was the overpowering figure in the camp. Any of these may have taken place—we just do not know. At any rate, the peasants did not hand over Müntzer.[59]

The contemporary sources provide sundry and colorful accounts of what happened. Hans Hut, the itinerant Anabaptist missionary, later reported that Müntzer's proclamation in the peasants' camp had been that "Almighty God wanted now to cleanse the world. He had taken the power from the rulers and had given it to the people. The rulers would become weak and ask for mercy. But they should not believe them, for they would not be faithful. God was with the peasants, for they had painted a rainbow on their banners." This rainbow was the covenant of God. According to another source, Müntzer preached for three days to the peasants and on each occasion a rainbow appeared in the sky, whereupon Müntzer pointed to this rainbow and comforted the peasants by saying that it was the covenant and the sign that God was on their side.[60]

The most melodramatic description came from Luther's *A Woeful Tale and Judgment of God over Thomas Müntzer,* according to which Müntzer incited the peasants by assuring them that "they were God's people. God himself was on their side and any one of them would kill a hundred enemies, indeed with a felt hat they would throw five men to death." *The History of Thomas Müntzer,* in turn, said that Müntzer told the peasants, "you will see that I will catch all bullets in my coat sleeve,"[61] and the Catholic *Trustworthy and True Instruction* added "and would return the bullets into the enemy's camp."[62] These are picturesque descriptions and make a melodramatic story, though one regrets that their drama is not matched by their authenticity.[63] Simpler, and thus more accurate, seems the report that Müntzer "always rode about the camp, emphatically shouting that they all should remember the power of God which would come to their aid." Perhaps Müntzer wanted to strengthen his own courage.

Philipp and Duke George of Saxony used the time of the peasants' deliberations to improve their own position. The peasants were surrounded on three sides and thus lost their strategic advantage. Philipp of Hesse put it this way: "But their answer was long in coming.

Therefore we moved our artillery close to the hill toward the town."[64] According to the *Trustworthy and True Instruction* the peasants intoned Müntzer's German translation of the ancient hymn *Veni creator spiritus* when the first rounds were fired by the rulers' forces. Another report of the "battle" mentioned that this first round did not reach the peasants, prompting Müntzer to exclaim: "I told you: no bullet will harm you," a statement which should probably be understood as referring to the presumed strategic safety of the peasants' position.[65] But then came the second round of fire and many more—and these hit the bull's-eye. Confronted by a well-trained army, the peasants must have realized then that victory could not be theirs. Frantically they sought to reach the safety of Frankenhausen, but in vain. The city, too, was quickly overrun by the soldiers of Philipp and George. When night fell, some five thousand peasants had been killed. Müntzer, however, had escaped the massacre by hiding in the attic of a house. A nobleman of Philipp's forces found him in a bed, and the story is a bit pathetic. Müntzer pretended to be sick. The nobleman, more interested in spoils than in the identity of the man in bed, concentrated on the contents of a bag in which he found a letter addressed to Thomas Müntzer. At first Müntzer denied his identity, but then confessed it. "A Saxon nobleman came into this house to stay there. One of his servants went up to the attic and saw somebody lying in a bed. He called his master and they approached the man. 'Who is lying there? Who are you?' The man replied: 'Why, I am a poor sick man.' Then he found his traveling bag. It was the habit of these people to search everything and thus they saw letters written by Count Albrecht to the peasants. The nobleman said: 'Whence come these letters? I surmise you are their preacher.' "[66]

And so Thomas Müntzer was taken prisoner. Duke George turned him over to Count Ernst, who gave him the treatment proper for a heretic. Under torture Müntzer made a lengthy confession which admitted anything and everything. Though some of the biographical detail of his confession is otherwise corroborated and thus useful, it is obvious that some of his confession—"he had incited this rebellion so that all Christendom should be equal and that the lords and nobles who would not stand by the Gospel should be expelled and killed"—is altogether useless as it finds no substantiation in the records of his life. In this confession, incidentally, Müntzer alluded to Acts 2:44 by stating that *omnia sunt communia*—"everything should be held in common," all the evidence we have for Müntzer's Communist orientation—rather meager, once we think of it. It deserves to be noted that Müntzer only theorized about what the elect should do and did not speak about society in general. Perhaps Müntzer deliberately used the Latin to show that he was really quoting only the Vulgate.

On May 17 Müntzer signed a four-paragraph recantation which conceded that God-ordained governmental authority should be obeyed. Further, he wanted to keep the Sacrament of the Altar as the Christian church had always kept it. The same day he wrote a touching letter to the people at Mühlhausen, exhorting them to abstain from the shedding of blood and asking that his wife be given his property, books, and clothes. "This I want to say, departing from this life, lest burden and weight are upon my soul, that you do not continue in rebellion so that innocent blood may no more be shed."

Ten days later, on May 27, 1525, Müntzer and Pfeiffer, who had in the meantime been apprehended, were executed outside Mühlhausen. According to *The History of Thomas Müntzer*, Müntzer exhorted the rulers present that fateful day to read *Libros regum*—the Books of Kings.[67] Even in his dying breath he could not desist from exhortation. Obviously he died a sober person.

So ended the life of Thomas Müntzer. His head was put on a pole, presumably as perpetual warning to all that insurrection, identified with godlessness, would not escape its due reward, and six years later Luther observed that Müntzer's head could still be seen—a rather unlikely possibility.[68] But Müntzer's memory lived on in the awesome recollections of Luther and Melanchthon, and in the steadily increasing throng of Protestant radicals. Luther blamed Müntzer for the repudiation of the Bible, indeed, for causing the failure of the Reformation. Across the dinner table the reformer observed that "the Gospel was advancing beautifully—but then came Müntzer."[69] The Protestant radicals, on the other hand, saw Müntzer, though erroneously involved in the Peasants' Rebellion, as a profound propagator of the Christian gospel. The Hutterite *Chronicle* wrote many years later:

Thomas Müntzer of Allstedt, in Thuringia, was a highly intelligent and eloquent man who proclaimed many a profitable doctrine based on the Sacred Scriptures against the Catholic and the Lutheran church. He taught of God and his quickening Word and his heavenly voice against all scribes. The people quickly accepted this teaching and opposed the Catholic priests. At that point the peasants rebelled in the land and he could not keep them in Christian peace. He was blamed by those who willed him ill for this rebellion and indicted as its originator, was captured and beheaded by the Duke of Saxony. His head was placed on a pole. God, however, has declared and confirmed his innocence in many a pious heart.[70]

There can be no doubt that many of those who had been swayed by Müntzer's proclamation subsequently sought—and found—their greener pastures in the emerging Anabaptist movement. Several Anabaptist leaders—such as Hut or Denck—show their indebtedness to Müntzer.

The Measure of the Man

What kind of a man was Müntzer? He was a learned man, no doubt. His writings show him conversant with the Bible, but indicate little of the academic training which must have been his. One is impressed by the clarity and the coherence of his writings, though Hans Hut, the Anabaptist, himself no mean writer, intimated that "he had heard him preach several times, but had been unable to comprehend him." Toward the end, Müntzer's language became increasingly abusive, though this point must not be overstressed. Sixteenth-century ears were accustomed to many a word now deemed shocking. Müntzer was a man of "words rather than deeds." His capture in bed or his confession may be taken as expressions of cowardice. Perhaps we should see them as indications that in retrospect he saw his involvement with the peasants as a nightmare—a terrible involvement made possible by his theological dualism.

Müntzer's concern was not practical, and thus political and social considerations were secondary for him. To be sure, he wrote about the "hungry" people, said that "the creatures must be free," or that "power shall be given to the common people," but all this—and, incidentally, these are all the pertinent comments—must either be understood in a spiritual sense or traced back to his basic religious concern. Müntzer indicted the rulers and their exploitations—not to prepare the ground for an overthrow of the existing order, but in order to repudiate the "Christian" character of these rulers, whose godlessness he himself had experienced.

Thomas Müntzer was one of the first sophisticated and erudite exponents of the view that Luther's reformation of the church was haphazard and itself in need of being reformed. His two tracts of early 1524 constituted the first battle cry from within the Reformation camp against Luther. Müntzer argued vehemently that Luther was profoundly in error. And for his polemics Luther had supplied the arguments. Only in part, however, for Müntzer had also imbibed Tauler and Joachim of Fiore, even though he himself claimed that "my teaching is from high above." Luther had taught him to reject Catholicism, and Tauler and Fiore, in turn, had confronted him with the mystic and the apocalyptic traditions of the Middle Ages. The evasive imagery and terminology of his writings—the *Verwunderung, Langeweile, Bewegung*—which (like an Ingmar Bergman movie) can so easily mean all things to all men, clearly shows his theological ancestors. From all this emerged a pattern of salvation, somewhat eclectic, but creative enough to constitute a viable delineation of the gospel.

Müntzer never forgave Luther that he repudiated one external authority (the Pope) only to accept another one (the Bible). He spoke of the Bible as "paper pope" and this was more than one of those clever phrases which he so easily coined; it was an indictment of a religious orientation which favored, like Catholicism, external norms rather than inward ones. Not that Müntzer did not think highly of the Bible. This he did and he could prooftext like an orthodox divine from the seventeenth century. But the Bible was only the record of the Spirit's communication with man, and Müntzer made a point that the prophets had always asserted: "thus *saith* the Lord" and never "thus *said* the Lord."

His great antagonist Martin Luther was content to let the details of man's reconciliation with God be clouded underneath the great postulate of *sola gratia,* by grace alone. Müntzer supplied the details—what man must do, how he can prepare himself, how he can attain communion with God. Since Müntzer's evasive style and his ever new and bewildering images got the better of him—all of his major pronouncements were written in great haste—this pattern may not be so clear as he himself thought. But there it is. Müntzer called for abnegation, for the repudiation of all creaturely desires, for the proper preparation for the Spirit. Like many mystics before him, he affirmed what might be called a "theology of grace," where man declares himself utterly unworthy to receive God's gift of salvation, which he does receive through grace. To this was added the apocalyptic orientation which had been in the air for some time and which the Reformation intensified a hundredfold. That these were the last days before the end of all things seems to have been a widely held belief, shared by most contemporaries—one Michael Stiefel even suggested a date. Thomas Müntzer, influenced by the tradition of the Spiritual Franciscans, provided an impressive theological framework, for which the reformation of the church in the early sixteenth century seemed to be a telling evidence.

Müntzer was a man with a dream, a dream of a church restored to its biblical pattern, arising out of the ashes of the old. Only serious Christians should be the members of this new church, men and women who knew how to walk with God, who knew how to listen to his voice, who had experienced in their own lives bitter despair, resignation, and deliverance, and who were willing to acknowledge the validity of the Law. At a different place, even during this turbulent time—one thinks of Zürich or Scotland, where the constellation of political power by the nature of the situation was different—Müntzer might have become a respected reformer, or perhaps a revered martyr.

Perhaps we may liken Müntzer to John Knox, for he shared with Knox not only an unfailing conviction of divine election, but also that profound understanding of God's rule in history which has thrones and men and empires shattered into dust to achieve God's noble purpose. Like them, he lived in the Old Testament. Its ideas and its men were his company. There was his paradigm. Müntzer's failure was not so much that he proclaimed the wrong thing, but rather that at the wrong time and place he said the right thing—or at least what some men would not be indisposed to call the right thing—that God, the Lord of history, would yet accomplish his worthy purpose and that man can do no nobler act than to aid its speedy realization.

2. The Lonely Individualist: *Sebastian Franck*

> I am part of this invisible church and I inwardly long for it, wherever it may be found among the heathen. I cannot point to this church, but I am certain that I am part of it, wherever I may be, and therefore I seek neither this church nor Christ at any specific place.
>
> —SEBASTIAN FRANCK, *Paradoxes*

An Ambiguous Reputation

Monk, priest, disciple of Luther, spiritual reformer, geographer, writer, translator, historian, soapmaker, book publisher and printer, theologian and philosopher—Sebastian Franck was all these, and perhaps much more. Since his time men have tried to assess him, but Sebastian Franck has evaded them all. In a way, he lost his intellectual respectability in the process; among the professional academicians who preside over the establishment of historical reputation, a jack-of-all-trades is seldom impressive.

At times Sebastian Franck appears a typical littérateur, endlessly thrashing out books on an equally endless variety of topics. In the process he failed to harmonize his prolific output—and he strikes us like a child on Christmas morning overcome by the variety and multiplicity of things. Moreover, he relied copiously on others for literary and religious inspiration, and thus is naturally suspect of being devoid of profound personal conviction. All the same, there is a serious note of personal engagement in Franck's writings. He struggled through the religious issues of his time, bravely attempting to find a more perfect way. And he found it—a way not altogether original, not completely integrated, but still of sufficient significance to make him one of the more interesting figures of the sixteenth century. Sebastian Franck admirably illustrates that influential ideas can be presented in many ways. As Franck's history and thought unfold, it will become obvious that this man did possess some creative insights and that the diversity and universality of his interests made for a persuasive interpretation of the gospel.

Very much like the others in this volume, Franck came in for a formidable share of denunciation. Luther thundered that Franck had written his histories only so that he could spread "his poison, mingled with honey and sugar," among the people, knowing that "history books are very popular."[1] From Franck's books, Luther said, one could not learn what a Christian should believe or even what Franck himself believed. As usual, the Wittenberg reformer was astute in his judgment, but utterly biased. Calvin called Franck "brainless and altogether insane," and thereby helped to inaugurate a lengthy line of criticism too boringly repetitious to follow here.[2]

Franck compiled anthologies of proverbs, translated books into German, and wrote one history after another. It is only behind the façade of these works, in their introductions, in the changes and paraphrases of the original text, that Franck's own view does come through. Franck did not trumpet his views into the world; he only played little songs. Reflecting on his function as writer he remarked that he did not want to convert or to persuade—but to give a testimony. In his *Chronicle* of 1531 he wrote that "this history was related as a judgment and a witness over man. Not that he would change or improve; I am certain that this will not happen for things will become even worse. We need to be aware that the end is near and that the Lord will bring the world to its end. This I say against the foolish eagerness of some, who sing, talk, and write vehemently hoping to convert the world to piety which will nevermore take place."[3]

Thus wrote a man who had given up proselytizing and who wished to be neither prophet nor reformer, but a simple witness. In the postscript to his *Sealed Book* of 1539, Franck observed that he never "dreamt that through my writing special followers, a sect, or church would be established."[4] Franck was an individualist; he would not and could not persuade. He wrote about history, compiled anthologies of Scripture passages or proverbs to let these speak for themselves. Only toward the end of his life he wrote three tracts in which he boldly used his own words—*Concerning the Kingdom of Christ;*

Concerning the World, the Kingdom of Satan; Concerning the Communion of Saints.[5] He said little in these tracts that he had not said before, but the form was now different.

A Simple Life

Sebastian Franck was born in 1499, probably on January 20, the day of St. Sebastian, in Donauwörth on the Danube. The day of his birth determined his baptismal name, which seems singularly appropriate for Franck, because like the martyr of old, he also stood at the stake of the world exposed to the "slings and arrows," a sad and pathetic figure. We know nothing about his youth. The first evidence comes from March, 1515, when "Sebastianus Frannck de Werdae" was matriculated at the University of Ingolstadt, paying the reduced fee for students of poor background. Ingolstadt was, at that time, one of Germany's most respected institutions of higher learning. Johann Eck, later Luther's theological opponent, had come to teach there in 1510; Conrad Celtis, the great German humanist, had been teaching there since 1492. To what extent Sebastian assimilated the intellectual influence must remain an open question; he himself was dubious. In his Latin paraphrase of the *German Theology,* he lamented that in his youth he did not participate in the humanist revival of learning.[6] This, of course, may have been as much his fault as that of his teachers.

Franck took the customary course in the liberal arts, and in December, 1517, he received the baccalaureate degree. Afterward he transferred to the University of Heidelberg—but nothing is known about the length and nature of his studies there. Since Martin Luther was at Heidelberg in April of the following year to participate in a meeting of the Augustinian order and in a theological disputation, chronology would suggest that Sebastian met the Wittenberg professor at that time, even as he must have encountered two other men—Martin Bucer, later the reformer of Strassburg, and Martin Frecht, later reformer at Ulm.

Then we lose track of Sebastian for almost a decade. He was ordained to the Catholic priesthood during this time and carried out his ministerial responsibilities somewhere in south Germany. He came under Luther's influence, for when we pick up his traces again, in the spring of 1526, Franck was a minister of obviously Lutheran propensity in a small village near Nürnberg, employed by the Nürnberg City Council. In a letter of April, 1526, he mentioned his low salary and also that he "was not sure, for more than one week at a time," whether he would be allowed to stay. For some reason, the City Council was unwilling to agree to a more permanent arrangement. Two years later Franck had moved to Gustenfelden, another village near Nürnberg. That year an ecclesiastical visitation committee examined the belief of the ministers in Brandenburg-Ansbach, the area near Nürnberg. Sebastian Franck's examination revealed only that "Sebastian N. has a wife, and answered well."

In 1528 Franck's name appeared in print for the first time—characteristically enough as translator. The Nürnberg minister Andreas Althammer had published a Latin pamphlet called *Diallage*. Against the new Protestant radicals who argued—rather like the Catholics—that the Bible was a book where certain passages were enigmatic, Althammer asserted Luther's hermeneutical principle that the Scriptures were clear and self-evident and could easily be understood. The tract listed one hundred pairs of Scripture passages which, as the title stated, "on first glance seem to contradict one another." Althammer's procedure was to quote additional Scripture passages which resolve the seeming contradiction.

Sebastian Franck translated this work. Here and there he made changes in the text and added a preface of his own—sharply echoing Luther's position in his denunciation of the "enthusiastic radicals." But his preface also included a concern for the ethical fruits of the Christian faith—not alien to Luther but far stronger in emphasis than anything the Wittenberg reformer had ever uttered. "Let us beseech God," Franck wrote, "that he may awaken his work in us, create life and spirit so that we are not only learned, but also god-pleasing . . . that is not faith which does not bring forth fruit."[7]

Also in 1528 Franck published the first book from his own pen—*Concerning the Cruel Evil of Drunkenness*. His ethical concerns found here a concrete expression. "Drunkenness is today so widespread that it is greater than at any time in history," Zwingli wrote in 1525, and pointed thereby to a widespread and characteristic phenomenon.[8] Sensitive contemporaries were appalled at this abuse of food and drink. Particularly the custom of drinking, which required that a toast be returned in identical quantity—with rather disastrous consequences—was a barbarous practice. Of course, one must keep the peculiar situation of the time in proper perspective. The lack of convenient substitutes, such as coffee or tea, virtually forced the thirsty souls to wine and beer. Franck must have experienced the consequences of excessive drinking in his parish. And this prompted him to take to the pen and venture the first serious discussion of the problem. Others had written before him, but they had contented themselves with describing the situation, rather than insisting on a cure. The humanist Christoph Gegendorf wrote two pamphlets—*The Praise of Sobriety* and *The Praise of Drunkenness*. Franck was concerned about a change of life and the new morality resulting from the proclamation of the gospel. "When will we take the Gospel seriously?" he asked. "Christ does not trust any believer unless he is serious."

The tenor of the pamphlet was obvious. God gave man his commandments; man must obey them. "Condemned be he who says that it is impossible for a Christian to keep the law and all that God requires, for this would be blasphemy against the Holy Spirit who moves and rules us." Franck wanted to improve man. It is revealing that he should devote his very first independent literary effort to a problem of ethics rather than theology. The cure of drunkenness was the ban. Those who transgress God's commandment by their drunkenness are to be excluded from the church. "Such public vice should be punished; the preachers should do it with word and the ban, the rulers with sword and law. Since there is no ban, there is no Gospel or Christian church."

One cannot easily discern Franck's place in the bewildering spectrum of diverging forms of Protestantism at that time. Was he still a good Lutheran? Luther's *German Mass* of 1526 advocated the use of the ban in the church. Or was he, as has been suggested, in a transitional stage from Lutheranism to Protestant sectarianism?[9] Franck's radical insistence upon newness of life suggests the latter. Judging from his tract on drunkenness, Franck was a bit more radical than Luther. Thus he wrote categorically: "If a minister observes that there is no improvement of life through the Gospel, but beholds that the Gospel is abused to the glory and cover of the flesh, he will fulfill God's purpose by leaving. He will cherish the pearl of great price which he will not cast before swine. Nor will he give holy things to pigs. Therefore he will become silent and go his way." The exuberant call to newness of life turned into dire pessimism.

Franck soon practiced what he preached. Not long after the publication of his tract he gave up his pastoral responsibilities and moved to Nürnberg. He had married and, in one respect at least, he was fortunate: his wife's ample dowry made possible a life without economic hardship. Otherwise, we know little about his wife, unless we take a comment about the fair sex in Franck's booklet on drunkenness as an indirect bit of information about her. "Something should be said about the precious and superfluous ornamentation of women's clothes," Franck wrote. "A woman is truly a vain creature if she thinks highly of herself. Husbands and civil authorities should not allow extremes of fashion and should assure that in all things order and decency prevail." One suspects that a man writing such words must have chosen a spouse whose beauty was on the inside—though, of course, the opposite could be equally true!

Franck's exodus from his pastoral responsibilities constituted a turning point in his life. He had endeavored to put the new Protestant proclamation into practice. The two small Franconian villages may have been ill-chosen places of activity for a literate and sensitive man—they spelled out failure all the same. More than that, Franck became convinced of the impossibility of changing the people and began to devote his time to writing, publishing, soap-making, or translating—but no longer to preaching. He was dismayed at the fruitlessness of the Lutheran efforts. The proclamation of the Word had not brought about the results that he had anticipated—and he despaired. Possibly, he was familiar enough with the Anabaptist conventicles—his *Chronicle* of 1531 shows an amazing conversancy—to have considered the Anabaptist alternative of gathering the true Christians in small congregations. Perhaps he even flirted temporarily with the Anabaptists—later on he was accused of having had to leave Gustenfelden "on account of the Anabaptists"—but we do not know.

No doubt, Luther and the other reformers experienced a similar disappointment in their efforts to deepen the moral consciousness of the people. Countless are the expressions of despair that the proclamation of justification by grace falsely meant the disregard for a new life. But the reformers overcame their disappointment and persisted in their efforts to educate the people. Franck was different. His life became an unsteady pilgrimage—two years at Nürnberg, two at Strassburg, one at Esslingen, five at Ulm, a few years at Basel, and then his early death.

During his stay in Nürnberg, Franck translated two books into German. One was a *Chronicle or Description of Turkey,* written by someone who had been prisoner in Turkey in the middle of the fifteenth century. Franck translated the work more or less faithfully, but exhibited what was to become a lifelong habit, namely, to add his marginalia and commentary to the translated text. He added an epilogue to contrast the simplicity of the morals of the Turks with the divisions of Christendom. He decried the improper attitude toward faith and works among Protestants who "shout, have a good drink and say, it is a joyful thing to be a Christian; I am no work saint."

In 1530 Franck left Nürnberg and went to Strassburg, which was, in those days, a spiritual Eldorado for dissenters. The list of men who sought refuge there—Denck, Bünderlin, Schwenckfeld, Servetus, Hofmann, to name but a few—reads like a who's who of sixteenth-century Protestant radicalism. Franck must have been aware of this situation when he directed his steps there. But Strassburg boasted another attraction—it was a publishing center and Franck had with him the voluminous manuscript of a new work which he had mentioned on the last page of his Turkish *Chronicle*. He published the manuscript in the fall of 1531 and gave it the title *Chronicle*, to which we have already referred. It is a formidable tome of more than a thousand pages and one can well understand how its several unorthodox passages escaped the censor's eyes, which may have tired after the first several hundred pages. This voluminous book was not altogether original with Franck: the facts and lengthy quotations he had obtained elsewhere. He has been chided for this, but he himself was open and frank about his sources, for on what we today would call the copyright page he enumerated in neat alphabetical form no less than 111 sources utilized by him, from Augustine to Zwingli.[10]

The *Chronicle* made Franck widely known. It consisted of three parts, the first of which—the *First Chronicle*—narrated the history of mankind from Adam to Christ. The second—the *Emperors' Chronicle*—dealt with emperors and political rulers. The third part was divided into three sections: a chronicle of the popes from Peter to Clement VII, of Franck's own time; a chronicle of the councils of the church; and a chronicle of heretics. The latter listed, in alphabetical order, a multitude of heretics from the medieval dissenters to Luther, Erasmus, and the Anabaptists.

The material for this Chronicle of Heretics came from Bernard of Luxembourg, a Dominican monk, who in 1522 compiled a *Catalogus haereticorum,* an alphabetical catalogue of all heretics condemned by the church, including a summary of their errors. Franck copied rather extensively from Bernard's book, but he made changes, which entailed a radical shift of perspective. His descriptions of the various heretics sought to be objective—so much so that the heretics, ordinarily despised and rejected, impress the reader as sober and serious individuals.

The *Chronicle* involved Franck in serious trouble. Franck had observed in the preface to the *Emperors' Chronicle* that emperors display an eagle in their escutcheon and, borrowing heavily from one of Erasmus' *Proverbs,* "the eagle does not look for flies," he launched into a lengthy comparison of the robbing and plundering qualities of both rulers and eagles.[11] In November, 1531, Ferdinand of Austria complained to Emperor Charles V about this derogatory comparison and the Emperor lost no time in protesting to the Strassburg City Council. A second demurrer came from Erasmus, whose annoyance over the use of his book on proverbs was intensified when he discovered that he himself had been numbered among the "heretics." He overlooked, in his sensitivity, that Franck considered such inclusion virtually as a place in a hall of fame—at one place Franck commented actually on "Erasmus and other scholars and God-fearing men." But here, as always, Erasmus was sensitive. He formally registered a complaint with the Strassburg City Council, which met in the middle of December to consider the matter. It decided "to put Sebastian Franck into the tower, read Erasmus' letter to him, examine him concerning the matter, find out who had allowed him to print the book and send his response to Erasmus."[12]

Franck was arrested. With the threat of expulsion hanging over him, he appealed to the City Council for permission to stay in Strassburg as well as to print a new book. Just before the turn of the year the Council ruled that Franck had written against the Emperor and governmental authority and that he had "promised in the title and preface great things which he did not present in the book." The city fathers also claimed that Franck had added new material during the printing—surely a chronic temptation for all authors who would rewrite their book on the galley proofs—but here a convenient explanation designed to relieve the Council from the embarrassment of denouncing *ex post facto* a book which had previously passed its censorship. Franck's books were not to be sold in Strassburg.

Early in 1532 Franck was released from prison and expelled from the city. For a short time he settled at Kehl, across the Rhine from Strassburg. Here he engaged in what was to become a characteristic pastime—namely, to address supplications to governmental authorities. He petitioned the Strassburg Council to permit the publication of a new work, "a description of the world," and to allow him to return. In May the Council decided not to honor Franck's requests.

We lose sight of Franck for several months afterward, until we find him, in the fall of 1532, at Esslingen, an Imperial Free City, some eighty miles east of Strassburg. No longer was he a writer, but he pursued a strikingly different activity: he was a soapmaker. The reason for this vocational reorientation is enigmatic. Soapmakers had no guild in Esslingen and Franck may well have selected a trade in which he would be free from close supervision. And there is the possibility that resignation had overcome him, and that he hoped for tranquillity through the pursuit of manual labor. In the sixteenth century the Protestant stress on the biblical legitimacy of all human endeavor added an attraction of its own. Another sixteenth-century radical, Andreas Cralstadt, who called himself "Brother Andrew," helped to spread manure in the fields of Orlamünde. All the same, the picture of Sebastian Franck pushing his cart with homemade soap, trying to convince housewives of the advantages of cleanliness as being second only to godliness, suggests that this was the wrong calling for the man.

Sojourn at Ulm

The following summer Franck moved southeastward to Ulm. Here, as he wrote in his petition for admission to the city in August, 1533, he had been blessed by God in selling soap, whereas in Esslingen "only the nobility and not many burghers wash with soap, but mostly with lye." Franck must have been quite serious about his soap-making endeavor, for he declared that he wanted to earn his living by the work of his hands. He announced that he did not want any ministerial responsibility: "What I have from the Lord I want to pass on to the people by way of writing, which requires a free man who is not tied up in an office." Probably in the fall of 1533 Franck took up his residence at Ulm, and for six eventful years this town was his home.[13] In October, 1534, he received citizenship; everything pointed to a permanent residence. We do not know for how long Franck continued, through making and selling soap, to contribute to the cleanliness of Ulm housewives, but he soon found a more congenial pursuit—writing and working with a local book printer, by the name of Hans Varnier.

At Ulm, Sebastian Franck wrote and published most of his works and thus these years were the most significant ones in his life. In 1534 appeared in rapid succession several works from his pen. The beginning was made with *World Book,* originally intended as the concluding section of a comprehensive tome which was also to include the *Chronicle* of 1531. The idea was to compile a one-volume encyclopedia dealing with sacred as well as profane history and geography.

The *World Book* is an interesting work, not only because it ambitiously undertakes to sketch "a mirror and picture of the entire world, namely, Asia, Africa, Europe, and America," but also because it is based, as Franck expressly stressed in the title, "not upon fables, but scrutinized, trustworthy and experienced writers."[14] Franck's impartiality, so eagerly sought in the realm of religion, was here applied with equal persistence to the realm of geography. But impartiality meant more than the distrust of fables; it also meant a disregard of what we might call "parochial" history, the self-glorification of so many writers of history. "The Venetians, Italians, Romans, Greeks, Frenchmen, Bohemians, Swiss, indeed all countries and rulers want their histories written their own way," Franck wrote. But he was concerned about truth and insisted "everybody should realize that there has been enough deceit and flattery."

Franck's very undertaking mitigated against parochialism of any sort. The world was thus for him the limit. There were great marvels, wonders, or beauty outside of Europe, even as absurdity, strange sects, and obscure behavior were no European prerogative but were found at many other places. The world, then, was not parochial, but universal, not multitudinous, but one. Accordingly, Franck's preface addressed itself to the "inner man" and wished him the ability to discern the works of God—to become aware of the essential unity despite external diversity.

Soon after the *World Book* came the publication of an anthology —*Four Crown-Books,* of which Franck observed in the preface that the four separate writings united under this heading "had one single argumentation and purpose, namely, to show that the course, essence, and purpose of the world is nothing but vanity, foolishness, sin, fable and abomination in the sight of God."[15] Franck derived the term "crown" from the mystic notion that God is praised, and indeed "crowned," by a truly spiritual person.[16]

The first of the four writings was a partial translation of Erasmus' *Praise of Folly;* the second came from Agrippa von Nettesheim and was called *The Praise of the Donkey*. Then followed Franck's own contributions—*The Tree of Knowledge of Good and Evil* and *A Praise of the Foolish Word of God.* All four writings were to express one single sentiment—to question the wisdom of the world. Erasmus' irony and Agrippa's skepticism were added to his own efforts. Franck battled against outward appearance, and called for true inward discernment rather than endorsement of externals.

Two more publications rounded out Franck's literary efforts for 1534: a slender tract entitled *That God is the One and Highest Good in the Hearts of All Men* and a formidable volume, *Two Hundred and Eighty Paradoxes.* The former argued, as the title set forth, "that God, the one and highest good, as well as his almighty, true, living Word, and will, knowledge, law, son, sense, character, light, life, image, rich, poor, spirit, power, hand, Christ, the new man and the seed of women along with the seed of the serpent are in the heart of all men."[17] The *Paradoxes,* in turn, discussed 280 *Wunderreden,* strange sayings or paradoxes, since "theology, the true meaning of the Scriptures, which is alone God's word, is nothing but an eternal paradox contrary to vanity, appearance, belief and values of the world."[18] Not all of the sayings cited by Franck were taken from the Scriptures; some were proverbs, others came from theological writings. Franck had traveled a long way between 1527, when he had translated Althammer's *Diallage,* and 1534, when he published the *Paradoxes.* In the former work he had lent his hand to the effort of synthesizing Scripture; in the latter, his pessimism that such harmony could be achieved without the guidance of the Holy Spirit shows through in every line.

The publication of the *Paradoxes* involved Franck in serious controversy. His opponent was Martin Frecht, the leading minister of the city, a good theologian, but also a somewhat quarrelsome spirit. Several years later Frecht recalled that when Franck had first arrived at Ulm he himself planned to write about paradoxical statements concerning God and man. Frecht, who knew Franck from his student days at Heidelberg, had shown him a copy of the *Paradoxa* of the Spanish humanist Ludovicus Vives, "hoping that Franck would write, after the example of Ludovicus Vives, or even Cicero, about paradoxes. But he sat down and fabricated them in his head."[19] Frecht's subsequent hostility toward Franck was surely in part a matter of hurt pride—that Franck had written a book after he had called attention to the topic.

Frecht was an arch-Lutheran who exhibited an almost pathological eagerness for the purity of doctrine. In many ways, Frecht was the prototype of the orthodox defender of the faith, not without integrity and conviction, nor even without willingness to suffer martyrdom for the truth. When, after the War of Schmalkald, Charles V sought to recatholicize the German Empire, Frecht put up bitter opposition. He was removed from his ministerial office and imprisoned for some time. Although he spent the last three years before his death in 1556 as a professor of theology at Tübingen, he suffered willingly for his conviction the fate that Franck in some measure had earlier undergone on his account.

On the last day of December, 1534, Landgrave Philipp of Hesse informed the Ulm City Council that Franck had "published many inappropriate things, in word and writing, especially against governmental authority; he was widely known as a revolutionary and an Anabaptist." Philipp asked the city fathers to expel Franck from the city. One wonders, of course, what Philipp had to do with Sebastian Franck, and the answer is that Frecht was the Saul behind the voice of Paul. Frecht had written to Martin Bucer in Strassburg about Franck, and Bucer had passed on the gossip to Philipp Melanchthon, who saw to it that word of the matter promptly reached the Hessian Landgrave. What persuasive evidence of a Europeanwide fraternity of reformers! Philipp acted promptly. So did the Ulm City Council. On January 25, 1535, Franck was called a revolutionary and an Anabaptist and ordered to leave the city within a month. Four days later, January 29, the minutes of the City Council mention a "supplication" from Franck requesting a reconsideration of his case. The City Council must have had second thoughts about its speedy decision and a meeting of the Council early in March discussed the matter. It must have been a lively session, for the minutes record two decisions. According to the first, Franck was allowed to stay in the city, with the obligation to submit future manuscripts to censorship. This decision, however, was crossed out in the minutes and replaced by a new one: Franck was ordered to leave Ulm by June; the taxes he had already paid were to be refunded.

Early in June, Franck countered this new decision with a new supplication. He asked not to be expelled without a proper hearing, insisting that his "heart is frightened when it comes to sects and groups." He volunteered to change his books if he were convinced of any error. Indeed, aside from a German history just about to be published, he would agree not to print anything of his own "and put down the pen since God has opened another door to provide a livelihood for me and my children." Franck's supplication was a moving plea to spare him and his family from economic distress:

> Therefore I beseech you, for the sake of the Lord who examines all hearts, to consider not only my innocence, for I am no evil doer but a Christian who cannot be truthfully blamed for vice or evil deeds, but also to consider my pregnant wife, my young children, and my pious creditors here and elsewhere, one of whom has advanced 700 guilders to me. He is well disposed to this city as will become evident after his death.

The unnamed creditor was an obviously influential Augsburg citizen, Jörg Regel, a former Anabaptist and a man of deep spiritual conviction. In January, 1535, Regel had written the Mayor of Ulm a letter in which he pointed out that he had heard of Franck's desperate economic situation: Franck has "always aided other printers so that they become rich and drink wine, whereas he must drink water."[20] Regel agreed to advance one hundred guilders to Franck to set him up in business. The Mayor's services were needed to obtain suitable rooms for the printing shop; permission was also needed to employ a Jewish printer to help Franck publish Hebrew books, "for these books are presently good money with which he hoped to make 100 guilders above expenses." Franck undoubtedly had kept his benefactor informed of the subsequent developments and in June at the height of the crisis Regel wrote once again, this time stressing the pecuniary argument. Regel recalled that Franck owed him 700 guilders, without having had opportunity to use the money for the purpose intended.[21] If Franck was expelled from the city, the 700 guilders would be lost.

On June 16 the city fathers showed that such argument was not beyond their comprehension. They decided that Franck's "books and writings, especially the two which he had published here, should be thoroughly and industriously searched and examined." Frecht was charged with the inquisitorial task and the outcome was obvious. Frecht found fault with numerous passages in Franck's *Paradoxes* and the *Praise of Folly,* found fault also with Franck's treatment of Luther in the *Chronicle* of 1531, and asserted that Franck misunderstood the proper relationship between Word and Spirit.

Frecht and his fellow ministers proposed simply that Franck should revoke six erroneous propositions found in the *Paradoxes:*

> 1. God's grace is given without external means. 2. Scripture is not God's Word. 3. Concerning the inner and the outer word, concerning word and spirit, Old and New Testament as well as its servants, he writes differently than Scripture and the pious learned fathers. 4. Scripture is not given for doctrine, but for a testimony, which is against Paul's explicit statement in II Timothy 3:16. 5. The godless do not preach the Gospel of Christ and have neither the vocation nor the office of a priest. 6. Concerning the establishment of peace and unity in the churches.

On July 4, 1535, the City Council ruled that Franck should answer the memorandum of the ministers and its six specific charges. Two months later Franck submitted his answer—a lengthy document which stated at the outset that it would discuss the following points:

> The ways in which Scripture is and is not God's word; concerning the distinction between the outer and the inner word, man, both testaments and the vocation and office of its servants; how godless and uncalled persons cannot preach and concerning the distinction between a sinner and a godless person; concerning the arts of man, how they are said to come from the devil even though they are gifts of God; concerning the description of Ulm and Augsburg in my *Chronicle;* concerning the community of goods; a suggestion concerning concord and unity of the churches.

The remainder of the document was typically Franck. He copiously cited other writers—such as Luther—to prove his point. He used enigmatic language to cloud his own position. Thus he wrote concerning the relationship of Scripture to the Word of God that he did not mean to take away the honor due to Scripture, for "I esteem it worthy of all honors and above all treasures, values, and creatures. However, it should not be given the honor due to God, nor should it be put alongside God or his word, be called God or his word."

Frecht and his colleagues, understandably, were not satisfied. Franck had answered their questions in his own way, had used his own language and thereby had evaded the issue, as far as they were concerned. Quite persistently the ministers tried again to ascertain Franck's orthodoxy, this time in such a way as to avoid semantic confusion: Franck should subscribe to a confession of faith, written by Martin Bucer for the city of Augsburg, as evidence of his belief, with an additional paragraph which stated that if Franck's books contained any material contrary to the confession this was to be revoked; the dark and enigmatic passages in Franck's writings were to be interpreted in light of Bucer's confession.

A neat noose had been placed around Franck's neck, but Franck's response showed that he could rise to the occasion. A moving letter, perhaps the noblest product from his pen, carried his answer. Here was a most personal document, the outcry of a man who found himself entangled in the web of inquisitorial orthodoxy, who could not understand why his desire to live a quiet and spiritual life was not honored. No mean diplomat, Franck stated that he had shown his earlier statement to several people in Augsburg who had indicated their approval; it could hardly be wrong. Franck volunteered "henceforth not to write, print or publish one single line" of his own, and publish only books that had been approved by the representatives of the City Council. He would promise not to write or publish anything against the faith of the city and asked, once again, for the sake of his family, to be allowed to stay in the city.

The point of the letter lay unmistakably in its promises regarding the future. The affirmation of his willingness to abide by certain conditions in the future must have appeared to him as the only solution of his difficult situation. "I beseech Your Lordships," Franck wrote in conclusion, "to give me the chance of another year or of two years. If I do not fulfill my promises Your Lordships have the power to punish me accordingly, to expel me, and even to kill me." One can hardly read these words without emotion, for it was surely the pledge of a man who, above everything, wished to live in peace.

The City Council was undecided and the observer suspects that more must have happened in Ulm during those weeks of early fall, 1534, than meets the historian's eye. Perhaps Frecht and his ministerial colleagues had become too painfully adamant in the matter; perhaps the city fathers knew of the personal integrity of Sebastian Franck; perhaps Franck had support in high places. Eventually Franck was told not to write anything against Ulm, nor to publish a manuscript without previous approval. Nothing was said about his expulsion.

Reprieve and More Books

Thus, after a controversy lasting for the better part of a year, Franck was allowed to stay in Ulm. He could pursue his book-printing and book-publishing ventures. Judging from the titles, the output was prolific—he published works of other authors and several of his own. In line with his favorite preoccupation, Franck translated copiously from others. The censors objected to the publication of several works from Franck's pen, but astutely Franck published two of these, the *Golden Ark* and the *German Chronicle,* elsewhere. The latter was a history of Germany, with special emphasis on the history of Ulm. Once again Franck followed his old habit of relying extensively on others and once again he conscientiously listed his fifty-two sources in his preface. Far more important was Franck's structure for his presentation, which departed from the traditional chronological scheme. He was concerned about the "inner" coherence of things; perhaps this was one of the reasons why Wilhelm Dilthey found Sebastian Franck so congenial—Franck, too, emphasized *verstehen.*

The *Golden Ark* was a collection of quotations on important theological subjects. The quotations came from Scripture and from other writers, both Christian and pagan. The importance of the work lay in the vigorous denunciation of the sophistication of the philosophers and theologians: "We are frustrated," Franck wrote, "with unprofitable questions and arts which do not contribute to eternal salvation and indeed hinder more than further us so that we stare and read, write and dispute until we are worn out. At the same time we fail to consider what is most needful to know."[22]

Little is known about the mundane side of Franck's life during those years. His professional activity suggests that he may have been able to attain some measure of economic success. On the whole, these years were the most peaceful ones in his life, though his wife was seriously ill for over a year, which prompted Franck to see her recovery as if "she had risen from the dead."[23] The size of his family increased; to the two children who had comprised the family when Franck moved to Ulm were added four more.

In the spring of 1538, the idyllic picture was disturbed. We cannot say from this distance if the turn of events came like the proverbial flash of lightning out of a clear blue sky or whether the storm had been gathering for some time. Probably the latter, for in June of 1537 the City Council heard the ministers' report that Franck had acted contrary to the decision of the Council by publishing books and behaving in an annoying fashion. Since Franck's earlier books had caused such commotion, he should be stopped. The Council decided that Franck could "translate histories into German, but is not to write anything out of his own head."[24] One year later, in July, 1538, the City Council decided that, since Franck had violated the previous mandate not to write or publish, he was to leave Ulm before the end of September.[25] Eleven days later Franck submitted a petition to the City Council. The laconic wording of the decision of the Council had provided no clue as to the reasons for his expulsion; Franck must have been at a loss as to the charges. He had kept the promise made in 1535 to the best of his ability. With the exception of a few incidental items—an almanac, a calendar for peasants, a satirical praise to St. Penny, and a few recipes—he had published nothing without the approval of the censor. As far as these unapproved publications were concerned, he had assumed that the ministers did not wish to be bothered with such trifles. He admitted that he had published his writings elsewhere without obtaining approval at Ulm, but his promise of 1535 pertained only to books to be printed at Ulm. Then he commented on the content of these books: "How could I possibly write something that pleases everybody in this dangerous time with its numerous sects?" Indeed, if his books were heretical, why was the *Golden Ark* published in Augsburg, a city concerned about the true faith, and why was it read by scholars and yet not refuted? His books were proper and his personal life was also above reproach. He had good friends with whom he enjoyed eating and drinking. But he hardly ever conversed about religion. "I have no special followers; I think highly of all who are serious about God and who live honorable lives. I do not inquire into anybody's belief but rather into his life. As a matter of fact, I moved to the market square so that everybody could know my life, my character, and my friends."

Franck's energetic document temporarily accomplished its purpose. On July 31, the City Council ruled that the committee which had investigated Franck in 1535 should be reconstituted to examine the new charges and Franck's defense. The committee found that it could not proceed without detailed evidence and asked the ministers to name the books Franck had published without permission since 1535.

The ministers responded with a detailed document, the content of which was somewhat beside the point. The committee had stated that Franck's "previous matter was, upon his supplication and request, forgiven and forgotten" and that the issue was, simply, whether or not Franck had abided by his promise made in 1535. The ministers, however, argued differently. Their concern was not had Franck kept his promise, but was he orthodox in his beliefs. The document announced at the outset—rather properly so for a ministerial exposition—that the ministers "wanted to have mercy upon Franck, his wife, and his children," but then followed words of violent denunciation. Franck had not revoked anything he had previously written! Frecht and his colleagues saw the problem not as a legal but as a theological one: Franck was the unorthodox dissenter and it was not difficult to support this charge. The old matter of Franck's translation of Erasmus' *Praise of Folly* was brought up, as was the publication of the *Paradoxes* which "filled the world with annoyance." Then followed a lengthy list of books prohibited by the censors: a *Chronicle of Venice,* "because there was nothing good, but only evil in it, for whoever writes history should write both good and evil"; a book "concerning passages of Sacred Scripture which are to be incompatible one with another"; a book on the Psalter "which was to be interpreted far worse than ever before"; a book concerning God's commandments and prohibitions "to which Franck added, at the end, such evil things that those in Strassburg prohibited their book-sellers to sell this book."

And so the document concluded: "In sum: Sebastian Franck, once a parish priest, ordained in the bishopric of Augsburg, later a Protestant minister, suspected of having had dealings with Anabaptists (which he now denies), behaved in such a way at Strassburg that he was expelled from the city after he had been arrested. How he has behaved himself here with his writing, printing, and in his life, we commit herewith to you."

The committee, suddenly involved in a theological tug-of-war, decided on September 23 that a verdict was really beyond its competence and informed the City Council that it could not bear the sole responsibility. "In matters of faith and religion it is difficult for us to render a verdict alone. Therefore, we request that the Council with its insight take the matter into its hand and render a decision with that sound reasoning so highly endowed by God." The City Council, however, appeared unwilling to make a decision and simply returned the matter to the committee; Franck's response to the ministers' charges should be heard to see if the charges and response could possibly be harmonized. This was in the middle of October. Seven days later the City Council ordered the ministers to take the place of the committee.

The issue had ceased to be Franck's obedience to his promise of 1535; the issue was his orthodoxy. Frecht once more submitted a detailed list of passages in Franck's writings which taught erroneous doctrine. Franck obviously had at least one ardent, albeit unimpressed, reader—Frecht, who must have gone through Franck's books with a red pencil, marking here and there and waiting for the right moment to pull out the evidence. Aside from objecting to questionable doctrine—such as the assertion that governmental authority should only punish public evil and leave conscience and the inner man untouched—Frecht went to great pains to chide Franck for factual errors—such as, that the pagan philosopher Hermes Trismegistos lived after, and not before, Moses. The document concluded with a scriptural repudiation of Franck's thought.

The next step was a meeting between the ministers and Franck, which must have taken place shortly before the end of the year. Franck's response and Frecht's charges were worlds apart. Franck stated that he had faithfully kept the agreement of 1535, had lived "according to this understanding and had published nothing whatsoever unless it had been seen." He refuted the specific charges against him. Two of the mentioned works had been published four years earlier, thus prior to the agreement; the others had not been published at all, because of the ministers' objection. Franck argued that he had abided by the stipulation of 1535 and had accordingly done nothing wrong. He had lived a quiet life, had refrained from talking "religion" with people, and had submitted his manuscripts to censorship.

There is an irony in Franck's experience which evokes sympathy. He was defeated underhandedly—was told one thing and then judged according to another. The bad stain of heresy had been put on him and he could not get rid of it. The ministers finally informed the City Council that Franck's writings would cause troubles and the Council decided early in January that "Sebastian Franck should be told that between now and the day of St. George (April 23) he is to leave the city with wife and children. He is not to request the City Council again for permission to stay. The Council is definitely resolved not to allow him here any longer."[26] On January 6 the City Council confirmed its decision. Something or somebody must have prompted the reconsideration. Did Franck submit a petition after all? Did one of his supporters on the Council request another hearing? We do not know. On the evening of Epiphany, 1539, Frecht was finally victorious in his battle against Franck.

It so happened—how this must have angered Frecht—that Franck and his family were able to stay beyond the day stipulated by the City Council. In the middle of July Franck was still in the city.[27] His wife was with child at the time and the City Council granted a temporary extension. In May Franck traveled to Basel in search of a new place to live. A letter he wrote at that time shows his state of mind, his experiences in the past and his hopes for the future. He was forty years of age, so he wrote, "by God's grace well and healthy." He had encountered difficulties in obtaining paper in Ulm and had found the censors "in that Lutheran town" rather unwilling to approve his books, which sold so well elsewhere. His labor had made others prosperous, while he remained a beggar; he was "befallen with children"[28]—three sons and two daughters. Berne would be his preference for a place to live, despite its distance from Frankfurt, bookselling center. Basel, another possibility, was oversupplied with rich printers and his "fate would be that of a fly in a boot." But, in the end, Franck decided to settle at Basel.

Last Days at Basel

The sources for his years there are scarce. We know that his wife died soon after their arrival, perhaps as a result of the strenuous trip so soon after childbirth. We also know that in 1541 Franck married a second time. His wife was Barbara Beck, whose father had published Franck's *Chronicle* in 1531. Franck became a citizen of Basel in May, 1541, and in July he purchased his membership in the guild of the saffron merchants—the guild of the book printers, a new genus of artisans created by the invention of the printing press, for whom the medieval spectrum of guilds afforded no place. According to the guild record for 1541:

> On Sunday before James in 1541 there appeared before My Lords, councilors, masters, and assistants the honorable Sebastian Franck who requested to be received into the guild and contributed his fee. Thereupon My Lords were favorably disposed to receive him into the guild according to custom, tradition, and order, for the amount of 41 pounds and 14 guilders which he paid in cash.

In the fall of the same year Franck purchased a house in Basel. Economically he must have been in a good position, but whether through his own efforts or through the dowry of his second wife we cannot say. He entered into a partnership with a Basel printer, Nikolaus Brylinger, with whom he published a Latin-Greek New Testament in 1541, and several other works.

Shortly after Franck's move to Basel came the official Protestant anathema against him. In March, 1540, several Protestant theologians —Melanchthon, Bugenhagen, Corvinus, Cruciger, Bucer, and others —met at Schmalkald. Frecht was sent there by the Ulm City Council to obtain a verdict concerning the two radicals who had caused difficulty in Ulm, Caspar Schwenckfeld and Sebastian Franck. The Protestant divines concurred with Frecht's denunciation, condemned Franck's *Paradoxes* specifically but otherwise limited the charges to his repudiation of the established churches. Protestantism and Franck had formally parted company.[29]

Franck continued his publishing efforts. In 1539 he brought out *Seven Main Points Briefly Brought Together from Scripture*—a concordance of scriptural passages on seven theological loci, slim in form and surprisingly simple in content. One almost suspects that Franck thrashed out this little pamphlet for economic reasons. The same year Franck published, under the pseudonym of Felix Frey, a tract entitled *Concerning the Saying: Faith Does Everything*. The preface informed the reader that the booklet was to help him understand the two divergent statements of Scripture: "Faith does everything" and "Faith without works is dead." Franck's discussion of the matter is concerned about a dynamic reality that defies static categories—concerned about faith as *imitatio Christi,* as implantation into God.

A third work from Franck's pen was the *Warring Book of Peace*. Published under the pseudonym of Friedrich Wernstreyt, it was a stanchly pacifist treatise. Peace has declared war against war throughout two hundred pages replete with the opinion of authorities, including the Bible, Augustine, and Luther, but especially Erasmus' *Querela pacis* of 1517. Once again, Franck was willing to use the authority of others, for this made the sentiment obvious, but left him out of the picture: "If they taught too much, then take their bones which have been long venerated as sacred from the altars and monstrances, burn them as heretics and scatter their ashes into the air."[30] The work denounced war categorically. Christ commanded that the sword be done away with. "Thereby he prohibits war for all spiritual persons who strive after perfection."

We can bypass several other works of Franck and simply speak of his last work, published shortly before his death—*Proverbs.* The book, of some 750 pages, considered proverbs and adages of all times and peoples. Erasmus' influence upon Franck was clearly discernible. Large sections came from Erasmus' *Adagia,* though proverbs are common possession and need to be collected somewhere. This Franck did, adding, however, extensively of his own. His arrangement was topical; related proverbs were put together to express their proper meaning. Here Franck's methodology found expression —to compare, to juxtapose, to put alongside one another: thus the true meaning will become obvious. Proverbs were for Franck an authentic expression of the divine spirit. They were, he wrote, "a firm word of God, which God has written and laid into the hearts and mouths of all men."[31]

In the prime of life, death came to Sebastian Franck. After a little more than two-score years, his sojourn on earth ended, though the exact time we cannot tell. Perhaps Franck died of the pestilence which raged through Basel, perhaps his was a less dramatic demise. On October 31, 1542, his property was assessed; probably he had died shortly before that date. The record reads that "on the last day of October inventory was made of the goods and property of Sebastian Franck, a deceased printer, and his wife, Barbara." This inventory listed not only the customary paraphernalia of home and profession, but also a lengthy number of books, most of which undoubtedly belonged to Franck's personal library, with a few perhaps destined for eventual sale. The scope of these books is fascinating—Bibles, Bible commentaries, theological and philosophical works of past and present, books on history, geography, folklore, medicine. The universality of Sebastian Franck is beautifully attested by the wide range of his library.[32]

The New Gospel

Franck's life was thus relatively brief, though by no means uneventful. His various bouts with the civil authorities were dramatic. After his brief parish experience had disillusioned him, Franck chose to live a life aloof from concrete involvements. He was, above all, a man of the pen rather than action, little inclined to change the course of events directly. Undoubtedly he was persuaded that he knew too much about history, and therefore too much about his own time, to do that. Yet his prolific literary output indicated that he did mean to pass something on to his contemporaries and what this was can be put simply: a strikingly new interpretation of the Christian religion.

Needless to say, Franck was deeply involved within the Christian tradition and remained ever, at least verbally, embedded in it. Nonetheless, his attack was radical and when he was done, little of the traditional faith remained.

Franck made the principles of the Christian faith, theretofore regarded as unique, to be the common expression of man's genuine religion everywhere and at all times. Sebastian Franck would have loved the parable of the three rings made so famous in the eighteenth century by Lessing—that fascinating story which tells of a man with three sons and one precious ring. He had two imitations made, lest he disappoint two sons. On his deathbed he called for his three sons and gave them each a ring, leaving each under the impression that he had the real one. Franck would have loved this parable, we said; only he would have insisted that the rings were genuine, indeed, that there were more than the three of Judaism, Christianity, and Islam. Sebastian Franck thought to have found genuine spirituality everywhere. He was not altogether novel in this regard. Some of the Italian Renaissance figures had denied traditional Christian precepts and others were wonderfully fascinated by the religious values of classical antiquity.[33]

Franck was persuaded that his approach was not incompatible with the Christian faith, but indeed its proper expression. He was not concerned primarily to show that heathens, too, are capable of genuine religious experience, but that the Christian faith, when properly understood, and such pagan religious experiences are one and the same. Franck meant to stand outside the established Christian churches but not outside a properly understood Christian faith.

Sebastian Franck argued that the precepts of the Christian faith need not be rigid. He insisted that a positive interpretation of the Christian faith can be found which recognizes diversity of religious belief, both within and without the Christian tradition, and acknowledges the validity of religious insight, no matter where it may be found. Obviously, Franck could not hold to such sentiment without discarding much of the traditional Christian faith. He knew this and yet was not sorry. In postulating this flexibility of the Christian faith, Franck was a herald of the future, for the development of Christian thought since the seventeenth century exhibits such flexibility in surprising fashion. How divergent are today the interpretations of the Christian faith! Barth, Bultmann, Tillich, Bishop Robinson and Altizer are but a few representative names on the rather complicated contemporary theological landscape which signify a wide divergence of orientation; yet they all claim to preach the Christian gospel. And most adherents of the Christian faith have become astoundingly broadminded in their willingness to accept these claims. One need not be a conservative to be able to claim the Christian label. Some will still argue that Adam was a historical personage, that creation took place in seven days, perhaps even that the devil might be combated, as was Luther's strategy, with inkpots. Others will view the creation story or the story of Jesus of Nazareth as symbols of an eternal truth. But, for better or for worse, the traditional rigidity of the Christian faith is gone.

In a way, Sebastian Franck has been vindicated by the development since the sixteenth century, though even today the alternative is still what it was in his days—orthodox Christian dogma or the expression of basic religious truth in new ways. Franck himself argued the latter and thus became the great herald of the future, and Wilhelm Dilthey wrote that Franck's ideas reach the modern world in a hundred different ways.[34]

The exact point at which Franck departed from the traditional Christian consensus is difficult to determine. The bewildering diversity of religious options, both present and past, was undoubtedly a major problem. It is one thing to be confronted with a single alternative, such as, perhaps, medieval man had experienced: one can take it or leave it. It is another—as was the case in the sixteenth century—if the options are manifold and, what is more, mutually exclusive. Sebastian Franck saw this as an inescapable problem. His *Chronicle* of 1531 indicated his encounter with such historical and theological diversity; his *Chronicle of Turkey* of the previous year similarly showed his awareness that the world did not end at the borders of Europe, that there were non-Christian religious traditions whose existence could be ignored, but never denied.

Franck might be called the first "reductionist" of the Christian faith, who reduced this faith to bare essentials. He was too steeped in the Christian tradition to avoid paying at least lip service to it. Moreover, since his time lacked a true historical-critical consciousness, certain matters, nowadays greatly contested, were beyond his concern. Thus Jesus' historicity was for Franck no matter for scrutiny, nor was Jesus' resurrection a special concern. But while he acknowledged the historicity of the Gospels, he discarded the supreme relevance of the historical events themselves. He did not doubt that the events happened as the narratives describe, yet their truth, and thus their significance, would be valid had they *not* so happened. What more revolutionary assertion could have been made?

To add a note of complexity here, one must observe that the

church fathers or even the mystics also emphasized a spiritual interpretation of the facts of the *Heilsgeschichte* long before Sebastian Franck. The point is well taken, of course, but still nowhere were the dogmatic statements made by the church concerning the historical facts questioned. The historical happening formed the backdrop against which the fathers insisted, for example, on the importance of a proper spiritual appropriation of these events. The events in themselves were regarded as unique and important. Franck's perspective was quite the contrary; he saw the events as unimportant, and by no means unique.

Franck's thrust caused the traditional structure of Christian doctrine to tumble like a house of cards—at least, so he thought. If we can trust him, he wanted to be an interpreter of the Christian gospel; nonetheless, it is quite clear that this his gospel, however Christian, in his own mind bore little resemblance to what had traditionally been so regarded.

The Question of Revelation

The first bastion to crumble under the attack was the exclusiveness of revelation. Natural theology had always had a place in Christian theology and no Christian theologian ever thought that the heathen was in complete religious darkness. But such affirmation of a natural knowledge of God was carefully circumscribed, and utilized mainly as a stepping stone to that which could be known all the more splendidly and brilliantly through Christian revelation. It was the exception rather than the rule. Even Zwingli, who among the sixteenth-century reformers was willing to make the greatest concessions in this regard—his sermon on divine providence mentioned Pythagoras, Plato, and Seneca as "pious" heathens—even he was ever cognizant of this basic distinction.

Franck argued, quite to the contrary, the equality of all religious insight. Thus he wrote in the *Paradoxes* that "God is also the God of the heathen," and added that "the impartial God has always held the world in identical estimate; the lover of man has always loved all men equally."[35] God was impartial—this was very important for Franck. "The impartial God is no respecter of persons but is well disposed to those, among all peoples, who do right and fear him. He is and always was also the God of the heathen and always bestowed, impressed and reflected his light, word, grace and Christ upon them." Such a perspective meant, of course, that the essential significance of the Old Testament and even of the New Testament—of relating the story of God's own people—was reinterpreted. "The gracious and impartial God loves, even today, the pagans as well as the Jews and disregards names, persons, and peoples."[36] The pagan philosophers were filled with the Spirit of God, and Cicero taught justification by faith.[37] The Mosaic law is valid, not because of its revelatory character, but because "it is written in the tablet of man's heart."

Revelation thus cannot be exclusive, but must be universal. "God," Franck wrote, "is a freely poured out indwelling goodness, an efficacious power which is in all creatures."[38] What is known to the Christian is potentially known to all men. Franck meant to say that there was no difference between general and special revelation, for both were reflections of God's communication with the spiritually alert person. Accordingly, neither the Old nor the New Testament conveyed a new message.

Franck almost sounded like a true Protestant when he emphasized that the source of religious insight was the "Word of God." But he was far from the early reformers and further yet from Protestant orthodoxy.

To possess the Word is a potential possibility for all men and not a biblical or even Christian prerogative. God has given his Spirit to all men. Franck never ceased to stress this fact and did so with an abundance of imagery that sometimes seemed to get out of hand:

> God has put a paradigm, tinder, sensitivity, light and image of his wisdom, quality and essence into the heart of man in which God sees himself. The Scripture calls this divine image and character the word, will, son, hand, light, life of God, the truth in us. Thus we are capable of God and are, in some measure, of divine quality. The light has been lighted in the lantern of our heart, the treasure lies already in the field, has been laid into the ground of our souls. Whoever allows the lantern to burn and does not prefer the lantern of the flesh, indeed, whoever moves into himself and looks for this treasure, will not find it above the sea nor must look for it in heaven. But the Word, the image of God, is within us.

God has given this Word to all men. The impartiality of God, so important for Franck, made this mandatory—as did the need for a criterion by which all men can be judged.[39] "All men are one man," wrote Franck in the *Paradoxes,* and continued, "the impartial God has created all things for all men in the same fashion and given them the same life and has made, with equal love, not one better or worse by one iota. Otherwise some could have occasion to complain of God."[40] Religious tolerance is one consequence. If genuine religious insight is available to all men, then the external differences prevailing between religious traditions are unimportant and the tolerant recognition of diverging externals is a mandatory consequence. Franck put it this way: "A papist, Lutheran, Zwinglian, Anabaptist, indeed a Turk is my good brother."[41]

Yet even though all men have the Word in their possession, not all are aware of it. The objective fact is of less importance than the subjective appropriation. "A hidden treasure," said Franck, "is of no use."

But what then of the Christian Scripture? If all men, regardless of their possession of Scripture, possess the Word, what function is left? Franck answered by stating that "Scripture will remain an eternal allegory."[42] The scriptural narrative has lost its significance of uniqueness, but its importance as example, paradigm, and illustration remains. Thus Franck wrote in the *Paradoxes* that "what happened in the past, according to the Scriptures, happens daily," and continued, "therefore the entire Bible must be repeated again and again and have one single meaning. Adam's fall, the tree of knowledge, repentance, Christ's death, life, suffering, resurrection do, in their own way, still happen today, as do all the stories of the Bible."

The allegorical interpretation of Scripture—the notion that there is a meaning of the text beyond the literal meaning—has always been afforded an eminent role in the church, especially in early and medieval history. Nonetheless, the point of departure was always the literal, historical meaning; the allegorical meaning was the second layer, the frosting on the cake to make the inside all the more attractive. Franck, on the other hand, was excited by the frosting. The allegorical meaning, abstracted from the empirical event, was for him the truly profound and eternal one. Eternal truth expressed itself in the historical event, but the truth rather than the event is important. Franck asserted that Scripture must be understood neither through the letter nor through unrhymed allegories. He rejected both approaches, for both stressed the priority of the historical event over eternal truth.

The Eternal Christ

Franck's general understanding of Scripture found its specific application in his view of Jesus. That there was a historical figure by that name whose life, death, and even resurrection are adequately described in the Gospels he did not deny. But Jesus' true significance is not found in this historical setting; the eternal truth is far more important. The consequences are crucial, for if the importance of the particular historical event is denied, the universality of redemptive insight can be stressed.

> The histories of Adam and Christ are not Adam and Christ. Therefore there are in all quarters and islands many who are Adam, his flesh and blood . . . though they do not know nor ever heard that there was someone on earth called Adam. Likewise there have been Christians among the heathens of all times . . . even though they do not know that there ever was, or will be, a Christ. Like Job they felt the power of Christ and the grace of God and his word and lived in it. This was sufficiently Christ for them, even though they never heard the history of Christ. The kingdom of God is a power, not a proclamation or the knowledge of a history.

Both Adam and Christ are found in the hearts of all men; both good and bad seed are in the field. Whether a man is called "Adam" or "Christ" will depend on which way he follows. Or to put it another way: "The external Adam and Christ are only an expression of the inward, indwelling Adam or the external Christ." Franck's argument was not, therefore, that unique historical events express eternal truths but, rather, that eternal truth finds illustrative historical expression, never more nobly than in Jesus of Nazareth. Franck always spoke highly of Christ. In him God was exceptionally discernible, he was the manifestation of God. Or, as Franck put it, "everything that God is, knows, wills, has, and can do, has in Christ been placed before us in human form" as the supreme example which illustrates, with exceeding clarity, what is universal. Jesus' history is thus universal history.

Franck was persuaded that the world "continues ever more to crucify the lamb which was killed in the beginning in Abel." Similarly he wrote in the *Paradoxes,* "Christ continues to be crucified daily to this very day; the world will ever remain the world."[43] "Easter and Pentecost do continue, as do Christ's suffering, death and ascension. The true New Testament is an eternal Easter, Sabbath and Pentecost." Man is everlastingly Adam—or Christ. "For what is said concerning God can truly be said concerning Christ, and what is true concerning Christ will not be found missing or fabricated in his members."

Obviously, traditional Christology has been discarded here. Adam's fall is not a historically unique event, but universal truth. Likewise, redemption is not based on a unique event; it is also universal truth. The restriction of redemption to a single event and, what is more, to its description in a single book, curtails and indeed denies the necessary universality of redemption. Those who have lived unaware of the Scripture, either before or outside of it, Franck argues, would then be condemned. Accordingly, "to know and believe the history of Christ is not justifying faith." Even as God does not condemn on account of the sin of someone else, so likewise will the righteousness of someone else—even Christ—not save us.[44]

Thus Sebastian Franck was at work with his ax cutting down traditional theological concepts. Even his concept of God was different. It was dependent in some measure upon the predilection of the mystic tradition to speak about God largely in negatives, though this was not the heart of the matter for Franck, who stressed God's immutability. God is without will and does not change. "God is and wills, what everybody is and wills and yet he is God in everything: will-less, name-less, affect-less, immovable. It only appears to us as if he willed this or that; he is in himself the immutable and will-less God."[45]

Franck made one important observation with regard to God's immutability: God is unchangeable love. "Even the furious Jove is good." Franck's strong affirmations rendered impossible the traditional Christian notions of God's wrath and God's love which underlie the soteriological drama described by Christian theology. God must not be satisfied—"the unchangeable God is not angry with anybody." If man had truly understood God as benevolent and loving rather than wrathful, it would have been unnecessary for God to send Christ. There was no necessity of a divine-human reconciliation initiated by God who canceled man's punishment because of the work of Christ. Nor is there a need for God to fight, in Christ, against the powers and principalities of this world. Such views were, for Franck, sophistry.

Man's redemption accordingly takes place not *extra nos,* but *in nobis*. Man is not credited with something which he lacks, but utilizes his potential. Clearly Franck's view of man formed the necessary corollary. Man has retained his freedom: in his translation of Erasmus' *Praise of Folly,* Franck wrote that "we have fallen in nothing, but we are somewhat weaker in strength, lazier in knowledge, more prone to evil." Man must be a free agent, for only if this is the case can God be cleared from the charge of being "the cause of all evil, an arch-sinner, the father of all the Godless." Man must accept or reject God's offer of freedom and redemption. "God is the one who sends his grace to our door, who knocks, woos and desires us. It is up to the bride whether or not she wants to let in the suitor and take him to be her husband." Much like the medieval tradition, Franck related human freedom to divine omniscience by observing that omniscience does not mean all-effectiveness. "If I stand on top of a tower and see a man go through a gate and see robbers on the other side who will kill him, I know that the man will be killed, but my knowledge has no effect upon the man."

Such was Sebastian Franck's contribution to the realm of theology. Hopefully the brevity of our exposition did not obscure its revolutionary character, though it may have passed over its inconsistencies rather glibly. But neither the details nor the inconsistencies are as important as Franck's departure from a common tradition. He may have been but a solitary voice in the wilderness, repudiated and all too quickly forgotten, but Christian theology was not to be the same thereafter.

The Writer of History

Before we take leave of Franck we need to recall that he also was a historian of stature. Melanchthon, no mean historian himself, called him "indoctae conditor historiae"—writer of an unskilled history—but that disparaging assessment may have been the result of professorial envy. Franck copied much from others, but despite such extensive plagiarization—or perhaps because of it—Franck advanced a number of important new insights. There was the "impartiality" of his historical writings: "I have written this history truly without affectation," he wrote in his *German Chronicle*. "All men are equally dear to me."[46] Franck seems almost a forerunner of Ranke in his concern to report history "as it actually happened." Thus he remarked, "I do not want to blame or praise anybody, chide him true or false. Nor do I want to announce or judge what I believe or think. I want to relate the facts as becomes a writer of history." Obviously he did not want to do away with the difference between true and false, good and evil. But he felt that precisely his impartial description afforded the best method for making the proper distinction.

Moreover Franck was the first person to apply the religious insights of the Reformation to historiography. His *Chronicle* of 1531 was a distinctly "Protestant" work, for the story of the church prior to the Reformation was not narrated as the visible manifestation of true religion on earth, but as the human, all too human, story of aberration, weakness, and corruption. The reader found little of pristine splendor, but much of latter-day apostasy in Franck's description of the medieval church. Historical evidence was marshaled to support the theological claims of the Reformation. But Franck did more than that. He formulated a hermeneutical principle for understanding the history of the Christian church. He argued that true spirituality is found in despised, condemned, and rejected form among the heretics, the outcasts, the dissenters. His point was subtle, but profound. He did not mean to say that within the institutional church, so often corrupted, true spirituality could be found. Quite to the contrary, Franck argued that precisely wherever there prevailed official condemnation and rejection, God was present. Thus he wrote in the preface to the *Chronicle of Heretics* that "one fears many pious Christians are found among the heretics"; or, a little later, "therefore they stand with great honor in this list."[47] Again and again Franck asserted in his *Paradoxes* that "figura contra veritatem"—appearance is contrary to truth. Thus his *Chronicle of Heretics* rather than his *Chronicle of the Popes,* is the history of the true people of God. Franck's history might well be called "metahistory," which is to say that for him the true meaning of events lies not in these external events but in something beyond them. Hermann Bischof, the first to examine Franck's stature as a historian last century, accordingly found a direct connection between Franck and Hegel's historical universalism.

One final comment remains to be made. Franck deserves credit for having delineated the structure of history not in terms of an external teleology—not even traditional Christian teleology for which the historical event of Jesus Christ is central—but in terms of the inner coherence of events and personalities. His *Chronicle,* a history of the world, was not structured along the lines of the Bible but along lines Franck found more congenial for his narrative. There is no uniquely Christian or secular motif that provides a grandiose teleological scheme.

Franck saw history as a continuing and, above all, unresolved struggle between good and evil. Thus all histories are, in the final analysis, only one history. "Vita una et eadem omnibus," Franck said at one place—and as there is only one life so there is only one history and indeed only one religion. The struggle between good and evil is a universal struggle, found at all times and all places, in the Old Testament as well as in classical antiquity. It is unresolved, for it ever continues with no hope of coming to a drastic and decisive end in time. Indeed, some of Franck's writings suggest that the forces of evil were growing ever stronger. "I see that the world has come to its end, that this aged, evil and concerned time has become so vile and bold that it has turned its ears away from truth, has become completely insane, and moves along the precipice."[48] In the *World*

Book Franck wrote, "It would not be surprising if he who looks at this matter seriously has his heart break in his body because of tears. . . . Thus the world jokes (*gaukelt*)—as a drunken fool."[49] Men are "laughter, Halloween prank and fable before God."

History, then, is not *Heilsgeschichte,* a comforting solace of soteriological meaningfulness. It is a reflection of man. Thus it is like the Bible—and Franck's title "Geschichts*bibel*" for his "history" was profoundly appropriate. To study history is to obtain wisdom, precisely because its happenings are so clear and stereotyped, because there is in history nothing new under the sun, or as Sebastian Franck puts it, "since nothing may take place which has not in olden days happened." Franck accordingly denounces—one is almost reminded of Nietzsche's attack upon "antiquarian history"—all those who "know only mere history, works and deeds."[50] The scriptural motto on the title page of the *Chronicle* was a quotation from the Psalms: "Come and behold the works of the Lord." History offers a profound insight into life and the historian is best conversant with the issues—to use Adolf von Harnack's famous phrase, the "royal judge." History is "the master of life."[51]

A Solitary Faith

Sebastian Franck—theologian and historian, or better: interpreter of life. We leave him with the feeling that, no matter how profound his understanding of a genuinely spiritual Christian religion, in the end he must be found wanting—and for a good reason. His disregard of the historical and empirical forms of Christianity meant that he had to go through life divorced from these empirical forms. Of course, he did so willfully and almost joyfully. His poem "concerning the four main churches of which one repudiates the others" makes it obvious that he attempted to label virtue what otherwise was considered vice. Wrote he, "we must unlearn everything which we have learned from the days of your youth from our papists, we must change everything that we have received, taken in and considered true from the pope, Luther, and Zwingli."[52] Similarly he wrote in his famous letter to his fellow radical, Campanus, "I am indeed persuaded that, after the death of the apostles the external church of Christ, with its gifts and sacraments, disappeared from the earth into heaven where it is now hidden in spirit and in truth. During the past 1400 years no true external church or efficacious sacraments have existed." Even as the empirical Jesus or the empirical Bible are only of secondary importance, so is the empirical church often the incarnation of evil rather than of good. Franck was persuaded that this was the lesson of history.

Perhaps Franck advocated a sixteenth-century equivalent of a community church, and this latter-day ecclesiastical innovation may owe an indirect measure of debt to Franck. In his letter to Campanus he wrote that "all outward things and ceremonies which were customary in the church of the apostles, have been done away with and are not to be restituted." Franck radicalized Protestantism because he categorically asserted the centrality of the individual. Any religious socialization he affirmed was the congenial friendship of impartial, that is, uncommitted, intellectuals.

Franck's attitude meant, of course, that his own interpretation and perspective were unable to become sociologically relevant. To put it succinctly, if everybody in the sixteenth century had been a Sebastian Franck, we today would likely be heathen. The tedious footwork of passing on the faith from generation to generation would have got lost in the shuffle. That is to say, for better or for worse, a faith needs to take on empirical form in order to survive; it must let itself become exposed to biting winds of time, to degeneration, decay, perversion—and revival. It must do so, for if it does not, it ceases to exist. Sebastian Franck was unable or unwilling to see this crucial point. Nor does he seem to have fathomed fully that it had been, after all, this empirical church, whose true existence for fourteen hundred years he denied, that had nurtured him and provided him with the tools with which to fashion his own faith. One must grant Franck that he was at least consistent in refraining from creating a new tradition. His prolific literary output must not be seen as a colportage effort, but simply as a move to put, as it were, the facts before the people. Wrote he, "I never sought any following, sect, disciples or group nor even wanted it, but a few, but good friends and acquaintances, honorable, impartial and courageous people."[53] And Franck was consistent in yet another way: since religious insight was universal, there was no need for a definite religious tradition—and certainly no debt to it.

These comments are not meant to give a brief for historical continuity. No doubt there are times when the disruption of the historical continuum is legitimate and no one standing in the Protestant tradition can deny this. But as long as men come to a profound religious experience within the context of such empirical reality, indeed, as long as even men like Sebastian Franck cannot deny their own debt to the institution which they despise, all Sebastian Francks of history must be found wanting—not because of their lack of ideas, brilliance, or thoughts, but because of their failure to recognize that in this world even noble spiritual truths must adjust themselves to the humdrum realities of everyday life.

Perhaps Franck sensed all this, for it must be more than mere coincidence that he is in the end a pessimist. Stadelmann's brilliant study of Franck painted too dreary a picture which suffered, above everything else, from the fatal error of placing Franck at the end of a waning Middle Ages, rather than in the middle of the Reformation.[54] But when all is said and done, the picture of Franck *is* dark and dreary. Thus, Franck delineated in his *Paradoxes* with ever new illustrations, suggestions, and descriptions, the irrationality of life. God can be Satan, and Satan, God; Christ can be Antichrist, and Antichrist, Christ—depending upon the vantage point. "God turns everything around," Franck wrote. "Thus one can speak as unrhymed or true as one wishes; it is both true and false depending on how it is viewed—against the judgment of God or the world."[55] Such paradoxical relativity remains as a darkening shadow. Spiritualism turns into pessimism; at the end of the insight that none of the existing forms of religion has the truth stands resignation. On the surface, Scripture fails to provide the answer in the quest for religious certainty; it is enigmatic, uncertain, contradictory. History likewise appears to be an inadequate guide; for too often have falsehood and evil triumphed over truth.

Franck's gospel was thus sad news rather than good news. Perhaps this is the price Franck has to pay for disregarding the traditional Christian dogma which knows, to be sure, of the profundity of man's evil—such as Franck was never willing to concede—but also knows of a power of victory that was likewise alien to Franck. By attempting to be all things to all men, by granting the possibility of authentic religious experience everywhere, namely, in man, history, and Scripture, Franck lost the certainty of religious experience where Christianity traditionally had known it, namely, in the church or in the Bible.

Franck's theology sought to be one of the "golden mean." Since it did not know of dark shadows, it could not know of brilliant light. There is a certain glow in Franck's religion, for man is still in the image of God and the stark gloom of human depravity is rejected; God is unchangeable and unerring love. But the backdrop to all this is pessimism, because it is none too easy to reach this understanding. Franck lacks the exuberance of Catholicism, which knows how to appropriate truth in the Church, or the certainty of Protestantism, which rests securely upon Scripture. For Franck truth is everywhere—in nature, history, Scripture—for those who know how to listen. Only those who know how to listen will hear the divine Word.

Perhaps we can call Sebastian Franck the Socrates of sixteenth-century theologians, if for no other reason than that such a combination of Athens and Jerusalem would be very much in keeping with his outlook. All his books and writings impress one, foremostly by their questions rather than by their answers. A Dutch scholar has called Sebastian Franck the "franctireur" of the Reformation—a guerrilla fighter—which is another way of expressing the same sentiment.

Franck asked many questions, but gave few answers. Since his time some of what he argued for has become theological commonplace. Such may not have occurred through his stimulus, but even if the causes were different Sebastian Franck would feel very much at home in the twentieth century. Or would he? Somehow or other one suspects that if Sebastian Franck were to live in our own day he would, once again, be the lonely outsider. He would dismiss, once more, the easy clichés rampant in the market place, university halls and pulpits, even though they might outwardly agree with what he himself stood for in his own time. But if history, and man, are ever the same—as he himself so tellingly argued—then he who walked the solitary road in the days of the sixteenth century would surely walk that same road in our day.

3. The Founding Father:

George Fox

> And the Lord opened to me at that place, and let me see a great people in white raiment by a river's side, coming to the Lord, and the place was near John Blaykling's where Richard Robinson lived.
>
> —George Fox, *Journal*

The Man in Leather Breeches

George Fox embodied a religious experience uncommon in Christian history and fashioned a new ecclesiastical tradition against the hostile opposition of the state and two established churches. He did so not by sophisticated theological argumentation, though he was no mean theologian, but by a tireless communication of his own religious experience wherever the opportunity presented itself—and for him this was always.

He was a remarkable man. Voltaire compared him flippantly with Jesus, as did William James, who, in his treatment of the *Varieties of Religious Experience,* placed both in the illustrious company of Buddha, Mohammed, and St. Francis. For Thomas Carlyle, in turn, Fox was the most remarkable phenomenon of modern history, more important, as a matter of fact, than "the Battle of Austerlitz, Waterloo, Peterloo, or any other Battle."[1] Carlyle's hero Diogenes Teufelsdroeckh—"devil's manure" in a somewhat literal translation of Carlyle's Germanism—was fascinated by Fox "making to himself a suit of Leather" and reflected that "working on tanned hides, amid pincers, paste-horns, rosin, swine-bristles, and a nameless flood of rubbish, this youth had, nevertheless, a living Spirit belonging to him." Macaulay in his *History of England,* on the other hand, spoke of

Fox's "strange theology" and of his mind as being "in the most unhappy of all states, that is to say, too much disordered for liberty, and not sufficiently disordered for Bedlam."[2] Such differing assessments of Fox could easily be multiplied, though the latest of the encyclopedic histories of England, Winston Churchill's *History of the English-Speaking Peoples,* discreetly omits Fox altogether.

When Fox appeared on the English scene, a theological free-for-all of considerable proportion was under way. The Anglican Establishment had been dislodged and a freedom of theological discussion prevailed which allowed everyone—the word must almost be taken literally—to get into the act. It still was illegal to interrupt a sermon in church, but afterward anyone could rise and present his dissenting point of view: shades of English democracy or the priesthood of all believers in action, though one suspects that Martin Luther would have raised his hands in horror. Such freedom to speak undoubtedly led to a willingness to listen. Fox found a fertile soil in England. The fascinating aspect of Fox's public ministry was that whatever response he encountered occurred on the grass-roots level. To be sure, the printing presses helped greatly to propagate Fox's message. But, above all, Fox's direct and personal contact with the man in the street proved to be utterly persuasive.

England, and perhaps the Christian church, had not witnessed anything like George Fox before. To the onlooker George Fox was a bizarre, eccentric, and strange phenomenon evoking pity rather than sympathy and curiosity rather than involvement. Fox's life was dramatic enough; his principles were sensational. He cheerfully "demythologized" everyday speech, cultural as well as ecclesiastical. The months of the year and the days of the week lost their pagan names and received simple numerical designations. No longer were Sundays —with the reference to the sun-god—or March with the reminder of the pagan war-god Mars—permissible. Quite prosaically Fox spoke of "First Day" and "First Month." Everybody was addressed with "thee" and "thou," as the plural "you" used for a single person was an expression of social hypocrisy as well as grammatically incorrect, a conviction Fox ventured to prove in a rather ambitious work.[3] Churches became "steeplehouses" and clergymen of whatever tradition were "priests"; men short on commitment but long on claim were called "professors." Social custom was unbiblical hypocrisy; Christendom was completely perverted. George Fox's brand of Christianity was, despite all its exuberance, austere. The quietness of a Quaker gathering in a plain meeting house graphically illustrates this point. Such a gathering expresses a deeply spiritual understanding of the Christian faith, though one that finds little worshipful meaning in a Palestrina mass, a Bach cantata, or a Gothic cathedral. George Fox could never have written the *Pilgrim's Progress;* he took life and himself far too drably and this was his strength as well as his weakness.

And yet there was more than eccentricity in George Fox, even though at first glance it may seem that here was but another addition to a religious scene already somewhat crowded with self-styled dissenters. The "man in leather breeches" contributed a dramatically new interpretation of the Christian religion.

We do well to remind ourselves that the historical residue of seventeenth-century religious England is astoundingly small in terms of new ecclesiastical traditions; aside from the Baptists, the Presbyterians, and the Congregationalists only the Quakers survived the biting winds of time. The reason is simple—the Quakers had a leader of outstanding proportions; the others who failed did not.

Fox's powerful and persuasive personality offers the clue to unraveling his movement—for a movement there was! How strange; one would hardly expect a spiritualistic interpretation of the Christian religion to lead to a new religious tradition. In Fox's case the combination of a spiritualizing religion and a new moral code provided the kind of elasticity which made it possible, a little bit like an inflated balloon, to bounce from one side to the other. If the insistence upon the "inner light" was sociologically destructive, then the simple precepts of Fox's moral evangel—the hat that remained immovable on Fox's head, the speech that would affirm nothing beyond the mere "yea" and "nay," the pacifism—always provided the empirical identification that made for a new tradition.

The Quest for Certainty

Basically, Fox's problem was neither how to find a gracious God, as it had been for Luther, nor even how to live the good life, as it had been for the sixteenth-century Anabaptists. His problem was to make the God of Scripture a living certainty and to make sure that his faith was authoritatively founded. He was not the only one in his day beset by such problems. John Bunyan, too, asked in his *Grace Abounding:* "How can you tell but that the Turks had as good scriptures to prove their Mahomet the Saviour as we have to prove our Jesus is? . . . Every one doth think his own religion rightest, both Jews and Moors and Pagans! And how if all our faith and Christ and Scriptures should be but a think-so too?"[4] Fox's solution pointed to "the light within," the immediate communication with God. It was not Fox, however, but the Scotsman Robert Barclay who in his *Apology for the True Christian Divinity* of 1670 developed in standard theological terms—even to the point of sounding like a true Scholastic—this notion. The credit for its initial exposition and formulation must go to Fox, who was overwhelmed by the light being in all men.

The emphasis upon the inner light was strangely juxtaposed with an emphasis upon the Scriptures. With the exception of the *Journal,* most of Fox's writings are almost biblical homilies, and the points he makes are, as a rule, supported by the kind of proof-texting that would become a Puritan divine. Indeed, a contemporary observer reported that if the Bible were lost one could reconstruct it through the mouth of Fox. The fact that Fox actively pursued the translation of Scripture into modern languages is yet another example of his trust in biblical authority.[5] Yet despite his concern for Scripture, Fox's connection to what might be called classical Protestantism is a tenuous one, for the true Protestant ever insisted that *Scriptura sui interpres*—Scripture interprets itself. Fox's contemporary, Richard Baxter, put the priority into classic words: "We must not try the Scriptures by our most spiritual apprehensions, but our apprehensions by the Scriptures."[6] Fox made the "inner light" autonomous only in unimportant matters, such as where to go on a given day, or what to say to a given person. In important matters the "inner light" was constrained and directed by the Scriptures. Fox found not only that his "revelations" agreed essentially with one another, but also that they agreed with Scripture. This substantiated his insights. Thus he wrote in his *Journal:* "And when I had openings, they answered one another and answered the scriptures; for I had great openings of the scriptures. And when I was in troubles, one trouble also answered to another."[7] For the observer, however, this raises the question of priority. One suspects that Fox's intense preoccupation with Scripture antedated what he subsequently came to understand as immediate divine revelation. At any rate, the two were identical in his mind.

Fox was persuaded that he had untied the Gordian knot of finding certainty in diversity, but his contemporaries failed to share his enthusiasm. He could point to the ancient Christian tradition that the Holy Spirit actively aided the believer in his understanding of the Sacred Writ. But he posited a priority that was unacceptable, inasmuch as it solved one question by raising a more serious one. In order to preserve the undisputed priority of the "inner light" over Scripture, Fox had to argue that it was in all men, not merely in those who had been in contact with the Christian gospel. But this raised the incisive question whether he was not merely talking about a natural light or conscience. Fox himself mentioned that in a conversation with Oliver Cromwell he "turned him to the light of Christ, who had enlightened every man, that cometh into the world: and he said it was a natural light." But Fox's response was unmistakable: "And he showed him the contrary and how it was divine and spiritual from Christ the spiritual and heavenly man, which was called the life in Christ, the Lord and the light in us." In refuting a Scottish minister by the name of Lodowick Simerell, Fox wrote pointedly that "the light which every one that cometh into the world is enlightened with, is not conscience, for the light was before anything was made, or conscience named."[8] One difficulty was that Fox commented on the content of this "inner light" in a way that—despite its nomenclature—was hardly christological, though Fox's references were directly related to Jesus' statements in the Gospel. "Every one of you hath a light from Christ," he wrote, "which lets you see you should not lie, nor do wrong to any, nor swear, nor curse, nor take God's name in vain nor steal. It is the light that shows you these evil deeds."[9] Fox was ready to give empirical proof for his contention of the universality of the inner light. During his visit to the American colonies he encountered a physician who denied that the inner light was in every man. Fox met an American Indian whom he asked if there was something in him that chided him for lying or doing evil. The Indian affirmed this and Fox was satisfied that he had proved his point.[10]

Fox shows that it is far easier to discern the weakness of the existing positions than to offer a constructive alternative. His theology indicated rather persuasively that he was unable to make his idea of the "inner light" constructive for a distinctly Christian theology and ethics without referring to the Bible. And thus he was back where he had started. The more profound "openings" of Fox—for example, nonswearing or pacifism—were but reiteration of what can be found in Scripture. Fox himself was not bothered by this dependence; for him the consensus authenticated both. It meant practically that Fox only appropriated personally, through his "openings," the Scriptures.

On the other hand, the autonomous character of the "inner light" could be stressed. But this raised at once the problem of distinguishing the "inner light" from conscience. Moreover the specifically Christian quality of the "inner light" could then not be properly established.

Fox's story is related, in large measure, in his *Journal*. The facts of his life could be picked up, easily enough, from other sources; the inner story, however, requires the *Journal*. Dictated at the age of fifty to his stepson-in-law, it is a lengthy account of his public ministry, interspersed with documents, personal reflections, and gleanings of spiritual truths. It has its own peculiar terminology—"steeple-houses," "priests," "professors," "convincements," and "openings."

Its style is racy, though frequently it reads more like a Baedeker than a work of spiritual provenance. The reader, confronted with a seemingly endless list of English villages and towns, with multitudinous and in a sense stereotyped instances of persuasive proclamation, wishes that Fox, as indeed Tolstoy or some other verbose writers, might have made the valid point in less space. The *Journal*, at any rate, is *sui generis*, though it could be called a combination of Augustine's *Confessions*, Francis Xavier's reports from India, and John Wesley's *Journal*. Keeping diaries or writing autobiographies was a favorite seventeenth-century English pastime, and was often pursued by religious men with great seriousness; Fox was here only a child of his time. But religious writers of autobiographies must be possessed by a conviction that their lives showed the presence and power of God; otherwise time, ink, and paper would be wasted. George Fox possessed that sense; it speaks in his actions and from every page of the *Journal*.

Fox wrote more than the *Journal*. He wrote voluminously, more than two hundred tracts and pamphlets. If we add to this a huge correspondence, we find that Fox, like other great figures in church history, was able to combine an extensive literary production with an indefatigable public ministry. Perhaps his literary efforts show a resultant wear and tear; there are probably few men in the history of the Christian church who are known so well and read so little. Fox's historical significance hardly stems from his literary production. If we seek it there, we shall be disappointed. George Fox caused no theological revolution, though not all theologizing is of one kind. Religious writings can convey a tightly knit theological argument—as illustrated by Karl Barth. They can also convey a devotional or practical mood or atmosphere. Fox's writings belong in this second category.

Unusual Beginnings

"I was born in the month called July in the year 1624, at Drayton-in-the-Clay in Leicestershire. My father's name was Christopher Fox; he was by profession a weaver, an honest man, and there was a Seed of God in him." Thus George Fox recounted, with characteristic language and attention to the essential, his own background. He passed over his childhood rather quickly; still the important elements stand out. George Fox must have been an unusual child, a boy of rare spiritual sensitivity, surely the result of the temper of his home. Too often a pious home only yields filial resentment; here it brought profound spirituality. Moreover, such domestic piety was no maternal prerogative, but was in both father and mother—his father was known as "righteous Christer" in the village and his mother was, as George reflected, "of the stock of the martyrs." At another place in the *Journal* Fox observes that he did "in verity love her as ever one could a mother; for she was a good, honest, virtuous and right-natured woman" (p. 673).

George Fox recalled his youth as having been rather exceptional. At an age when his peers probably played the seventeenth-century equivalent of cowboys and Indians, he had "a gravity and stay of mind and spirit not usual in children" (p. 1). At the age of eleven he knew "pureness and righteousness, for while I was a child I was taught how to walk to be kept pure" (p. 1). This comment on the opening page of the *Journal* supplies a characteristic of Fox's entire life. As Rufus M. Jones observed, Fox never appears to have undergone any travail over his shortcomings or sins.[11] If "sin" is thus absent from Fox's theological vocabulary, the corollary "grace" is not prominent either.

George Fox's spiritual pilgrimage was thus unlike that of many other figures in Christian history for whom a distinct "conversion" allowed a contrast between a spiritually empty life before this experience and a "new life" afterward. Fox tells the readers of his *Journal* that he knew "purity and righteousness" from his childhood. We will note presently that he, too, had a profound religious experience but that it was *sui generis*. There can be little doubt that Fox's theology was influenced by his own spiritual background. The Pauline tension between Law and Gospel, between sin and grace, never characterized him. The synoptic motif of discipleship is prominent in Fox's message—a profound motif of the New Testament.

Not surprisingly, this pious and sensitive boy was thought by his relatives to be proper material for the ministry. In the end, however, others—Fox leaves us wondering who they were—argued more tellingly for the economic side of life and young George was given as apprentice to a shoemaker who also "dealt in wool." This business association lasted for several years and is described by Fox in the *Journal* with an air of economic self-righteousness: because of him the shoemaker prospered; when he left, economic disaster struck. Such curious economic theory is, incidentally, characteristic of Fox. Throughout the *Journal* it appears to be the most natural thing for Fox that his enemies could not prosper, and one alternatively admires and denounces Fox for such uncomplicated sentiment.

At age nineteen George Fox left his "relations and brake off all familiarity or fellowship with young or old" (p. 3). We do not know what prompted this. George himself said that he did so "at the command of God"—but verifying this claim is obviously beyond the historian's competence. Evelyn Underhill's comment about Francis of Assisi and Richard Rolle that they "ran away to God as other lads have run away to sea" can be applied to George Fox. Fox sought spiritual certainty.

Fox's spiritual turmoil of that time is mentioned only briefly in the *Journal*. Fox speaks of his "great misery and trouble," mentions that he "was tempted almost to despair," that "all was dark and under the chains of darkness," that he spent many nights in walking (pp. 4 and 5). But he does not fully explain his problem.

His family, to which he returned after one year, suggested matrimony or the army—either apparently a timeless cure for despondent young men. George Fox responded that he "must get wisdom" (p. 4) and thereby presumably ruled out either suggestion. A clergyman in turn advised tobacco or singing but, as Fox wrote in the *Journal*, "Tobacco was a thing I did not love and Psalms I was not in an estate to sing" (p. 6). What made matters worse was the fact that this "priest"—at all odds a lonely or talkative soul—passed on Fox's troubles to his servants. Soon the "milk lasses," as George Fox called them, knew about his state of mind—a publicity which hardly helped him. He traveled seven miles to see another minister but found him "like an empty, hollow cask" (p. 6), and that was that. Undismayed, he sought out another divine with whom he conversed while walking in the man's garden. When Fox accidentally stepped on a flower bed, "the minister . . . flew into a rage as if his house had been on fire" (p. 63). Another "priest" suggested blood-letting!

A certain discrepancy in Fox's recollections must be noted. On the one hand, there are almost exuberant expressions of spiritual self-confidence with respect to his youth; on the other, one observes an element of seeking, of despair, of uncertainty. It is difficult to reconcile these two aspects. In no way was his an ordinary "conversion" experience; the insistence upon his righteousness from the days of his youth makes this obvious. All the same, Fox testified in the *Journal* to a profound spiritual experience:

And when all my hopes in them and in all men were gone so that I had nothing outwardly to help me, nor could tell what to do, then, Oh then, I heard a voice which said "There is one, even Christ Jesus, that can speak to thy condition," and when I heard it my heart did leap for joy. Then the Lord did let me see why there was none upon the earth that could speak to my condition, namely that I might give him all the glory; for all are concluded under sin and shut up in unbelief. . . . And this I knew experimentally (p. 11).

From the lengthy description in the *Journal*—repetitive, at times incoherent, with factual descriptions intermingled with mystic visions and devotional exclamations—several factors emerge. For one, Fox leaves little doubt about the profundity of his problem. He speaks about his "great trouble and temptation" indeed, about his "deepest miseries." Yet the problem was not, as one might expect, a deep cognizance of sin. Fox's description in the *Journal* suggests that he was profoundly perturbed that God was not a living reality in his life. This awareness was the cause of his troubles, and the pages of the *Journal* describe his quest. "There did a pure fire appear in me," Fox wrote, after he had crushed the thirst "after the creatures" and pursued only the thirst "after the Lord the creator." Fox felt a divine "spirit" in his life and he understood this "spirit" in christological terms. It was the "spirit of Christ" and it dwelt within him.

Fox looked for religious certainty and his discovery was the "experimentally" known Christ. Interestingly, he did not tediously cover the spectrum of ecclesiastical options in seventeenth-century England —he remarked coyly that "to be bred at Oxford or Cambridge was not enough" to make a man a minister (p. 7)—but resolutely adopted an alternative which was his own. Since it was his own, he was able to proclaim it with conviction.

Nonetheless, the question of possible influences upon Fox deserves consideration. William Penn, in his introduction to the first edition of the *Journal,* remarked that Fox was "no man's copy" (p. xliii), and Fox himself commented that he undertook to travel his path "without the help of any man, book, or writing" (p. 11). Perhaps one should take these comments at their face value, although, of course, historians have a professional interest in establishing lines of influence. The seventeenth-century English scene was replete with a bewildering diversity of sectarian groupings—all the way from the Baptists, Seekers, and Ranters to the Muggletonians, Sabbatarians, Millenarians, and Fifth Monarchy Men. Thomas Edwards' *Gangroena* of 1646 enumerated no less than 176 heresies in England, and John Milton reflected that "now the time seems come, wherein Moses the great Prophet may sit in heav'n rejoycing to see that memorable and glorious wish of his fulfill'd, when not only our sev'nty Elders, but all the Lord's people are become Prophets." In one way or another George Fox must have been influenced by the climate of opinion of his time. The German historian Theodor Sippell, who devoted a lifetime to the study of the backgrounds of Quakerism, called attention to John Everard, William Dell, John Saltmarsh, and the Ranters as the spiritual ancestors of George Fox. John W. Graham argued for parallels between John Wycliff and George Fox, and Paul Held pointed to the importance of the early seventeenth-century German mystic Jacob Boehme.[12] Sippell's suggestion, in particular, has much in its favor.

George Fox was undoubtedly aware of the religious ferment of his time; yet as he himself saw it, his tool was pre-eminently the Bible. In the *Journal* he asserted that among "priests" and "separate preachers" there was "none among them all that could speak to my condition" (p. 11), that he kept himself "much as a stranger" (p. 10) in his wanderings, that he "fasted much, and walked abroad in solitary places many days, and often took [his] Bible and went and sat in hollow trees and lonesome places till night came on; and frequently in the night walked mournfully about [by himself]" (p. 9). Fox's travail is reminiscent of the opening paragraph of Bunyan's *Pilgrim's Progress,* for he, too, was a "pilgrim" with a "book" to an eternal city.

The Public Ministry

At this point the story of George Fox could well have ended—if the inner experience had remained Fox's private affair. But it did not. And so the life of George Fox, shoemaker's apprentice, seeker and finder of God, became a chapter in the religious history of England. Fox proceeded to share his experience with others, persuaded that he had found the answer to the pressing religious problem of his day. Thus began his evangelistic mission which from that point on constituted his life. Fortunately he possessed, as he called it, "wherewith both to keep himself from being chargeable to others, and to administer something to the necessities of others" (p. 7), a happy and fortunate fact enabling him to pursue his evangelistic work, disregarding economic considerations.

What was George Fox's proclamation? The *Journal* indicates that Fox had both a message and also a way of proclaiming it: God forbade him "to put off my hat to any, high or low," to address with "thee" and "thou" "all men and women, without any respect to rich or poor, great or small." About the content of his proclamation Fox was equally clear. "I was sent to turn people from darkness to the light that they might receive Christ Jesus, for to as many as should receive him in his light, I saw that he would give power to become the sons of God. . . . And I was to direct people to the Spirit that gave forth the Scriptures, by which they might be led into all Truth" (p. 34). Or again: "Now, when the Lord God and his son, Jesus Christ, did send me forth into the world, to preach his everlasting gospel and kingdom, I was glad that I was commanded to turn all people to that inward light, spirit, and grace, by which all might know their salvation." This would mean separation "from all the world's fellowships," "from the world's religions," "from Jewish ceremonies and from heathenish fables" (pp. 35 f.).

The beginning of Fox's public ministry is described in the *Journal* with a characteristic air of self-confidence. The occasion was his presence at a meeting of Baptists at Broughton in Leicestershire. "And the Lord opened my mouth, and his everlasting Truth was declared among them, and the power of the Lord was over them all. For in that day the Lord's power began to spring, and I had great openings in the Scriptures" (p. 19). Afterward, Fox recalled "a report went abroad of me that I was a young man that had a discerning spirit; whereupon many came to me from far and near, professors, priests, and people. And the Lord's power brake forth; and I had great openings, and prophecies, and spake unto them of the things of God, and they heard with attention and silence, and went away, and spread the fame thereof" (p. 21). Fox mentioned in the *Journal* that a man named Brown "had great prophecies and sights upon his death-bed" of Fox (p. 20)—fortunate corroborating evidence for Fox's self-esteem. The result of this initial proclamation was, in Fox's language, "great convincement," including that of "one of the wickedest" men in Mansfield, "one who was a common drunkard, a noted whore-master, and a rhyme-master" (p. 27), raising at once the question of the relation of this last activity—in Fox's mind—to the other two!

Soon thereafter Fox had his first dramatic clashes with those of his contemporaries who were not under "convincement." One Sunday morning, in 1649, Fox found himself on a hill outside Nottingham and saw the "great steeplehouse," a "great and idolatrous temple" (p. 39). God told him "thou must cry against yonder great idol," and this Fox proceeded to do. The people he met "looked like fallow ground," and the minister "like a great lump of earth." The sermon pointed to the Scriptures as the "touchstone and judge" by which all doctrines were to be tried. Fox recalled:

> Now the Lord's power was so mighty upon me and so strong in me that I could not hold but was made to cry and say, Oh no, it is not in the Scriptures and was commanded to tell them that God did not dwell in temples made with hands. But I told them what it was, namely, the Holy Spirit by which the holy men of God gave forth the Scriptures whereby opinion, religions, and judgments were to be tried. Now as I spoke thus amongst them the officers came and took me away and put me into prison, a pitiful stinking place where the wind brought all the stench of the house of office in the place, where the stench of the place was in my head and throat many days after (p. 40).

Fox's first clash with the law, and his initial acquaintance with a prison! In both he was to become an expert.

No sooner had Fox been released from prison than a new and embarrassingly similar incident awaited him. The town was Mansfield and the place again a "steeplehouse." Fox eagerly pointed out in the *Journal* that "the priest had done" (p. 44) when he in turn declared "the Truth to the priest and people" (p. 44)—and after the sermon, anybody could propound such comments as seemed appropriate. In this instance the people in the congregation must have felt, somehow or other, that Fox did not mean to play by their rules and they let him have it. The rest is an incident from a late-late show.

> The people fell upon me with their fists, books, and without compassion or mercy, beat me down in the steeplehouse and almost smothered me in it, being under them. And sorely was I bruised in the steeplehouse, and they threw me against the walls and when they had thrust and thrown me out of the steeplehouse, when I came into the yard I fell down. . . . And I got up again and then they punched and thrust and struck me up and down and they set me in the stocks, and brought a whip to whip me, but did not. And as I sat in the stocks they threw stones at me, and my head, arms, breast, shoulders, back, and sides were so bruised that I was mazed and dazzled with the blows (p. 44).

Thus the stage was set for Fox's ministry. In October of 1650 came another clash with the authorities. This time a steeplehouse bell "struck at" Fox's life (p. 51). After the sermon Fox "was moved of the Lord" to speak concerning "the light in them" (p. 51)—and was promptly arrested. For eight hours he was examined, "backward and forward." At issue was Fox's violation of a legal provision of the same year which made it a criminal offense to claim to be God—a somewhat intriguing matter which suggests, once more, that there was more to the seventeenth-century English religious scene than meets the eye. The *Journal* recounts some of the questions put to Fox: "At last they asked me whether I was sanctified. I said, 'Sanctified? Yes,' for I was in the Paradise of God. They said, had I no sin? 'Sin?' said I, 'Christ my Saviour hath taken away my sin, and in him there is no sin' " (p. 52).

As a result Fox was committed to six months in prison. "Many came from far and near to see a man that had no sin" (p. 52). Such distinction brought opportunity for witness—and thus the time was hardly wasted. He heard the church bells in the depths of the dungeon and thus could not escape the ringing evidence of what was to him utter ecclesiastical perversion. To others this melodic sound might have proved an inspiration; but not so for George Fox. The bell-ringers in the "steeplehouse in Derby" got the following note: "Friends, Oh, take heed of pleasures, and prize your time now while you have it, and do not spend it in pleasures nor carelessness. The time will come that you will say you had time, when it is past. Oh, look at the love of God now, while you have time; for it bringeth to loathe all vanities and worldly pleasures. Oh, consider; time is precious! Fear God and rejoice in him who hath made heaven and earth" (p. 56).

In that same year, 1650, Fox and his followers received their label. "This was Justice Bennet of Derby that first called us Quakers because we bid them tremble at the word of God, and this was in the year 1650" (p. 58). The occasion is worth recalling. According to another description the Judge asked Fox: "What have you to say? Who are you? Why did you come here?" To this Fox replied: "God moved us to do so and to tell thee that all thy preaching, baptism, and sacrifices will never sanctify thee. Look unto Christ and not unto men." The Judge: "You're demented, taken up in raptures. You speak too freely of God." Whereupon Fox exhorted him, "Tremble and quake at the name of the Lord!" The Judge's reply has become classic: "You quake, do you? Quakers, eh?"[13]

The name stuck, for it was picturesque and also reasonably descriptive. Like most labels in ecclesiastical history—Lutherans, Anabaptists, Mennonites, Methodists—it was a name first given by opponents. Fox himself did not think that it was altogether an inappropriate one, and one of his Epistles formed a lengthy defense of what might be called the theology of trembling: "Moses . . . trembled, feared, and quaked. . . . David, a king, trembled. . . . The prophet Jeremiah trembled, he shook, his bones quaked, he reeled to and fro like a drunken man."[14] Though "Quaker" continued to be popular nomenclature among outsiders, "Friends of Truth" was the name Fox and the Friends greatly preferred.

In the winter of 1651 occurred the incident which is an indispensable part of all biographies of Fox. There is a problem of chronology here, for the three steeples at Lichfield mentioned in Fox's account were destroyed in the Civil War in 1643 and not rebuilt until 1669; thus the incident must have happened before or after.

> And as I was one time walking in a close with several Friends I lifted up my head and I espied three steeplehouse spires. They struck at my life and I asked Friends what they were, and they said, Lichfield. The word of the Lord came to me thither I might go, so, being come to the house we were going to I bid friends that were with me walk into the house from me; and they did and as soon as they were gone (for I said nothing to them whither I would go) I went over hedge and ditch till I came within a mile of Lichfield. When I came into a great field where there were shepherds keeping their sheep, I was commanded of the Lord to pull off my shoes of a sudden; and I stood still, and the word of the Lord was like a fire in me; and being winter, I untied my shoes and put them off; and when I had done I was commanded to give them to the shepherds and was to charge them to let no one have them except they paid for them. And the poor shepherds trembled and were astonished.
>
> So I went about a mile till I came into the town, and as soon as I came within the town the word of the Lord came unto me again to cry, "Woe unto the bloody city of Lichfield!"; so I went up and down the streets crying, "Woe unto the bloody city of Lichfield!"; and no one touched me or laid hands on me. As I went down the town there ran like a channel of blood down the streets, and the market place was like a pool of blood.
>
> And so at last some friends and friendly people came to me and said, "Alack George! where are thy shoes?" and I told them it was no matter; so when I had declared what was upon me and cleared myself, I came out of the town in peace about a mile to the shepherds: and there I went to them and took my shoes and gave them some money, but the fire of the Lord was so in my feet and all over me that I did not matter to put my shoes on any more and was at a stand whether I should or not till I felt freedom from the Lord to do so.
>
> And so at last I came to a ditch and washed my feet and put on my shoes; and when I had done, I considered why I should go and cry against that city and call it a bloody city; for though the Parliament had the minister one while and the King another while, and much blood had been shed in the town, yet that could not be charged upon the town. But as I went through the town there ran like a channel of blood down the streets and the market place was like a pool of blood; this I saw as I went through it crying "Woe to the bloody city of Lichfield."

But after, I came to see that there were a thousand martyrs in Lichfield in the Emperor Diocletian's time. And so I must go in my stockings through the channel of their blood in their market place. So I might raise up the blood of those martyrs that had been shed and lay cold in their streets, which had been shed above a thousand years before (pp. 71 f.).

Probably few men in the history of the Christian church have had this kind of an experience; fewer yet would have been willing to put it down on paper. George Fox alone had the boldness to be loquacious about the incident, though perhaps with some trepidation; even though the *Journal* does not say so, there can be little doubt that the meaning of the whole incident was beyond George Fox. The reference to the persecution of Christians is important and appears to have been a convenient explanation for what must have been an inexplicable experience. The incident, together with Fox's obvious embarrassment, indicates the uniqueness of his religious stature.

No doubt, it was a frighteningly strange incident, hardly "normal" and everyday routine; perhaps the psychiatrist should be called upon to give an explanation. We will need to keep in mind that the crucial aspect of the whole matter was not that bizarre shout one would expect from a noisy sailor, but rather what transpired in Fox's mind—the fire that made him comfortable though barefooted; the blood running down the streets and gathering in the market place. Moreover, for Fox the sequence of events was that the "word of the Lord" first came to him and demanded that he shout against Lichfield. Then came the vision of blood and, finally, the recollection of the martyrs.

Had Fox known about the martyrs beforehand? Did his obsession with the iniquity of the "steeplehouses" prompt his emotional reaction upon seeing the steeples of Lichfield? Did he really mean to say that he saw blood in the streets and market place or merely that he was reminded of blood while running through the streets? There is no answer to these questions, for the incident defies explanation.

The Gathering of the Flock

Afterward the details of Fox's ministry, as recorded in the *Journal,* became somewhat complicated, though the pattern was—and always remained—quite clear. Fox continued to make his way through the English countryside. He preached in steeplehouses after sermons and at times during them. He spoke, and more often argued, in houses and public squares, became involved with the zealots as well as the fellow travelers of Anglicans, Dissenters, Puritans, Baptists, and Ranters. He encountered profound "convincements" as well as solid opposition. He was thrown out of churches, over walls, and into ditches. He was hit with rotten eggs, stones, sticks—and Bibles (hardly appropriate equipment for true defenders of the Faith). Since he was still young—not yet thirty years of age—when he commenced his ministry he was put under lock and key at one place as "a young man that was made and was got away" from his family (p. 105), until his family had been notified. No authentic portrait of Fox is extant, but we can well envisage him, worn by the vicissitudes of the weather and the treatment received, in the leather breeches so admired by Carlyle, indefatigable in body and, above all, in spirit.

Fox's proclamation was, in both form and content, dramatic. But he did more than proclaim a message. Wherever he went, he gathered people, never in spectacular numbers, but always in spectacular fashion. The various conventicles which characterized the English religious scene were the tinder that lighted the spark. Here was the reservoir from which could be gathered new disciples.

In June, 1652, by one of those strange series of circumstances which seem so often to be the stuff of history, Fox directed his steps to Swarthmore Hall, the home of Judge Thomas Fell and his wife, Margaret. Both were religious persons and had a reputation for hospitality to traveling ministers, without regard for theological propensity. At first only Margaret seems to have responded to Fox's proclamation; her husband was more reserved. Away from home when Fox first arrived, he returned quickly because of Fox—and many years later Margaret recalled what had changed her critical husband into a sympathetic friend of George Fox. In her testimony to George Fox at the occasion of the publication of his *Journal* she wrote:

> So my husband came home greatly offended; and any may think what a condition I was like to be in, that either I must displease my husband or offend God; for he was very much troubled with us all in the house and family, they had so prepossessed him against us. . . .
>
> At night George Fox came: and after supper my husband was sitting in the parlour, and I asked him, If George Fox might come in? And he said, Yes. So George came in without any compliment, and walked into the room, and began to speak presently; and the family, and James Naylor, and Richard Farnsworth came all in: and he spoke very excellently as ever I heard him, and opened Christ's and the apostles' practices, which they were in, in their day. And he opened the night of apostasy since the apostles' days, and laid open the priests and their practices in the apostasy; that if all in England had been there, I thought they could not have denied the truth of those things. And so my husband

came to see clearly the truth of what he spoke, and was very quiet that night, said no more, and went to bed. . . .[15]

After several days Margaret Fell invited Fox to attend an Anglican service. He declined and after the household had left for church went for a walk across the fields. But "then the words of the Lord came to me to go to the steeplehouse after them and when I came the priest Lampitt was singing with his people" (p. 114). Such singing evidently sounded out of place to Fox's ears and what happened next had a familiar ring. "I was moved of the Lord to speak to him and the people after they had done singing" (p. 114). In the ensuing turmoil only Margaret Fell's intercession—"Let him alone, why may not he speak as well as any other" (p. 115)—calmed the churchgoers' minds. But only temporarily, for before long Fox was thrown out of the church. When he reflected on the incident in the *Journal,* Fox remembered some most uncomplimentary things about the arm of the law: "Justice John Sawrey," he wrote, "was a rotten professor who was full of hypocrisy, and deceit, and envy" (p. 115).

Judge Fell, while not exuberantly disposed to Fox's version of the gospel, permitted Swarthmore Hall to become the center of the growing movement. Margaret Fell was more enthusiastic, as was her daughter Mary, who in 1655, five years old, wrote a note to the local clergyman, a note characterized by disarming simplicity and a seriousness that must have been the result of juvenile eavesdropping: "The plaigues of god shall fall upon thee and the seven viols shall bee powered upon thee and the millstone shall fall upon thee and crush thee as dust under the Lords feete how can thou escape the damnation of hell. This did the Lord give mee as I lay in bed—Mary Fell."[16]

Subsequently Margaret Fell became a prominent follower of George Fox. Indeed, she was, as Isabel Ross's appreciative biography says, the "Mother of Quakerism." One may consider her devotion to Fox unduly exuberant; all the same, she was a glowing testimony to the effectiveness of Fox's message. Her devotion proved to be contagious and encompassed the entire household at Swarthmore. Thus several members of the household wrote Fox words of lavish admiration: "O thou bread of life, without which bread our souls will starve. O for evermore give us this bread, and take pity on us whom thou has nursed up with the breasts of consolation. . . . In thy presence is fullness of joy, and where thou dwells is pleasures for evermore, O thou fountain of eternal life, our souls thirsts after thee, for in thee alone is our life and peace, and without thee have we no peace: for our souls is much refreshed by seeing thee, and our lifes is preserved by thee, O thou father of eternal felicity."[17]

Women occupied an important role in Fox's movement and one might almost suggest that a characteristic feature of early Quakerism was the female participation. In his *Journal,* Fox recorded his repudiation of those who held that women lacked souls—a theological expression of the low place of women in society. Of course, the notion of spiritual inferiority of women has a long tradition in Christian history and is based upon a somewhat questionable interpretation of I Corinthians 14:34. When John Bunyan insisted—in line with a widespread consensus—that women "are not the image and glory of God, as the men are,"[18] George Fox asserted the contrary (p. 9). Subsequently Margaret Fell, Mary Fisher, Mary Dyer, Elizabeth Hooton, and others became important figures in the story of the early Quakers. One might say that Fox emancipated woman to religious respectability, though privilege meant here, as always, responsibilities. The several female Quaker martyrs show this quite succinctly. Twelve of the so-called "Valiant Sixty" were women, given the times an amazingly large proportion,[19] which showed that women could be rallied to Fox's cause as much as men and that Fox provided a unique opportunity for dedication in the realm of religion. Anne Knight, the writer of the first pamphlet on women's suffrage, was a Quaker, and this was surely more than coincidence.

Christ's atonement here made the difference. Fox wrote in one of his Epistles "after the fall, in the transgression, the man was to rule over his wife; but in the restoration by Christ, into the image of God, and his righteousness and holiness again, in that they are helps-meet, man and woman, as they were before the fall" (Epistle CCXCI). In another letter "relative to the station of Women in the Church" he reiterated his basic point: "And so now the end of all our men and women's meetings in the time of the Gospel (the power of Christ being the authority of them), is, that they may all labour in his power, and in his grace, and in his spirit, and in his light, to do his service and his business in truth and righteousness" (Epistle CCCXX).

And yet, Fox's proclamation was masculine; at least, looking at the heavy physical toll, the imprisonments, the beatings, the exposure to the elements, we are inclined to feel that Fox proclaimed—even as did Ignatius of Loyola—a religion for men, though the women in fact also suffered courageously.

The year 1652 is seen by Quaker historians as the birth year of Quakerism. Like all such dates it represents a certain measure of historical simplification, but from 1652 onward Fox's message was spread collectively and—what is more important—successfully. In the summer of that year Fox had come to Pendle Hill and climbed to the top. His vision is related in the *Journal.* It might well describe the remainder of his ministry:

> I spied a great hill called Pendle Hill, and I went on the top of it with much ado, it was so steep; but I was moved of the Lord to go atop of it; and when I came atop of it I saw Lancashire sea; and there atop of the hill I was moved to sound the day of the Lord; and the Lord let me see atop of the hill in what places he had a great people to be agathered. As I went down, on the hill side I found a spring of water and refreshed myself, for I had eaten little and drunk little for several days. . . .
>
> And the Lord opened to me at that place, and let me see a great people in white raiment by a river's side, coming to the Lord, and the place was near John Blaykling's where Richard Robinson lived (pp. 103–104).

The first four years of Fox's ministry—from 1648 to 1652—had hardly been successful. Indeed, judging by the brutal treatment Fox received, one might conclude the opposite, though empirical success provides no yardstick for spiritual profundity. The year 1652 proved to be of considerable importance to Fox because he then came into contact with groups of "Seekers" who found it possible to identify their search for true religion with his answer. The term "Seeker" must incidentally be used with considerable caution and merely denotes those Separatists who denied the ministry and the sacraments, thus anticipating Fox's propensity. William Penn reflected on the memorable happening by saying that Fox "saw people as thick as motes in the sun, that should in time be brought home to the Lord, that there might be but one shepherd and one sheepfold in all the earth."[20] Fox had climbed his Pendle Hill as a lone preacher; he left accompanied by a band of preachers who, in twos and threes, proclaimed the same message. Many, writes a contemporary, "believed in ye truth by him preached, & became obedient to the same, and lived & died faithfull witnesses & faithfull testemony bearers therto."[21]

The following year brought further activity and Fox's third imprisonment. This time the place was Carlyle, and the charges that Fox was a "blasphemer, a heretic, and a seducer" (p. 159). He spent two months in prison, a most unpleasant time. In those days, prisoners enjoyed—if this be the proper word—the dubious privilege of having to pay for their room and board. Fox informed his jailer that he would not do this, and found himself in the worst part of the prison, "a filthy, nasty place" without "even a house of convenience." The prisoners there were "exceedingly lousy; and there was one woman almost eaten with lice" (p. 162). In the end Fox once again had his way, and without paying he was moved to a better part of the jail. Since several of his fellow prisoners "were convinced," the time was not wasted.

As the number of Quakers increased, the question of their political loyalty became more and more important. In 1655 Fox was arrested by one Colonel Hacker at Whetstone, about five miles from Leicester, and examined at length about his views. In the end the Colonel ordered him to go home and stay there. For Fox such a command was obviously impossible. It was rather like asking a man to stop breathing—he could not do it if he tried. "Well, then," said Colonel Hacker, "I will send you tomorrow by 6 o'clock to my Lord Protector by Captain Drury, one of his life-guard" (p. 192). The next day, George Fox was on his way to meet Oliver Cromwell, who with sword and Bible sought to transform England. In those days the rumor of a plot against the Protector was in the air; Fox and his followers were implicated. Cromwell, at first disinclined to go through the superficialities of a personal encounter, wanted to take care of the matter in writing. He demanded that Fox "would promise that he would not take up a sword against the Lord Protector or the Government as it is now; and that George Fox would write down the words in answer to that which the Protector required, and for George Fox to set his hand to it" (p. 197).

Fox penned a note that left no uncertainty about his position:

> I, who am of the world called George Fox, do deny that the carrying or drawing of any carnal sword against any, or against thee, Oliver Cromwell, or any man. In the presence of the Lord God I declare it. . . . Therefore with a carnal weapon I do not fight, but am from those things dead; from him who is not of the world, called of the world by the name of George Fox. . . . From him who to all your souls is a friend, for establishing of righteousness and cleansing the land of evil doers and a witness against all wicked inventions of men and murderous plots, which answered shall be with the light in all your consciences, which makes no covenant with death, to which light in you all I speak, and am clear.
>
> F. G. who is of the world called George Fox, who a new name hath which the world knows not (p. 198).

The note made Cromwell curious to see Fox. Early in the morning of March 6, 1655, the two men met in Cromwell's bedroom. It must have been a fascinating scene: attendants walking to and fro, Cromwell getting dressed, and Fox talking religion. Fox's recollection in the *Journal* provides us with his version of the incident: "And I spake much to him of Truth, and a great deal of discourse I had with him about religion, wherein he carried himself very moderately" (p. 199). Surely Fox sought to make the best of the occasion and, judging from the *Journal,* his performance must have been impressive. At their parting Cromwell "said with tears in his eyes, 'Come again to my house; for if thou and I were but an hour in a day together we should be nearer one to the other'" (p. 199). Fox's recollection was accurate. He and Cromwell shared a common seriousness about the Christian faith and Fox recorded, not without pride, Cromwell's words of esteem: "He said that there was a people risen, meaning us, that he could not win either with honour, high places, or gifts, but all other people he could" (p. 200). Cromwell and Fox met again later on, the last time shortly before Cromwell's death in 1658. Fox wanted to see the Protector about the treatment of the Friends. Their meeting was brief and Fox was to come back for a more extended conversation. When he returned "the doctors were not willing I should come in to speak with him. So I passed away, and never saw him no more" (p. 350). In Fox's recollection of the incident is an authentic spark—the close proximity of the irrelevant and the spiritually significant: "Before I came at him," reads the *Journal,* "he was riding in the head of his lifeguard, I saw and felt a waft of death go forth against him, and he looked like a dead man" (p. 350).

Following his first encounter with Cromwell, Fox was released from jail and took up once again his itinerant ministry, but before long came his fourth imprisonment, of all he suffered undoubtedly the worst. He was thrown into "Doomsdale" dungeon, commonly reserved for murderers and witches "before their execution" (p. 252). Fox's description of the place is rather horrible and need not be recounted here—it was not unlike Dante's *Inferno*. Even at that, Fox appears not to have reported all that happened, as is evident from his remark—one still feels the innocent indignation—that the jailer called them "hatchet-faced dogs and such names as we never heard in our lives" (p. 253). Fox's spirit was undismayed by this experience, and he spoke here the famous words that he "was never in prison that it was not the means of bringing multitudes out of their prisons."[22]

In March, 1656, the trial was held. What a scene! Fox and two

Friends stood before the Judge with their hats firmly on their heads. The Judge, uninformed of Fox's principles, asked why the prisoners did not take off their hats.

> And then I replied and said, "Where did ever any magistrate, king, or judge from Moses to Daniel command any to put off their hats when they came before them into their courts amongst the Jews the people of God or amongst the heathen, or where did any of the heathen command any such thing in all their courts or their kings or judges? Or show me where it is written or printed in any law of England where any such thing is commanded; show it me and I will put off my hat.
>
> And then the judge grew very angry and said, "I do not carry my law books on my back."
>
> Then said I, "Tell me where it is printed in a statute book that I may read it."
>
> Then said the judge, "Takc him away, prevaricator, I'll firk him."
>
> Then they took us away and put us amongst the thieves; and presently after he calls to the gaoler, "Bring them up again."
>
> "Come," said he, "where had they hats from Moses to Daniel? Come, answer me, I have you fast now," said he.
>
> Then I said, "Thou mayest read in the third of Daniel that the three children were cast into the fiery furnace by Nebuchadnezzar with their cloaks, hose, and hats on." And you may see that Nebuchadnezzar was not offended at their hats.
>
> He cried again, "Take them away, Gaoler" (pp. 243–244).

Thus Fox and his friends were back again where they had come from and they "were kept a great while" (p. 244). Afterward Fox penned a little treatise on the subject of swearing—the court experience must have suggested its urgency to him. Before long they were in court again; again the hats remained firmly on their heads; again the hats were forcibly removed. But no sooner had they been received back, than they were put on again. "So we were kept in prison," wrote Fox, "and divers people came far and nigh to see us, and several people of account. It was the talk of the town and country that never men answered so as we did, and that the judge and justices were not able to answer us one word in twelve" (p. 250).

The Quaker Jesus

That same year occurred the Nayler episode and near disaster for Fox, whose remarks in the *Journal* are brief but reveal the seriousness of the happening: "James Nayler ran out into imaginations, and a company with him; and they raised up a great darkness in the nation. And he came to Bristol and made a disturbance there" (p. 268).

This James Nayler was, at all odds, the most brilliant, most spiritual, and most renegade follower of George Fox. That bizarre incident described so detachedly in the *Journal* by Fox earned Nayler the hardly complimentary title "Quaker Jesus"; yet a winsome and lovable character he was. First a farmer, then a soldier in the Civil War, then again a farmer, Nayler was typical of those of his sensitive contemporaries who had been touched by the turbulent religious ferment of the time. In 1651 Nayler's life took a dramatic turn. He himself recalled later on that he "was at the plough, meditating on the things of God, and suddenly I heard a voice saying unto me 'Get thee out from thy kindred and from thy father's house.'"[23] At first Nayler hesitated and agonized; then he decided to obey the voice —to leave wife and children. What followed next, we do not know. Probably it was Fox, when Nayler encountered him, who gave him the spiritual certainty he was seeking, for he soon became an outstanding figure in the movement. Richard Baxter felt Nayler was its "chief leader." Truly, he was a gifted man and, though untrained, competent to write theological treatises. Thus the very first printed Quaker pamphlet, *Spiritual Wickedness,* came from his pen. His writings—Emilia Fogelklou's admiring biography quotes therefrom at length—were not what we would call the most significant theological exposition to come from the seventeenth century, but they exhibit a disarming simplicity and show him as a clear head and solid theological mind.

He was a powerful preacher and winsome personality, and naturally attracted a group of devotees. Some of these—they were women—became increasingly exuberant in their devotion to Nayler. Nayler himself was too innocent to note what was happening and thus was little more than a sheep being led to the slaughter. His strenuous activities, long periods of fasting, a chronic physical ailment, the periods of imprisonment, and a sensitive spirituality had undoubtedly undermined his inner equilibrium. He began to issue forth with ecstatic statements, parroting his followers' praise, with the result that his own person assumed increasingly prominent spiritual significance. He willingly went along with the exuberant expressions of his devotees, who had called him "Son of Zion, whose mother is a Virgin and whose birth is immortal."[24] He had revived an unconscious woman by the name of Dorcas Erbury—the allusion to the Dorcas of the Book of Acts was telling—and had not objected that this incident made the rounds as a spectacular tale how the woman had been raised from the dead.

Fox was terrified. But since he was in jail at Launceston and Nayler was arrested on his way to see him, there was not much he could do. When the two men finally met, it was too late. Fox had stiffened in his opinion of Nayler who, in turn, was shocked by Fox's hostility. The encounter between the two men was dramatic, for Nayler sought the kiss of fellowship from Fox who—whether through practical circumstances or theological intent we do not know—offered his foot to be kissed. The *Journal* reports laconically, "But I seeing he had turned against the power of God, it was my foot, and so the Lord moved me to slight him and to set the power of God over him" (p. 269). Fox may have felt that he had to make a theological point; but surely what he possessed by way of theological incisiveness, he lacked in charitable warmth; a positive response to Nayler might have done wonders.

Afterward he wrote a letter to his erstwhile companion and left no doubt that their ways had parted: "Thou hast satisfied the world, yea their Desires they looked for, and thou and thy Disciples, and the world is joined against the Truth." At this point, however, Nayler was beyond hope. In October he was released from prison and together with a small band of followers he made his way to Bristol. There the drama took place.

Those who stood along the road leading to Bristol that cold and rainy day in October, 1656, saw a curious scene. A group of travelers, four men and three women, together with a horse, slowly approached the town. Once inside Bristol, the women took off their wrappings, threw them in the path of the horse, and chanted, "Holy, holy, holy, Lord God of Israel." They were obviously re-enacting Christ's entry into Jerusalem. Unlike the biblical event, however, the procession failed to catch the people's imagination. Few, if any, must have taken the happening seriously—though the inclement weather may have kept the people inside. Nayler and his followers had no sooner arrived at an inn to dry their wet clothes than the arm of the law arrived and arrested them. The theophany of James Nayler had come to a sudden though perhaps not altogether unexpected end.

This melodramatic incident might have concluded then and there, with some sort of stern admonition and a sharp rebuke to go home. What made the matter important and so sensational was the incriminating evidence found in Nayler's pockets—letters which called him "the only begotten son of God" and asserted "Thy name shall be no more James Nayler but Jesus." During the initial investigation

Nayler might have seized the opportunity to avoid trouble. But, when the question was asked if he were the son of God, his answer was affirmative. To be sure, he added—and this addition makes theologically all the difference—that "he had many brethren" but this elaboration must have got lost in the uproar following the first part of his sentence. In response to a similar question during his subsequent trial Nayler made an identical assertion: "Where God is manifest in the flesh, there is the everlasting Son, and I do witness God in the flesh; I am the Son of God, and the Son of God is but one."[25]

Did Nayler take himself seriously? We wonder. No doubt, the ecstatic frenzy of some of his female devotees egged him onto the slippery ice of messianic speculation and caused him to push a biblical literalism—one need only mention the Johannine Gospel or Galatians 4:7—to its extreme. The matter was made worse by Fox's insistence on the inner "light of Christ." The difficulty is, of course, that the theologian has the option of spelling "son" either with a capital or a small *"s"*—a differentiation with far-reaching theological consequences. Nayler's tragedy was that such semantic subtlety got lost in verbalization. The Johannine soteriology of man's divinization has a long history and is, in itself, not problematic. If, however, the stress on the inner "light of Christ" is added and the whole matter pushed to the extreme, then there is theological trouble. Nayler was the unfortunate victim. Fox had the simpler—and thus more profound—understanding of the theological issue. Wrote he in the *Journal,* "then was I moved of the Lord God to stand up upon the table in the eternal power of God and tell the people, that Christ was in them, except they were reprobates; and that it was Christ, the eternal power of God, that spake in me at that time unto them; not that I was Christ" (p. 95). Yet he also called himself "son of God" (p. 197).

The remainder of Nayler's story need not concern us here in detail. Nayler and several of his devotees were sent to London, where oil was added to the fire. Nayler's devotees continued their expressions of reverence for him. Then a committee of the House of Commons investigated the case and found that Nayler had assumed "the Gesture, Words, Honour, Worship, and Miracles of our blessed Saviour, and the names and incommunicable Attributes and Titles of our blessed Saviour." Eventually, the entire House discussed the matter, with a thoroughness and sophistication that would have become a council of theologians. Carlyle's *Cromwell* described the situation with characteristic candor:

To Posterity they sit there as the James Nayler Parliament. Four hundred gentlemen of England . . . to sit in solemn Debate on this terrific Phenomenon: a mad Quaker fancying or seeming to fancy himself, what is not uncommon since, a new Incarnation of Christ. Shall we hang him, shall we whip him, bore the tongue of him with hot iron? Shall we imprison him, set him to oakum, shall we roast or boil or stew him? Shall we put the question whether this question shall be put? Debate whether this shall be debated?—in Heaven's name, what shall we do with him?

Parliament debated the matter for three months with typical British seriousness. The sessions were many and the argumentation tedious, prompting one member to observe to his colleagues that there was danger that "you should kill yourselves by voting by what death Nayler should die."[26] Others were more adamant. A member warned that "the eyes of the nation are upon you. This whole matter touches the safety of the nation," a comment seconded by another member, who found that here was "the greatest matter that ever came before a Parliament."[27] After all words had been spoken, after heaven and hell, the past as well as the future, had been evoked, Parliament sentenced Nayler to be whipped through the streets of London, to have his tongue bored with a hot iron, to have a *B* for "blasphemer" branded on his head, to have him sent back to Bristol, there to enact his entry, only this time riding backward on a horse without a saddle. Then he was to be whipped again on the market square. And if that were not enough, he was to be brought back to London and kept imprisoned until such time as Parliament decreed his release.

The twentieth-century observer will find it astounding that a legislative body should so extensively concern itself with a theological issue, particularly at a time when weighty political matters demanded consideration. But in those days religion was an explicit prerogative of temporal authority, and Parliament jealously guarded its privileges. Yet, not the exercise of political prerogative is so amazing here, but that Nayler's neck escaped the noose. Though some diehards in Parliament argued that God's honor would be irreparably violated if Nayler were not punished by death, the moderates won the day. A new wind was blowing, and thus the case of James Nayler, blasphemer, has relevance not only for the story of George Fox but also for the larger story of religious liberty. The absurdity of the case must have indicated to many members of Parliament as well as the English people that verification of messianic claims really lay outside the competence of a legislative body.

Nayler suffered the inflicted punishment manfully and awakened from his own nightmare. His public confession, *James Nayler's Recantation, printed and directed by himself to all the people of the*

Lord, gathered and scattered, deeply bewailed what happened "in the sight of temptation and the hour of darkness." "Dear Brethren," he soon wrote to his fellow Quakers, "my heart is broken this day for the offence I have occasioned to God's Truth and People, and especially to you who in dear love followed me, seeking me in faithfulness to God. . . . I beseech you, forgive me wherein I evilly requited your love that day."[28] In the end Nayler was reconciled to Fox and until his death in 1660 again played an important role in the ongoing proclamation of Fox's message.

The moral of the Nayler episode was a simple one. Nayler introduced—as Geoffrey F. Nuttall's little study, *James Nayler: A Fresh Approach,* tellingly suggests—the concept of sin into the Quaker vocabulary.[29] Fox had been silent on this point, but Nayler showed that the claimed possession of the "inner light" did not mean that sin was absent from the lives of the faithful.

There was yet another consequence. The knotty problem was how to keep the "inner light" in proper control. To insist on the Bible would have led Fox back to where he came from; the church was likewise unacceptable. So Fox formulated the notion of the "collective" inner light—that is, the individual's direct religious experience was to be authenticated neither by the Scriptures nor by the church but by its agreement with the consensus of other "inner lights" in the congregation. For Rachel Knight this was Fox's original contribution.[30] One can argue that the locus of authority was once again the church, albeit defined differently as in Roman Catholicism. It was understood by Fox not as a hierarchical church, but the gathering of believers; the meeting of Friends was to procure a meeting of spiritual minds. This was, no doubt, an exciting variation of the quest for authority, though one not quite so new as Rachel Knight, and perhaps even George Fox, thought it to be; sixteenth-century Anabaptist ecclesiology—and Congregationalists and Baptists as well—exhibited a similar orientation.

The End of the Struggle

In 1660 came the Restoration and King Charles II—but little changed in the life of George Fox. He was arrested that year at Swarthmore, despite the fact that Charles had declared a "liberty to tender consciences." In his *Journal* Fox recalled, probably not without irony, that in the first night of his arrest some of his guards "sat in the chimney; they were afraid I would go up the chimney, the Lord's power so terrified them" (p. 375). After four months, on

Margaret Fell's pleading with the King, he was released from imprisonment—it had been his fifth.

Soon thereafter Fox's life intersected a final time with the larger course of religious and political events. In January, 1662, England witnessed the spectacular uprising of the Fifth Monarchy men who believed, on the basis of the arithmetic of the Book of Daniel, that the time of the Fifth Monarchy of the King Jesus was imminent—and that they were called upon to help usher it in. The uprising was sternly crushed and this fact proved persuasively that the calculation had been in error and the Fifth Monarchy was not yet at hand. George Fox and his followers felt the consequences of the uprising in painful fashion, for persecution intensified throughout England. "And all the prisons were soon after filled with Friends and many died in prison, they being so thronged up" (p. 395). This course of events brought forth a vigorous statement, drawn up by Fox and signed by eleven of his associates, concerning their attitude toward war and peace. "Our principle is, and our practices have always been, to seek peace and ensure it and to follow after righteousness and the knowledge of God, seeking the good and welfare and doing that which tends to the peace of all. . . . All bloody principles and practices, we, as to our own particulars, do utterly deny, with all outward wars and strife" (p. 399). The principle of pacifism delineated here marks one of Fox's major characteristics. It was supported in the document with the classical biblical passages—Matthew 5:21, 26:51; Micah 4:3—and showed the fascinating relationship between biblical literalism and the spiritualism of the "inner light." The *Declaration* said quite plainly that "the spirit of Christ, by which we are guided, is not changeable, so as once to command us from a thing as evil and again to move unto it" (p. 399). Here, at least, the priority of the Word over the "inner light" seemed obvious. Such pacifism was expounded, not by a group of otherworldly dreamers and idealists, but by men who had experienced the grim realities of brutal force and were yet persuaded that the spirit of Christ required nonresistance rather than force.

By that time the Quakers had become a national phenomenon; indeed, Fox's message was being spread across the seas and in faraway lands. The number of Quaker evangelists was legion; their zeal was exuberant and their experiences dramatic. One Mary Fisher traveled first to America and then to the Turks, for whom she had, so she said, a special message from God. Two other Friends undertook to convert the Pope, though with negative results; one of the two was hanged. Fox provided the Quaker missionaries with literary support. He wrote letters to the crowned heads of Spain and France, to the Pope, to the emperors of Austria and China, and one "To all the nations under the whole heavens." His communication to the Pope was telling, for he, too, was addressed, as was everyone else, with "Friend."

Friend, read this over and the said lamentation that's over thee thou maist behold, how that thy field is a field of blood, and how that thou art naked, thy Emperors and thy Princes from the Spiritual Weapons, and the Armor of God. . . . Therefore and all the Emperors and Princes, and thyself, having not the Spiritual Weapons, and not the Armor of God, ye have been faint to set up your Inquisitions, your Racks, your Tortures, your Prisons, your Banishments, and this showeth you have no Rule nor Government by the Power of God.[31]

The results of such vigorous activity were numerically meager. The otherworldliness of the Quaker missionaries as well as the ever present persecution of the movement must be counted as important reasons.[32]

In 1664 Fox was arrested again. The confinement turned out to be the longest and most trying one he experienced, lasting for two years. The charge was that he had refused to swear the seventeenth-century "loyalty oath" of allegiance to the King. Fox refused to swear it and gave a simple explanation: "I never took oath in my life" (p. 481). As weeks turned into months, and months into two years, Fox's physical condition became increasingly miserable. At times the smoke in the jail almost smothered him: "It rained in also upon my bed, and the smoke was so thick as I could hardly see a candle sometimes. . . . I was almost smothered with smoke and so starved with cold and rain that my body was almost numbed" (pp. 484–485).

Freedom came in September, 1666—just before the Great Fire broke out in London. Fox, never slow to see divine Providence at work round about him, related the fire to his own misfortune and concluded that it was a divine punishment. "The people of London were forewarned of this fire; yet few people laid it to heart but grew rather more wicked and higher in price" (p. 503). With even greater zeal, Fox resumed his evangelistic activities. In 1669 he went to Ireland, and described his decision to go in typical fashion: "I was moved of the Lord to go over into Ireland, to visit the Seed of God in that nation" (p. 536). Yet, aside from the new names of towns and places in the *Journal*, the story is the same one.

On the heels of his return from Ireland came what at least on the surface appeared a romantic matter. George Fox, forty-five years of age, married Margaret Fell, eleven years a widow and ten years his senior, three of her six daughters already married. After his wedding Fox departed for another evangelistic mission. Margaret in turn was soon arrested, and at her release George was about to depart for a lengthy voyage to America. This state of affairs remained typical; there was little togetherness in this marriage. George and Margaret were rarely together. However, one must not make a principle out of expediency, as Margaret pointed out in a letter: "We were very willing both of us to live apart for some years on God's account and His truth's service, and to deny ourselves of that comfort which we might have had in being together for the sake of the Lord and his Truth."[33] George Fox chose a companion ten years his senior; as far as he was concerned, he took this step in obedience to a divine call —"I had seen from the Lord a considerable time before that I should take Margaret Fell to be my wife . . . it opened in me from the Lord that the thing should be now accomplished" (p. 554). Moreover, Fox meant to demonstrate that among believers marriage could be observed in its pristine form, cleansed from the baser considerations of fallen man. George Fox wanted his marriage understood in a spiritual sense. An Epistle, to be read in meetings of Friends everywhere, pointed out that his matrimonial bond was a symbol of Christ and his church—a mystical spiritual union. It was a "figure of the Church coming out of the wilderness."[34] In the *Journal,* he wrote that his was to be a marriage such as existed in the beginning. When he was told that marriage was for the procreation of children, Fox remarked that he "judged such things below" him (p. 557). He was a typical Puritan who sought to combine spiritual eminence with romantic affection, for the "spiritual" side of Fox's marriage must not be unduly stressed. Margaret addressed George as "Dear Love," and George addressed her as "Dear Heart." Once, when Margaret sent the imprisoned George a large sum of three pounds—one could travel to America on five in those days— George used part of it to send her "as much black cloth as will make thee a gown."[35]

George Fox and Margaret Fell were determined to make their wedding a spiritual feast. Appearing before a gathering of Friends they stated their intention of getting married. "George Fox and Margaret Fell have this day proposed to this assembly of the people of the Lord their intention of being joined in the honourable marriage which, in the power and presence of the Lord, they have both declared to have arisen and to stand in the everlasting Seed, in the Covenant of Life which is from everlasting to everlasting." What happened at another meeting is also recorded or, rather, nothing could be recorded because of the enthusiastic atmosphere of the occasion: "But the life and power of the Lord were so over all that the words were not written, Friends being so filled and overcome with the power of the Lord, and testimonies that arose in themselves to the honourable marriage then made mention of, that they could not write George Fox's words." There seems to have been some grumbling from the rank and file over the marriage, for Fox wrote in the *Journal* that there "was some jumble in some minds about it, but the Lord's power came over all and laid all their spirits, and some after confessed it" (p. 557).

After his wedding came Fox's most significant missionary venture. Accompanied by a party of ten men and two women, Fox sailed for the American colonies in August, 1671; seven weeks later their vessel reached the West Indies, not without the customary difficulties. The voyage was truly one of faith; the boat was so leaky "that seamen and passengers do for the most part, day and night, pump" (p. 585). There were the inevitable pirates; when a pirate vessel chased them and the ship's master turned helpless, George Fox was called upon to act as a seasoned navigator, which he did with great skill (p. 592).

For the better part of two years Fox and his group traveled both in the West Indies and in the American colonies, preaching to settlers, Indians, their "emperors and kings," and organizing Friends' meetings wherever they went. In June of 1673, Fox was back in England. No sooner had he set foot on English soil, than he was arrested—for the eighth time—and he served nearly fourteen months at Worcester jail. A lengthy period of recuperation at Swarthmore followed; the spirit was still willing, still eager, but the body was getting weak. At Swarthmore he devoted his time to the collecting of his papers and correspondence. After more than two decades of unceasing activity George Fox began to rest from his labors.

In 1677 came a visit to Holland and Germany—a final burst of activity. Eight Friends made the trip with him, and one of them was William Penn, son of a distinguished family and known as a vigorous writer of Quaker pamphlets, such as the famous *No Cross, no Crown, or several sober reasons against hat-honour, Titular respects, You to a single Person, with the Apparel and Recreations of the Times*. Also in the group was another recent convert to Quakerism, Robert Barclay, author of the *Apology for the true Christian Divinity,* then just published. The trip was brief, lasting only the better part of four months. After his return to England, Fox continued to guide the affairs of the Society of Friends. The groundwork had been laid, the seed sown, and others could take over. In 1677

Fox paid his last visit to Swarthmore and then settled down to spend the final years of his life in London. In May, 1689, the persecutions which had put many of the Friends into prison ceased. The *Toleration Act* marked the end of the long battle in which Fox and the Friends had fought as vigorously as had the other dissenters. From that time comes another claim of Fox to a sixth sense which allowed him to anticipate the dramatic changes of the Glorious Revolution. Wrote he, "I had not been long in London before a great weight came upon me, and a sight the Lord gave me of the great bustles and troubles, revolution and change, which soon after came to pass." Or again, "About this time great exercise and weights came upon me (as had usually done before the great revolutions and changes of government) and my strength departed from me, so that I reeled and was ready to fall as I went along the streets."[36]

Death came on January 13, 1691. A testament contained a nondescript enumeration of his few worldly belongings and their requested disposition:

> I do give to Thomas Lower my Sadle and Bridle . . . and Spurrs and Bootts . . . and the New England Indian Bible and my Great Book of the signifying Names and my Book of the New Testament of eight languages and all my Physical Things that came from beyond the Sea with the outlandish Cupp and that thing that People do give Glisters with And my two Dials the one is an Equinoctiall Diall and all my Overplus Books to be divided among my four Sons in Law and also my other Books . . . And Thomas Lower shall have my Spanish Leatherhood and S.: Meade shall have my Magnifying Glass and the Tortoiseshell Comb and Case.[37]

The testament also contained comments concerning the "printing of my books" and instructions for charitable benevolence, the latter written in such a way as to provide proper ammunition for all those who prefer to look upon Fox as an illiterate eccentric: "And my Chest in Benjamin Antrobus his Chamber there is a little Gilt Box with some Gold in it. Sarah Meade to take it and let it do service among the rest so far at it will go the Box is sealed up."[38] Here, as well as in the *Journal,* we realize that even though George Fox had profound religious insights, he never fully penetrated the mystery of English grammar.

William Penn assumed the task of informing Margaret of her husband's passing. The letter which conveyed the news is moving, and very much to the point:

> With the dear remembrance of my unfeigned love in Christ Jesus, I am to be the teller to thee of sorrowful tidings as I may call it in some

sense, which is this, that thy dear husband and my beloved and dear friend, George Fox, has finished his glorious testimony this night about half an hour after nine, being sensible to the last breath.

Oh, he is gone, and has left us in the storm that is over our heads, surely in great mercy to him, but as an evidence to us of sorrows to come.[39]

A simple funeral followed, attended by two thousand Friends. Today the visitor to Bunhill Fields cemetery in London can see, amid factories and houses, a parcel of ground and thereon a simple epitaph: "George Fox, Born 7th Mo. 1624, Died 13th of 11th Mo. 1690, Aged 66 years."

The Legacy

What a remarkable man he was! Expert in disturbing church services, in sleeping out of doors; expert also in English prisons, in making few friends outside the Society but in influencing many people; acquaintance of both Oliver Cromwell and the inmates of prisons; powerful proclaimer of the gospel and silent meditator on the "inner light." George Fox hardly fits a prescribed pattern.

What shall we make of him? The answer is not easy, for historical assessments have varied far and wide. Some, from William Penn to W. C. Braithwaite, Geoffrey Nuttall, and Henry J. Cadbury, have seen him as reviving primitive Christianity. The title of Penn's famous work of 1696 is thus quite apropos, *Primitive Christianity Revived in the Faith and Practice of the People Called Quakers*. Even Lewis Benson, a 20th-century Quaker, means to do the same, although Fox in the process becomes a seventeenth-century Barthian. Most of those outside the Quaker fold, such as the witty, not unsympathetic, but theologically hostile Monsignor Ronald Knox, have grave reservations.

George Fox was persuaded that God had in a special way chosen him and that he therefore possessed God's Word and his opponents did not. In the *Journal* he noted quite appropriately "the Lord's power broke forth; and I had great openings, and prophecies, and spake unto them of the things of God, and they heard with attention and silence, and went away" (pp. 20–21). This quotation could easily be multiplied. Time and again Fox indicated that his unequivocal possession of the divine truth influenced the course of historical events. The world was black and white—he was on the right side and knew it. Fox's exuberance in this respect even led him to conclusions about the mind of God. Thus he wrote concerning the "image" of

Oliver Cromwell lying in state, "men were standing and sounding with trumpets over his image, after he was dead. At this my spirit was greatly grieved, and the Lord, I found, was highly offended" (p. 356).

Fox, and many early Friends with him, were "moved of the Lord" to do certain things—and the practical consequences were as a rule rather spectacular, though theologically quite harmless. Fox's screams against Lichfield could be multiplied in their own way by many other examples—as, for instance, by the statement of a Friend who poured out her indignation against a minister with these words: "I, Jane Withers, was moved of the Lord to go to the Steeplehouse of Kellit, to speak to Priest Moor these words. Thou art the beast that all the world worships and wonders after; the plagues of God must be poured upon thee."

One stands in awe before this unusual personality, and Fox himself seems to have sensed his uniqueness. One incident can stand for many: "As I was going towards Rochester I lighted and walked down the hill; and a great weight and oppression fell on my spirit. So I got on my horse again, but my weight and oppression remained so as I was hardly able to ride. So we came to Rochester; but I was very weak to ride, and very much loaden and burdened with the world's spirits, so that my life was oppressed under them" (p. 569). And a short while later: "And I saw all the religions and people that lived in them, and the priests that held them up, as a company of meneaters, and how they ate up the people like bread, gnawing the flesh off their bones. And great sufferings I was under at this time beyond words to declare, for I was come into the deep" (p. 571). When Friends suffered martyrdom for their faith in faraway New England, Fox "had a perfect sense of their sufferings, as though it had been myself, and as though the halter had been put about my own neck, though we had not at that time heard of it."[40]

The other side of Fox's self-confidence was the ease with which he could denounce those who did not respond to and even obstructed his proclamation. To others this certainty expressed itself in sternness. When James Nayler came to see him before the dramatic Bristol incident, Fox was cool and would not accept "his show of kindness"; indeed, he said, "The Lord moved me to slight him" (p. 269).

There was no doubt in Fox's mind that the "vengeance of the Lord" was upon his enemies. In 1652 he reported that one of his foes was drowned and "the vengeance of God overtook the other justice, Thompson, that he was struck with the dead palsy" (p. 140). At another place in the *Journal,* Fox cited no less than eighteen men and women who had opposed him, and concluded: "All these aforesaid were dead and ruined in their estates and several others of our persecutors whom the Lord blasted and ruined; and though I did not seek to execute the law upon them for their acting contrary to their own laws against me, yet the Lord had executed his vengeance upon them" (p. 505).

Some of the biographers of Fox have been uneasy about this particular trait. Rufus Jones remarked that Fox could have shown more "gentleness and tender sweetness," and John Sykes, in turn, called it an "over-narrow, compulsive" orientation. But we must not forget that to look for, and rejoice in, divine judgments, is a biblical notion and many leading characters in the history of the Christian church were characterized by it. Fox surely considered himself "unique" only because he saw God at work through him. The same must be said about the knowing and fulfilling of God's will—a standard Christian activity, assumed by all prayers and sermons. Thus Fox was noteworthy only because he accentuated and intensified common Christian notions.

Fox's *Journal* abounds in visions and premonitions. At the onset of his public ministry, in 1648, Fox reported that he "saw there was a great crack to go throughout the earth, and a great smoke to go as the crack went" (p. 22). In 1670, while riding toward Rochester, "weight and oppression" fell on Fox's spirit and when he arrived at his destination, he was "very much loaden and burdened with the world's spirits" (p. 569). In 1667, London in ashes after the Great Fire, Fox commented that he had been aware of such a disaster all along "as the word of the Lord came to me concerning it several years before" (p. 510). Closely related is Fox's peculiar vocabulary describing his spiritual pilgrimage. It abounds in visual terms which can hardly be coincidence. George Fox remarks that he "saw light," "the nature of dogs, swine, vipers, of Sodom and Egypt, Pharaoh," that he "saw into that which was without end," saw "the mountains burning up and the rubbish, and the rough and crooked ways and places made smooth." At Lichfield he saw "like a channel of blood." Some of the customary mystic nomenclature is absent in Fox's writings, but his mystical streak is beyond question.

Then there are Fox's healings. One almost expects them from him, and as far as Fox was concerned they were nothing spectacular. His followers took the "signs and wonders" for granted. Thus at Ulverston in 1652 Fox was so thoroughly beaten that he fell unconscious. When he awoke, he challenged his attackers to hit him some more—which they promptly did, pounding his hand which appeared smashed. Fox recorded afterward that the power of God came so through him that his hand was restored. Of his other healings a few random examples must suffice. At the age of twenty-five, Fox healed a woman who "had been possessed for two and thirty years." In 1675 Fox met a woman who had had "the King's evil" and "when I was there, before, she desired me to lay my hands on her and pray for her, which I did, and it was immediately made well" (p. 707). An even more spectacular case had occurred three years earlier in America.

George Fox was perhaps one of the last Christian thinkers who lived in the world-view of the Bible. He was still profoundly persuaded of the immediacy of God's rule in this world. Thus his constant declarations of direct divine guidance, thus his healings or his invocation of God's wrath. The pages of the *Journal* convey ever anew the image of a man who lived in the Bible. This was his paradigm and his handbook; what happened then could happen in his day. His was a God who was willing to intervene directly in his affairs, who heard prayer, gave his power to his own, slew his enemies, in short, a living God as the men of the Old and New Testaments knew him.

And, finally, George Fox holds the distinction of being one of the few radicals who succeeded in their quest for true Christianity—if the establishment of a new religious tradition can be said to constitute success. At any rate, George Fox showed what commitment and determination, coupled with a reasonably opportune time, can do.

4. The Private Scholar:

Thomas Chubb

> If anything is offered to us under the character of divine revelation, it calls for our most careful inspection, as well as our serious attention, lest we should be misled thereby.
>
> —THOMAS CHUBB, *The Author's Farewell*

Again: An Ambiguous Reputation

There is curious significance in the fact that Thomas Chubb, an eighteenth-century radical, was neither a very learned man nor even a trained theologian—and yet theologically he was the most radical one of our list. He was of *docta ignorantia,* which his age was beginning to love. His education did not go beyond the elementary level; universities he saw only from the outside, theology he never formally studied, and all foreign tongues were equally Greek to him. Chubb, though conscious of his demonstrable lack of formal learning, was nonetheless persuaded that his insights were valid as well as important. In the preface to his essay on the *Supremacy of the Father Asserted* he acknowledged his inadequate linguistic competence, but insisted that since the scriptural verdict on the matter at hand was so clear and obvious, he could well argue his case without knowing the biblical languages. What is more, Chubb did not let his simple background cloud his sense of self-importance: thus, he remarked at one place that he wrote "to the pleasure of the intelligent part of mankind."[1]

Discovered by his contemporaries—as well as by himself—almost by accident, Chubb quickly followed established precedent and published with obvious enjoyment rather indiscriminately and prolifically.

His writings comprised some two dozen volumes; his *magnum opus* —*The True Gospel of Jesus Christ Asserted* of 1738—had two editions. Yet such fame was transitory. Most of the contemporaries rejected him—his *True Gospel,* as a matter of fact, evoked ten responses—and posterity forgot him. Perhaps this is the proper verdict on Thomas Chubb, even though it does not quite agree with the exuberant sentiment of the anonymous "muse" who on the occasion of Chubb's passing penned an ode of which the following are typical lines:

> Let Envy die, let Calumny be dumb
> Chubb triumphs where Detraction cannot come;
> Aloft He soars to REASON's native Sphere,
> And quaffs rich Draughts of boundless Knowledge there;
> Where Bacon, Milton, Locke and Newton shine,
> Mingles high Converse, built on Truths Divine. . . .
> Virtue, like CHUBB's, must suffer by Extreams,
> To gild the Brilliant clouds its radiant Beams,
> His WORKS, the mirror of his nobler Mind,
> Thro' latest Ages shall instruct Mankind.[2]

The chronicler must report that such well-meant enthusiasm proved to be unwarranted; mankind has preferred not to be instructed by "His WORKS, the mirror of his nobler Mind." As a matter of fact, a less benevolent contemporary penned a response to this ode, and we quote a few lines:

> Go forth, says Jove, to Sarum's mitred Sire,
> Pour my just Vengeance on that Trayt'rous Head.
> The Chief obeys, inflam'd with sacred Fire,
> And with deputed Thunder strikes him dead.

even adding an epigram:

> When Thomas sunk down to the Regions below,
> Whither sooner, or later, all INFIDELS go;
> Quoth Satan, Friend Chubb, I am sorry thou'rt come;
> Fain would I have much longer protracted thy Doom.
> Thy scheme, like my own, my high Foes would have brav'd,
> And, if possible, damn'd more than Jesus have sav'd.[3]

Clearly, most folk viewed Chubb with a combination of anger and disgust. One contemporary remarked "many women"—and everyone knew how low their estate—"without taking half the pains Mr. Chubb did, both think more justly, and deliver themselves in a much better stile; but it passes for no wonder in them, because they think it (and no doubt it is) a more rational way of spending their time in knotting, or making a housewife, than in starting difficulties and quirks to puzzle the minds of mankind, or in working up old threads of Libertinism into new Deistical books."[4] No doubt, our author considered Thomas Chubb above all a nuisance and could not quite make up his mind as to whether there was enough substance in Chubb's "difficulties and quirks" to warrant serious attention. John Leland, another seventeenth-century writer, was slightly more positive: in his *View of the Principal Deistical Writers* he noted, though with charmingly English restraint, that "among the deistical writers of this present age, Mr. Chubb made no inconsiderable figure."[5]

Who, then, was this Thomas Chubb—according to our anonymous muse peer of Bacon, Milton, Locke, and Newton?

A Life Hardly Exciting

Thomas Chubb was born at East Harnham, near Salisbury, on Michaelmas—September 29—in 1679, youngest son of a village maltster by the name of Henry Chubb, who died when Thomas was still young. His education was simple and elementary, comprising the three "R's" and nothing more. At the age of fifteen Thomas was given as apprentice to a glover; he learned the trade and pursued it for several years, until poor eyesight forced him to give up glovemaking about 1707. Finding a benefactor in one John Lawrence, a "tallow chandler," young Thomas began to assist Lawrence "in his own business"—and this association enabled him to earn his livelihood. At about this time came his first literary effort; it was somewhat cautiously pursued and resulted in a tract entitled *The Supremacy of the Father Asserted*. The circumstances of its writing as well as of its publication were rather dramatic. In 1711 Chubb had come across William Whiston's *Primitive Christianity Revived*. Fascinated particularly by the "historical preface" of Whiston's work, Chubb put his own thoughts on paper, for "his own satisfaction," as he himself remarked. The very fact that Chubb would take to the pen suggests his intellectual alertness; after all, he was but a common laborer, as were countless thousands. The manuscript found its way to Whiston, who proceeded to undertake its publication. Once published, Chubb's work evoked bitter controversy. His first biographer assures us that this work "gave great Offence to many warm Zealots in this Neighbourhood, from whom the Author met violent Opposition and much Scurrility."[6] Chubb's basic assertion was rather simple: straight Arianism—"the son is a Being inferior and subordinate to the Father, and that the Father is the supreme God." Chubb survived the storm of protest—which assured him, at all odds, of his ability to write. Needless to say, not all of the response was negative. A word of approval came from none other than Alexander Pope, who called Chubb a "wonderful phenomenon," adding that he read "through his whole volume, with admiration of the writer, though not always with approbation of the Doctrine."

One of the repudiations of his work came from the pen of a certain John Claggett, and his title denoted his thesis: *Arianism Anatomized.* Unwilling to let his opponent have the last word in the matter, Chubb promptly issued a second work, entitled *The Supremacy of the Father Vindicated,* which reiterated the theological contentions of the first, adding that Claggett's argumentation was based on "base insinuations, falshood [*sic*], and slander."

Rather like a gambler after the first sweet fruit of success, Thomas Chubb was ostensibly under the spell of his successful invasion of the realm of theological writing. From then on, Thomas considered himself self-appointed spokesman on the theological issues of his day. Or, as his opponents had it, "no Controversy can arise, but He must have an Hand in it, tho' He knows no more about it than a wild Ass's Colt."[7] In 1530 he published a collection of no less than thirty-seven essays, some of which probably had been printed before. A random list of topics shows the range of his interest—and claimed competence: *An enquiry concerning property, wherein is considered liberty of conscience; An enquiry concerning sin, in which is considered original sin; An enquiry concerning faith and mysteries; a discourse concerning persecution; the glory of Christ; some short reflections on virtue and happiness; some short reflections on virtue and vice; reflections on national punishments;* and—last, but by no means least—that intriguing sequence of four tracts: *An enquiry into that important question, whether Christ is sole King in his own kingdom —in a letter to a gentleman; Part of a letter to another gentleman, relative to the foregoing enquiry; The previous question, with regard to religion; A supplement to the previous question, with regard to religion.*

The following year, in 1731, Chubb published *A Discourse concerning Reason, with regard to Religion and divine Revelation,* and shifted his concern and interest. The sentiment of the tract appeared on its title page: "Reason either is, or else that it ought to be, a sufficient Guide in Matters of religion." With this publication Chubb entered, as his earlier tracts had already anticipated, the arena of the Deist controversy by addressing himself to the question of revelation. The response was as could have been expected, and in 1532 Chubb—never at a loss to express his sentiment—ventured to set the record straight with a second tract, entitled *The Sufficiency of Reason in Matters of Religion farther considered.* He argued rather cautiously here, dealing mainly with the "sufficiency of reason" wherever there was no divine revelation, wherever "natural man" and his potential had to be considered.

Two years later came a tract entitled *An Enquiry concerning the Books of the New Testament, whether they were written by divine inspiration, according to the vulgar use of that Expression.* Chubb's answer to his own question was negative and people threw up their hands in horror, though, of course, Chubb could take refuge in the fact that he had defined, once again, his terms rather carefully. He was concerned about what he called the "vulgar use" of revelation and insisted that he denied only such vulgar understanding of revelation.

There is no necessity to list all of Chubb's prolific production; only the more important tracts need a passing reference. In 1737 Chubb published *The Equity and Reasonableness of the divine Conduct in pardoning Sinners;* as the subtitle indicated, this was to be a rebuttal of Butler's famous work on the *Analogy of Religion natural and revealed to the Constitution and Course of Nature.* In 1738 came his *magnum opus, The True Gospel of Jesus Christ Asserted: wherein is shewn, what is and what is not that Gospel,* and two years later *An Enquiry into the Ground and Foundation of Religion.*

These writings involved him in running controversy, for opposition was widespread and formidable. But sprinkled among a host of antagonists were a few supporters as well as some benefactors. A certain Mr. Cheselden, a surgeon, thus provided him with "suits of clothes, which had been little worn, and which Mr. Chubb was pleased to accept."[8] Eminent among the benefactors was Sir Joseph Jekyl, Master of the Rolls, to whom Chubb had been recommended by Whiston. Chubb stayed for the better part of two years in Jekyl's household. Though the exact nature of Chubb's role in the household is uncertain, there is a tradition—apocryphal, to be sure—that Chubb "sometimes waited at his patron's table." Some of his adulant biographers found such mundane activity rather unbecoming, though it was admittedly a less risky pursuit of happiness than that undertaken by Thomas Müntzer and radicals of earlier generations. Moreover, this sojourn introduced Chubb, according to an early biographer, "to the personal Knowledge and Intimacy of many Gentlemen of Letters and Eminence; and from them this late Ornament of our City received such Kindnesses as, we may presume, originally enabled him to live, in some sort, independent of Labour"[9]—for eighteenth-century man, and perhaps most men, surely the apex of good fortune!

The last few years of his life were spent at Salisbury. There must have been a generous offer to move elsewhere, but Chubb preferred to stay—which evoked well-nigh ecstasy on the part of his first biographer: "Oh Salisbury," wrote he, "could Plenty and Grandeur have seduced him from thy Habitations, he had been lost to himself, his happier humble State, and thou wouldst have long since been deprived, in him of a Spirit, whose rich Qualities outvied all the Wealth thy Walls could boast to contain besides!" Chubb continued his literary production, some of which was published after his death under the title *Posthumous Works,* in 1748. At Salisbury he seems to have participated in a theological discussion group, a sort of drawing-room radical group that propounded on the theological issues of the day.

Chubb never married; as far as he was concerned "matrimony increased the cares and anxiety of life"; in light of the lack of regular employment on his part, perhaps not an altogether inaccurate description. Death came to Thomas Chubb on Sunday, February 8, 1747, at almost seventy years of age.

His first biographer attributed his demise to a "dis-use of his accustomed Exercise, which was much walking, and . . . an imprudent Indulgence of Milk-Diet, at an improper season." The opponents were not so charitable: one observed that his demise occurred just after he had "returned from the Necessary-house" and added "and pity indeed it is, as his Fate was so near at hand, that he had not staid where he was a Minute or two Longer, that his End might have been of a piece with his Beginning, and that he might have died as He had lived, in a Stink."[10] The noise of controversy sounded beyond his grave. Shortly after his death, a rather partisan account of his life appeared, entitled *A Short and Faithful Account of the Life and Character of Mr. Thomas Chubb*. Such glorification of a man so deviate in proper religion provoked a cleric by the name of Joseph Horler to present the other side of the story: *Memoirs of Mr. Thomas Chubb, Late of Salisbury*—with the subtitle "A fuller and more faithful account of his life, writings, character, and death"—but then posterity began to cloud its ignorance and nescience.

The New Theology

We see his life was rather uneventful, though the example of Thomas Woolston or Peter Annet shows clearly enough that even in those days it was still risky business to be heterodox. He was not a great man and perhaps even he himself would have conceded the point. Nor was he a hero of the faith, or a bold churchman, or a profound theologian. He was a popularizer of religion, and a radical one at that; there was little sympathy between him and the religious establishment. One wonders if Thomas Chubb ever attended church at Salisbury, though habit may well have turned into convenience—or convenience into habit. Above all, Thomas Chubb was an opponent of the ecclesiastical status quo.

Forerunner of "religionless" Christianity he was, and thus he reminds us at once of Sebastian Franck. The sixteenth-century radical stood aloof from the empirical church because he was persuaded that the proper primacy of the inward over the outward was not safeguarded. Thus one kind of worship, or even one creed, was as good as the other. Franck insisted that he did not want to be a Catholic, or Lutheran, or Anabaptist because all of these stressed externals rather than true inward piety. But not so Chubb. He opposed the religious establishment, unable to acknowledge even the possibility of a spiritualizing consensus. Christendom perpetuated a false interpretation of the gospel and accordingly had to be repudiated. It was as simple as that.

Such perspective raises the crucial question whether or not Chubb considered himself a Christian and thought within the Christian tradition. For better or for worse we must allow him the privilege of his own definition of terms—and on this basis the answer is affirmative. "I am a believer, and a Christian," Chubb wrote, adding thoughtfully, "but whether it will be allowed that these appellations are properly applied to me, I know not, nor am I at all solicitous about it."[11]

One supposes that Chubb acknowledged frankly that with respect to the prevailing definition he had to be excluded—yet it was the very core of his argument that this prevailing understanding was abominably erroneous and must be supplanted by the genuine one. One of his contemporaries volunteered the observation that "if the essence of Christianity consists in an exact rectitude of mind and life, and worship of the supreme God, through Jesus Christ our Lord," then he was a Christian.[12]

Others, in turn, were unwilling to grant this point; Edmund Law, for example, contended that Chubb "seems to have fallen at last into an almost universal scepticism; and quitting that former serious and sedate sobriety, which gave him credit, contents himself with carrying on a mere farce for some time; acts the part of a solemn grave buffoon: sneers at all things he does not understand; and after all his fair professions, and the caveats he has entered against such a charge, must unavoidably be set down in the seat of the scornful."[13]

Such divergence of opinion and sentiment about Chubb—by this time a somewhat standard ingredient of the stories related in these pages—demands all the more urgently an examination of Chubb's role and significance: What was his concern? What his contribution? These are the questions; before they can be answered, several more general matters must be considered.

In order to understand Chubb's significance we must, before speaking of his thought, speak about his time. When Thomas Chubb was born, in 1679, a new day had dawned—such as neither Martin Luther nor Thomas Müntzer, neither Sebastian Franck nor George Fox, had dreamed of. The issues confronting Christianity were, in some measure, still the old ones: Protestantism had experienced periods of spiritual vitality as well as periods of spiritual ebb—a rather telling evidence that no Christian tradition could escape what appears to be an iron law of ecclesiastical history: *ecclesia semper reformanda* —the church must ever be reformed. Certain issues facing early eighteenth-century Christianity, however, were new. From the early seventeenth century onward new forces began to exert their influence upon Western Christianity. The rise of natural science, the reorientation of philosophical thought, the broadening of the geographic horizon meant developments which changed the face of European Christianity—whether rightly or wrongly is still debated, though that this has been unalterable seems beyond dispute.

For centuries Western civilization had been a relatively static society. The old was perpetuated and the new was questioned. What was handed down from the past was tried, and thus good; the new was untried, and thus questionable. The rise of natural science disrupted not only cherished concepts, but the underlying presuppositions. In the realm of the natural world, at least, it became obvious that the old was false. Slowly the tables were turned. The old became questionable, and good was only what had been examined, proved, and not found wanting. Man looked with new eyes at his world. And in so doing, he looked with new eyes at his religion—and he found problems. Some of us may find these problems self-imposed and the result of an eager identification of the Ptolemaic world-view with the Bible; yet that the time labored under these problems cannot be doubted. The issue at stake was simple: the new insights of science clashed with the traditional view of the Christian religion and of the Bible.

Scores of polemical treatises appeared. Some defended the traditional position with striking arguments. Others sought to utilize the new insights for a reinterpretation of the Christian faith. These are important for understanding Chubb.

The number of such pertinent volumes is legion and a few random illustrations must suffice: Louis Cappel asserted in his *Arcanum punctationis revelatum* of 1624 that the Hebrew vowel signs of the Old Testament, theretofore regarded as divinely inspired, were a later addition to the scriptural text. Spinoza's *Tractatus theologo-politicus* of 1670 argued that the Old Testament books from Genesis to II Kings were the work of a later writer, and the Richard Simon *Histoire critique du vieux testament* of 1678 saw the Old Testament as a product of postexilic Judaism. Suddenly, the very truth of the Christian religion was called into question.

Traditionally, this truth had been supported by the claim of Scripture to be divine revelation and by recourse to the occurrence of miracles and the fulfillment of prophecy. In the course of the seventeenth century these traditional supports became questionable and some argued that they could no longer be sustained.

Yet the point of all this revoluntary theologizing—and we do well to keep this in mind—was to strengthen the Christian faith and effect a *rapprochement* between this faith, properly understood, and the new world-view. And in this respect, at least, the success was noteworthy. Though some might want to object that fundamental affirmations of the Christian faith were surrendered in the process, the "new" theology prevented the split between "religion" and "culture" for a century.

England was in the very forefront of such theologizing; the theological debate in England in the latter part of the seventeenth and the early part of the eighteenth century was of a considerable vehemence and breadth. Shades of the days of George Fox—though we suspect that he would have turned in his grave upon reading some of the new theological pronouncements! Most men did indeed throw up their hands in horror and resolved to oppose the "new theology." "We cannot," wrote the author of *A Representation of the Present State of Religion with regard to the late excessive growth of Infidelity, Heresy, and Profaneness,* "without unspeakable grief, reflect on deluge of impiety and licentiousness, which hath broke in upon us, and overspread the face of this Church and kingdom, eminent, in former times, for purity of faith and sobriety of manners." But this lamentation over the "deluge of impiety and licentiousness" must not mislead us: the "new theology" was hardly a popular phenomenon—and a coherent movement it never formed. For this, it was too revolutionary and, moreover, too intellectual.[14] There were a few dozen pamphleteers, that was all. Most Englishmen preferred to stay on the side of the angels; the "new theologians" were the theological avant-garde, small in number, a bit self-conscious and, above all, without religious warmth. Historical nomenclature refers to this "new theology" as Deism—Toland, Woolston, Annet, Tindal, and all the rest. Yet since Deism has a broader and more specifically philosophical definition—which allows Voltaire and Diderot to be subsumed under it—we do well to refrain from using the term.

This, then, was the world of Thomas Chubb. Not completely, of course, for there were other sides to it: the London coffeehouses, outgrowth of the latter-day introduction of coffee, where the "smart set" gathered to talk politics, literature, and religion; the time of William Hogarth and his wonderfully satirical engravings of London life—such as "The Enraged Musician," that chaotically crowded London street scene where an honorable musician has to behold from his window a weird beggar playing the recorder, a boy beating his drum, a "woman" with child shrieking "The ladies Fall," a knife-sharpener, a beadle blowing his horn, and a little boy, unperturbed by it all, using a little hole in the ground as toilet. What a seething and facile, exuberant and stately as well as naïvely bawdy life it must have been! Richard Steele, illustrious publisher of *The Tatler,* no one to bypass needlessly the pleasures of life, wrote *The Christian Hero* in 1701 in order to moralize that only the Christian religion could save a man from the temptations of London.

Thomas Chubb lived and wrote in this time. He was one of the "new theologians," concerned to propound the proper understanding of the Christian faith or of, as his *magnum opus* calls it, "the true gospel of Jesus Christ." His necessary presupposition was that the traditional understanding of the Christian faith was perverted, and thus inaccurate.

The Examination of Revelation

Chubb argued that it cannot be "defined or determined what Christianity is," that "nothing but contention and confusion has attended it from its first promulgation," that the New Testament is a "fountain of confusion and contradiction."[15] Accordingly his avowed purpose in the *True Gospel* was to separate from the gospel "those things which have been blended with it, and which thereby have laid a foundation for most of the difficulties and objections which have been urged against it."[16] Quite properly, Chubb remarked at another place that he meant to restore Christianity "to its original native purity and simplicity."[17] What underlay his presupposition can be simply stated: Christianity, as presently conceived, as well as the Scriptures upon which it is based, forms a heterogeneous mixture of genuine elements and subsequent perversion, a motley of accurate and inaccurate descriptions. The urgent task of the theologian, therefore, was to distinguish properly between the two.

The point of departure for such an effort at reconstructing the "original native purity and simplicity" of authentic Christianity was the Bible—for him, as we noted, a heterogeneous collection of documents. "Alas," he lamented, "it is as easy to make the two Pole-Stars meet in a point, as fairly to make all the parts of this composition center in any one of the many systems that have been grounded upon it."[18] Scripture had only brought confusion: numerous contradictory teachings have been based upon it; certain teachings, such as "unconditional election and reprobation, religious persecution, and the like," supposedly found in the Scriptures, are actually "most dishonorable to God, and most injurious to men." What is more, Scripture contains matters "greatly below, and unworthy" of God; indeed, it taught different precepts at different places: what was required at one time was forbidden at another. In sum, Scripture is incoherent, "the books themselves are not quite clear."

And yet this very Scripture claims to be divine revelation. Chubb is willing to acknowledge the claim—but nothing more. The very heterogeneity of the Bible and the existence of other, competing claims of divine revelation outside the Hebrew-Christian tradition, do not allow that the claim itself be considered the authentication. Chubb insisted that revelatory claims cannot be accepted by faith, but must be critically examined in order to be authenticated.

"If anything is offered to us under the character of divine revelation, it calls for our most careful inspection, as well as our serious attention, lest we should be misled thereby." Such is Chubb's categorical dictum; examination is necessary in order to distinguish between an authentic and a spurious revelation. Thus Chubb wrote concerning a point of the christological dogma: "to say, that the new Testament writers referred to, received the aforesaid doctrine (of Christ's making and upholding the world) by divine inspiration, is begging the question; because this is a point which is not to be presumed, but proved." "It becomes our bounden duty, because our interest and safety are embarked in the case, to examine carefully and cautiously the grounds upon which they are built, and the channels through which they have passed."

Thus, speaking about the Gospel according to Mark, Chubb raised one question after the other: How do we know, he inquired, that Mark was the author? How do we know that Mark knew what he related? How do we know that this book has been faithfully transmitted to us? There must be critical scrutiny and the three questions just cited denote the scope of verification considered mandatory. Chubb seems to say that verification of revelatory claims must investigate the form of Scripture, its content, as well as its transmission. The student of Scripture must establish, first of all, what the Gospel writers actually wrote; he must, moreover, establish their credentials with respect to their accounts; he must, finally, examine if their writings have been accurately transmitted through the centuries.

The second and third aspects deserve additional comment: Chubb contends that the Gospel writers included materials which upon close scrutiny cannot be considered valid—as, for example, the description of certain happenings at which the writer himself was not present. Joseph's dream in the nativity story is here a case in point for Chubb: "And though the historian has given an account of the dream, yet that Joseph told this dream to him, or how he otherwise came by this information, this he saith not." The scope of authentic description is limited, therefore, to what the writer himself saw and experienced. This must be what Chubb had in mind when he spoke at one place of separating the "probable from the incredible." And then the third aspect: not only must there be a proper examination of the revelatory claims but there must also be the acknowledgment that a revelation may have been altered in the process of its historical transmission. It may have become perverted and lost its pristine glory. "Revelation, like a pack of cards, is capable (perhaps more capable) of being shuffled and cut, compounded and divided, and so dealt forth, as to answer all the purposes that the depraved appetites and the various instincts of men may direct it to." This aspect is of fundamental importance for Chubb; as a matter of fact, it constitutes the very heart of his contention: divine revelation, no sooner given, was perverted and this perversion is even in evidence in the Scriptures: certain writers, instead of confining themselves to an accurate description of what actually transpired, were wont to add hearsay and personal opinion—thus perverting the authentic message.

Chubb's major concern is verification of scriptural claims. But by way of parenthetical remark, we must point out that traditionally, too, the claims of biblical revelation were subjected to verification; the function of apologetics was to do precisely this. Accordingly, the basic effort of Chubb was not unique; the way he went about it was.

Traditionally, verification took place in a definite and circumscribed setting which we might label "intra-scriptural": the starting point was the scriptural record and its authentication was sought in it. Thus the descriptions of miracles and the fulfillment of prophecy constituted the two cornerstones. In other words, history recorded in Scripture was cited to prove Scripture. As long as the former was not questioned with respect to its accuracy, there was no problem. However, as soon as an "extra-scriptural" perspective arose, which questioned the scriptural as such, a precarious difficulty was introduced. This is the situation confronted by Thomas Chubb. His examination purports to be radical inasmuch as it does not acknowledge any incisive quality of Scripture.

Fundamental to Chubb is an important presupposition: if the examination of a revelatory claim is needful, man must have available a tool enabling him to undertake this examination. Clearly enough, this tool will determine the nature of the examination. The character of revelation must correspond to a faculty of man, for otherwise man would not be able to discern a revelation nor adjudge it. No valid decision could be made between a spurious and an authentic revelation. "Without this," Chubb observed, "the written word of God is but as of so many words or empty sounds which to us are of no signification. And if we should admit the Pope, or any other man, or body of men, to be the infallible interpreters of Scripture, which we deny, yet still the case is the same; because we must exercise our reason to discern and judge which is the sense and meaning of their interpretation. Or, if we should suppose a divine assistance, by which the spirit of God informs us what is the mind of God contained in his revelation; then this assistance, or work of the spirit in us, is either an assistant of our reason in its use and exercise, as aforesaid, or else it is an immediate informing of our understandings, by inspiration or other ways, of those truths which are contain'd in that revelation."[19] Man's reasoning faculty constitutes the touchstone by which revelation is adjudged. Reason is superior to Scripture; that which is outside of man receives its authentication from man. But, even more significantly, the content of revelation and man's reasoning are positively related.

The Sufficiency of Reason

In his *True Gospel* Chubb remarked that he "rendered the gospel of Christ defendable upon rational principles."[20] His language was somewhat careless here, for his use of the term "gospel" was unique: what he meant to say was that he so reinterpreted the gospel as to make it conformable to rational principles. His treatise on *The Sufficiency of Reason,* of 1532, defended reason as "sufficient guide" in religion. From the perspective of the traditional understanding Chubb was walking on thin and slippery ice. But he was going to make the best of it. The subtitle of the tract indicated Chubb's concern; he meant to establish the sufficiency of reason in religious matters—for every man "whether he resides in China, or at the Cape of Good Hope." He was concerned about delineating what might be called minimum standards of comprehending the divine purpose; enable man everywhere—outside or inside the context of "biblical revelation"—to discern God's will. Men, of all times and all places, must be able to know God and his commandment. A common denominator must embrace all men—and Chubb contended that this common bond is reason. Yet, he added, reason is only a sufficient guide, not a full one. Chubb would have thrown up his hands in horror had we charged him with denying revelation. He did not, though revelation was for him rather like the icing on the cake, the "extra" not really necessary, though quite helpful. His *Enquiry Concerning the Use of Reason in Matters of Revelation* distinguished between truths "which are in reason's province" and truths "which are in faith's province." As example for the former, Chubb cited the assertion "that there is a God."[21] Man's "reasoning faculty" allows him to obtain a satisfactory answer. On the other hand, "in faith's province" is the assertion, for example, that "the bodily part of our Saviour was not produced into being by the agency of man, in the ordinary course of generation; but by the power of the Holy Ghost." Chubb says here that with respect to such questions revelation can provide the proper and satisfactory answer—one that is helpful, but rather superfluous. Chubb shows himself a disciple of John Locke by acknowledging that revelation can be "a-rational," but that it never can be "ir-rational"; it can be above reason, but never against it. Moreover, where "revelation" conveys propositional truth, such truth is not essential to man's eternal happiness; it cannot be, since it would put the recipient of revelation into a superior position.

At any rate, Chubb circumscribed his sentiment carefully. Reason, he claimed, "when carefully used and followed is sufficient to guide men to God's favor, and to happiness of another world: in opposition to that absolute necessity of a divine revelation, which supposes, that it is impossible or at least that it is exceeding difficult, and next to impossible, for a man to obtain God's favor, and the happiness of another world, who has only his reasoning faculty to guide him, and who has not the help of a divine revelation."[22] The point was obviously to provide man everywhere with the possibility of obtaining God's favor. The complete sufficiency of reason—as, for example, for the establishment of a system of morality—was outside Chubb's concern.

Chubb insisted rather pointedly that he did not deny revelation and declared that the recipients of revelation enjoy a "very great favour and advantage." The nature of this "favour and advantage" was spelled out in exuberant detail; "to rouse up men from their sloth and security; to bring them to consideration and reflection; to assist their enquiries, and to facilitate that work; to present to their view that rule of action, which the reason of things requires they should govern their behaviour by; to awaken in men a just sense of the trust that is reposed in them and the obligations they are under both to God and to each other; to call those who live viciously, to repentance and reformation of their evil ways; and to represent to them the certain consequences of a good and a bad life, with regard to divine favour or displeasure."

While the traditional concept of revelation is retained by Chubb—though its certainty is cautiously left undecided—the traditional content of revelation is called into question: essentially revelation does not proclaim something new, but confirms the old and, moreover, obtains its authentication from its content.

In his *True Gospel,* Chubb remarked quite appropriately that "the certainty which revelation affords, that God will judge the world, does not barely result from the divine declaration, but from the ground or reason of that declaration, viz., the rightness, or fitness of the thing declared."[23] His opponent Hallett, on the other hand, saw it quite differently and found that the scriptural declaration made all the difference. The question arises why Chubb sought to reinterpret the traditional content of revelation: it can hardly have been the need for rationality; if so, his acknowledgment of "a-rational" revelation certainly complicated his case. The need for universal principles allowing all men a proper understanding of God must have been important. Chubb is concerned about those outside revelation. "Are they to be considered as accountable creatures," he asked, "and yet destitute of ability sufficient to render them pleasing to their Maker? No, surely. The very supposition is monstrous, and carries with it a most horrid reflection upon the moral character of Almighty God."[24]

The moral character of God is at stake for Chubb, who cannot imagine that God would leave some men without the "sufficient" means to walk the more perfect way.

The Inquiry Concerning the Gospels

With such considerations Chubb approaches the New Testament and he accepts the essential accuracy of the biblical narratives concerning Jesus' life and ministry. Still, the key word is "probable": "It appears improbable," Chubb wrote, "that Christianity should take place, and prevail in the way, and to the degree that it did, or, at least, that it is represented to have done, supposing the history of Christ's life and ministry to be fiction."[25]

Chubb's argumentation is historical pragmatism. The rise and expansion of Christianity—a historical fact—finds its explanation in the assumption of the historical accuracy of the Gospel accounts. There must be a concrete event at the beginning—and Chubb is willing to assume the historicity of this event as described in the Gospels. All the same, he is cautious; the possibility of a faulty description of the rise and expansion of the Christian faith—which constitutes the cornerstone of his willingness to accept the historicity of Christ's life and ministry—is mentioned, yet not carefully examined. Only the assumption of a general accuracy of the Gospels affords a satisfactory explanation for the subsequent history of Christianity.

The gospel as originally conceived was quite different from its later expressions. Christianity was clear, Chubb assured his readers, "of all that mystery and darkness, that his pretended successors have since introduced, to raise their superstructures of wealth and power upon." Such original clarity did not prevail, however; the Christian faith was not transmitted in pristine form. "Christ's message has been so loosely and indeterminately delivered to the world that nothing but contention and confusion have attended it, from its first promulgation down to this time; insomuch that what has been deemed to be Christianity in one age, and by one people, has not been so in, and by another." We are faced, once again, with the postulate of a mixture of perverted and authentic materials in the New Testament which in principle demands the same measure of verification as Chubb desires of the traditional position. "Mystery" and "darkness" are Chubb's watchwords, the elements to be eliminated from the Gospel accounts.

Chubb stated the purpose of Christ's mission simply: "It is probable that Jesus Christ was sent of God to be an advisor and an instructor to mankind, by communicating such useful knowledge to them as otherwise they might not have attained to, and by refreshing their memories, and awakening their attention to such propositions as otherwise might have been greatly neglected by them." Jesus was the great teacher and his "great end and the professed design" were to "save men's souls." One must not be misled here: such traditional terminology did not mean orthodox theology. By "saving men's souls" Chubb meant that Jesus wanted "to prepare men for, and to insure to them the favor of God, and their happiness in another world, and to prevent them from bringing great and lasting misery upon themselves."[26] This was done, as we shall see, by his teaching, rather than by his life.

The denial of the uniqueness of Jesus' proclamation raises questions about the need for his coming. Chubb sought to explain the reason for Jesus' coming into the world and even for the subsequent perversion of his message. Mankind was "generally corrupt and vicious," he declared in the *True Gospel,* and he added that "men, from a false and unworthy sense of God, went into false ways of pleasing him; and upon a sense of their guilt, they took wrong measures to recommend themselves to the divine mercy."

Describing the nature of Jesus' mission, Chubb used the term "undeceive" to suggest what Jesus did—he "undeceived" men. "Our Lord Jesus Christ took upon him to be their reformer." Jesus made men aware of their perversion and gave them the proper understanding. "Mankind in general were grossly corrupted."

The True Gospel of Jesus Christ

If Jesus' gospel was not more than a "republication of the religion of nature," to use Tindal's words, the question arises why it was not universally received. Here was indeed a crucial question, and an entire section of the *True Gospel* is devoted to it; intriguingly enough, the Duke University Library copy of the work contains the marginal annotation of an eighteenth-century writer, "worthy to be read." Several reasons are cited for the limited appeal of Jesus' "natural religion": first of all, the wickedness of men who were disposed to oppose everything that checked their enjoyment; the gospel needs seriousness of purpose. Second, the gospel of Jesus "lays the axe to the root of the tree, and (if I may so speak) it gives no quarter." The gospel, in other words, requires moral virtue, conformity of mind and life, repentance. Third, there are man's prejudices "arising from education, preconceived opinions and the like." Since Jesus' proclamation was contrary to that which had been known, men were unwilling to embrace it. Religion, Chubb assures his readers, "with many becomes hereditary, and like men's estates descends from father to son." Fourth, governmental jurisdiction in religious matters prevented men's free decision, as did the fact that religion helps many people "to build a profitable trade upon." This has been the case in all ages, Chubb remarks, but "it is notoriously so at this day." Finally, "the gospel itself very soon corrupted," and one can hardly expect men to accept such aberration.

What was the content of Jesus' proclamation? According to Chubb, three truths were proclaimed by Jesus—or, as his picturesque language has it, there were three truths "which Christ has thus recommended to public consideration." Jesus insisted, first of all, on conformity "to that eternal and unalterable rule of action which is found in the reason of things (which rule is summarily contained in the written word of God)." Several observations follow: there exists a "rule of action," eternal and unalterable, which is found in "the reason of things." Thus Jesus merely called attention to this rule and insisted on its realization. "Christ's doctrine was exactly conformable to our natural order of things,"[27] Chubb opines, and adds that Christ did not "deliver any new body of laws" but recommended "that law of reason which they were antecedently obliged to govern their behaviour by." As contents of this law or "rule of action," Chubb notes "the doing as one would be done by, the loving God with all our heart, soul, mind and strength; . . . the loving our neighbor as our selves." Chubb acknowledges that Jesus exhorts men to believe in him for their salvation, but he argues that to believe in Christ "is the same as to believe the gospel or the good news which Christ proclaimed." Faith, accordingly, is redefined as obedience, rather than trust or humility, and the object of such obedience is not Christ, but that eternal law to which he directed men's attention. Second, Jesus proclaimed that deviation from this law must lead to "repentance and reformation" as the "only and the sure fount of the divine mercy and forgiveness." And third, Jesus affirmed that God has "appointed a day in which he will judge the world in righteousness, and that he will then either acquit or condemn, reward or punish them according as they have, or have not, conformed their minds and lives to that rule of righteousness."

This, in essence, was Jesus' message and thus formed his gospel: there is a moral law which man is called upon to obey; deviation from this law must lead to repentance if divine mercy is to be obtained; a judgment day will confront all men. Most contemporaries found these postulates embarrassingly commonplace and without distinctive Christian propensity. To Chubb himself this was, all the same, signal virtue: the harmony between the principles of the "true gospel of Jesus Christ" and the "natural order of things" constituted proof for the authenticity of both.

Chubb asserted these principles to be the "gospel of Jesus Christ," yet clearly enough, this was not the "gospel" which had been found traditionally in the New Testament. Thus he had to delineate a hermeneutic principle allowing the rejection of the traditional interpretation and the embracing of a new one. The question was where and how this "true gospel of Jesus Christ" can be discerned in Scripture. Chubb's answer was categorical: not all of the New Testament, not even all of the written Gospels, contains this "true gospel." The New Testament is a mixture and conglomeration of the authentic gospel and perverted views and interpretations. How can we know what is what?

Chubb asserted that only Jesus' life and words constitute this true gospel: this is his major methodological and hermeneutical assertion. He distinguishes between two kinds of New Testament materials: the "gospel" in the strict sense—what is extant "at first hand, as from Christ himself, without anyone's comment upon it, supposing those records to be originally true history, and to have sustained no injury thro' its conveyance to us." On the other hand, there are those who describe the happenings "at second hand, as from Christ through them, who, to say the least, were liable to misunderstand their master."[28] In the *True Gospel* Chubb contends that the gospel of Jesus Christ "is not any particular private opinion" of the evangelists, who were sent out to proclaim his gospel.[29] Their "private opinions" are useless for the delineation of the "true gospel." True enough, the Gospel according to John describes Jesus as the logos of God, as pre-existent, as agent in making this visible world. But, Chubb argues, these assertions are "of no consequence to us" because they are not part of Christ's gospel. In this way Chubb was able to dismiss the entire epistolary part of the New Testament as well as some of the dramatic assertions of the Gospels, since they cannot be ascribed directly to Jesus. Where a saying of Jesus expressly countered the general tenor of his proclamation, such as Mark 4:11 f., Chubb was bold enough to insist that "it cannot be true; or, at least, it is very unlikely to be so. And this, I think, will justify me in pronouncing this to be a branch of history, that is either false in itself, or else that it is falsely related to us." Who were the men who proclaimed Jesus' message? Chubb says that the apostles "are not only proved to be fallible, peccable men, and, as such, are not fit absolutely to be relied upon; but also their errors of judgment and practice seem to stand upon record."[30] They cannot serve, therefore, as trustworthy guides.

At any rate, Chubb's acknowledgment of a general accuracy of the Gospel accounts, which we have already noted, does not remove the fact of error in specifics. "The gospel historians give a relation of things, which took place many years before those histories were written; things they could have no personal knowledge of, but must have taken them upon trust from others, no one knows who." Here Chubb shows clearly that in principle the Gospel accounts in their entirety have become questionable historically speaking; no longer does the clear or unanimous testimony of the Gospel writers suffice, for the very accuracy of this testimony is being questioned. Accordingly, Chubb countered the assertion that Jesus performed his miracles, according to the Gospel writers, "in the open day-light and before a multitude of spectators" with the observation that "we have no other authority for it than the bare testimony of the historian; so that the circumstances referred to; namely, that Christ's works were performed before a multitude of spectators, amounts to just nothing at all. The multitude referred to have left no testimonies concerning those facts; and therefore the case is the same to us as if they had not been spectators of them. Witnesses without a testimony are in fact but so many mutes, and are not witnesses at all."

There is only one testimony and that comes from the "historians." While this does not "sink the credit of those histories; yet, surely, it weakens that credit." Uncertainty prevails and while Chubb shows himself willing to accept the general tenor of the Gospel accounts, he does no more than that—and even relegates that which he accepts into the realm of probability.

But Chubb eliminates not only "private opinion" from his definition of the "true gospel" but also what he calls the "historical account of matters of fact" relating to Jesus—that Jesus "suffered, died, rose from the dead, ascended into heaven, etc."[31] Chubb does not at all question the historicity of these "historical accounts of matters of fact," but he rejects the utilization of these "recorded facts" for the construction of the gospel of Jesus. This he considers not legitimate. He repudiates thereby any doctrinal significance of Jesus' death and resurrection. And his authority for rejecting the traditional emphasis is none other than Jesus himself: "That Christ hath by his sufferings and death made satisfaction to God for the sins of the world, and thereby merited the sinners discharge from condemnation, this doctrine Christ did not preach."

The "true gospel" is comprised of that "which Christ was specially appointed of God to preach to the Jews"—above all his own words, his message. Moreover, it is comprised of his life, insofar as this life constituted a perfect manifestation of his teaching: "Christ preached his own life if I may so speak, and lived his own doctrine."[32] Word and deed were here in perfect harmony. From this perspective Chubb is willing to concede a certain importance to Jesus' death—but not *that* he died is significant, but *how* he died is worthy to be recalled: Jesus exercised "such patience and resignation under the severest trials and mosts painful afflictions and persecutions" as to become worthy of our imitation.[33]

Jesus lived an exemplary life and Chubb describes this life in colorful and moving terms: "In him we have an example of a quiet and peaceable spirit, of a becoming modesty and sobriety, just and honest, upright and sincere, and above all of a most gracious and benevolent temper and behaviour. One who did no wrong, no injury to any man, in whose mouth was no guile, who went about doing good. . . . His life was a beautiful picture of human nature, when in its native purity and simplicity."

One may, of course, heap theological scorn upon this humanitarian image of Jesus and, no doubt, it is a far cry from the orthodox portrait of the redeemer engaged in cosmic conflict. All the same, there is a profound religious sentiment even here—and we do well not to overlook it. Chubb's opponents charged essentially that he restricted unpardonably the fullness of the gospel; what he asserted was not false, but incomplete and not the "full gospel of Jesus Christ."

Jesus Christ is, at all odds, a unique person—a man, to be sure, of the same species as all other men, not pre-existent but, so Chubb acknowledges, "under God the greatest benefactor to our species." Probably Christ's mission was divine; probably he "was entrusted with a superiority of power"—and yet this, he adds with cautious and restrained skepticism—"is the utmost that can be inferred." The sources are too evasive, the distance of time too great, the possibility of false representation too formidable to allow more than such tentative and haphazard conclusions.[34] The case for Jesus' divinity cannot be examined exhaustively; what can be ascertained and examined suggests only a measure of probability.

Such "superiority of power" may have enabled Jesus to perform miracles. Chubb admits the possibility of miracles—and this admission relieves him from the burdensome obligation to make a case against them. All the same, he is rather cautious: "That God upon some extraordinary occasion and to answer some great and good ends immediately interposes and by his power produces, or causes to be produced such effects as would not be produced in the course of his general providence . . . by the settled laws of nature were they left to take their course; this is such a particular providence as I have no objections against, and therefore have not opposed." Again, he wrote: "I do not hereby charge myself with the proof of the facts before-mentioned," adding, "admitting they were really wrought as the history sets forth."[35]

But his admission of the possibility of miracles constitutes only part of his argument. Miracles as such, he argues, are "natural marks" and "give a sensible proof of a superiority of power"; the point of the Gospel accounts of miracles is not that they were performed in a vacuum, as it were, but rather that they were meant to authenticate the proclamation of Jesus. These two aspects must be clearly distinguished. The acknowledgment of the miracles described in the New Testament does not, therefore, entail the verification of Jesus' message.[36] Accordingly, miracles can render only probable proof: "Miracles, under the most advantageous circumstances cannot, in the nature of the things, offer certain, but only probable proof that a revelation is divine."[37]

Two considerations are of substantive importance for Chubb for assessing the character of an occurrence. One is that the act itself needs to be examined from various perspectives—if it is above the natural ability of man to cause; if it is above the ordinary course of nature; if it is produced by God; if it is annexed to truth. The other is that a completely different problem arises from the chronological distance of the "objective" viewer and the presumed miracle. It is one thing to acknowledge the probability of a "miracle"; it is quite another to allow for the accurate transmission of such "probable" opinion through the centuries.

Applying these considerations to the "miracles" found in the Gospel accounts, Chubb finds that persuasive evidence is lacking. There are no genuine witnesses of miracles in the New Testament materials, only historians—namely, the Gospel writers—who report witnesses. Thus, Chubb argues, the "witnesses" of Thomas Sherlock's famous tract on *The Trial of the Witnesses of the Resurrection of Jesus,* namely, the apostles, are not really witnesses in the proper sense of the word, and Sherlock's case thus remains unproven. Such is the case, even if the various discrepancies of the Gospel accounts are resolved and their difficulties eliminated. The conclusion is simple enough for Thomas Chubb: "Thus stands the case with regard to those miracles that were wrought by Christ himself, they come to us under such circumstances as leave room for doubting whether they did really take place, or not."[38]

The problem of Jesus' resurrection is seen in this perspective. The historicity of this miracle is outside Chubb's concern—not, of course, because he would not be interested in its verification or repudiation, but because he sees no possibility of doing either. "The present question is not," Chubb writes, "whether Christ did really rise from the dead. That may have been the case." And he continues that the only question is "whether we have proper proof that he did." It is hardly surprising that Chubb gives us a negative answer. His arguments are not exactly new but stem from the arsenal of the Deists of the time, though Chubb hardly bothers with details of exegesis, which, of course, was in a way parenthetical to his argument anyhow, since he was persuaded that the "historians"—the Gospel writers—were hardly accurate and sufficient witnesses. Christ appeared only to a few persons who were hardly objective witnesses; these persons, according to the scriptural accounts themselves, were unable to identify him properly, suggesting the possibility of allusion and deception. As a matter of fact, "those whom he did appear to have left no testimonies upon record with regard to this fact (except St. Peter and the historians); and therefore, with respect to posterity, they are no witnesses at all. The historians, indeed, say that Christ, after his resurrection, appeared several times to several persons; but then it does not appear that those persons themselves have made any such declaration."

This is the crucial point for Chubb: whatever the actual happening, the sources are inconclusive. Accordingly, Chubb replies to the argument that, according to the second chapter of Acts, Peter and several of the brethren were witnesses of the resurrected Christ, "that St. Peter delivered such a discourse to the Jews, rests only and wholly on the authority of one single nameless Historian, the author being unknown." The New Testament writers made observations and offered comments "of which it does not appear that they had anything to ground those assertions upon."[39]

We are back again at the simplicity of the "true gospel of Jesus Christ"—not that which is clearly evidenced and beyond doubt, but that which is probable and thus can be accepted.

We need not rehearse here the possible objections against Thomas Chubb. Most of his contemporaries delighted to do so whenever the opportunity presented itself. Such repudiation took varied forms: the anonymous "Antichubbius" preferred to level enigmatic charges against Chubb's personal morals and Joseph Horler penned a massive 565-page *Vindication of the Gospel of Jesus Christ* which he concluded with a personal appeal to his antagonist to mend his ways and be converted. Since these men defended the status quo, they could do little more than reiterate the traditional position; this they did—Hallett with more incisiveness than Horler—without following Chubb onto the slippery path of his methodological distinction. They never entered into a real dialogue. Edmund Law thought he could sum it all up by observing that "by ever aiming at things far beyond his reach; by attempting a variety of subjects, for which his narrow circumstances, and small compass of reading and knowledge had in great measure disqualified him; from a fashionable, but fallacious, kind of philosophy (with which he set out, and by which one of his education might very easily be misled), he fell by degrees to such confusion in divinity, to such low quibbling on some obscure passages in our translation of the Bible, and was reduced to such wretched cavils as several historical facts and circumstances, wherein a small skill either in the language, or sciences, might have set him right; or a small share of real modesty would have supplied the want of them."[40]

Chubb's most formidable opponent was none other than Jonathan Edwards, whose treatise on the *Freedom of the Will,* of 1754, included some frontal attacks upon Chubb's tract *Vindication of God's Moral Character,* which he published in his *Collection of Tracts on Various Subjects.*[41] Edwards was persuaded that the postulate of the freedom of the will meant the dislodging of the full compass of the Christian faith; Chubb's deviation from the orthodox faith was only the result of his false teaching concerning the freedom of the will.[42] Paul Ramsey, the present-day editor of Edwards' treatise, has suggested that Chubb's view on sin led to his Pelagian view of the human will. This may well be, though it must be more than coincidence that Chubb's views are found within a discussion—or rather, as he would have it, a "vindication"—of "God's moral character." Perhaps this constitutes Chubb's starting point; he reinterpreted man's potential *ad majorem Dei gloriam:* God's moral character required that man's eternal fate be the result of man's free action rather than God's arbitrary fiat. Edwards was, no doubt, a brilliant protagonist and marshaled the full force of the traditional anti-Pelagian argument against Chubb. Yet the disagreement between the two men remained unresolved—as theological controversy often is;

Ramsey acknowledges that Edwards did not succeed "in refuting Chubb's position because he does not effect a meeting with it."

The Measure of the Man

What manner of man was Thomas Chubb? One might call him a skeptic with respect to the traditional precepts of the Christian faith. He meant to be a theologian, yet he was a theologian of a newer sort, such as we today have come to know rather well, but such as an earlier time did not know. For one, it deserves to be recalled that while Chubb's thought was radical, his life assuredly was not. Thomas Chubb was the paradigm of a new breed of radicals who combined the amenities of bourgeois existence with shockingly radical theological pronouncements. It goes without saying that some of the radicals of earlier generations, involved in turbulent controversy and strife, would have much preferred to do the same, but they could not. Thomas Chubb heralded a new age.

Thomas Chubb made bold to look at things his own way; he would have hardly felt comfortable in the company of Origen, Thomas, Luther—or Müntzer, Franck, and Fox, for that matter. Yet his orientation was indicative of the change in the theological climate of Western Christendom. With the exception of his trinitarian—or rather Arian—reflection, Chubb did not address himself to the traditional themes of theology, but dealt instead with new ones. He was not the first one to do so; his Deist peers did the very same. The new theological concerns of the day were the problems of revelation, God's relationship to the world, and miracles, and they were argued with passion and acumen. The defenders of the status quo marshaled the conglomerate insight of 1,600 years of Christian history; the proponents of the "new theology" sought their strength in the application of the new insights of their day to the Christian faith.

The trouble with Thomas Chubb was that he meant to be on both sides of the fence at the same time; one can do that, however, only by assuming a rather painful and hardly impressive position. Chubb affirmed the possibility of miracles, yet denied their practical significance. He affirmed the reality of revelation, yet he so redefined its content to render such affirmation without practical significance. One suspects either ignorance or insincerity here; either or both are possible. Yet we must not chide him all too naïvely. By introducing the term "probable" to the contested issues of revelation, miracles, and Jesus' resurrection, Chubb carefully avoided the metaphysical noose around the necks of either the Deists or their opponents. And his ambivalence constituted a most intriguing solution, one which should have merited better attention.

One should note Chubb's methodology. He shared with the other Deists the desire to reconstruct the "historical" or original gospel. Their underlying presupposition was that the pristine splendor of the "historical" event had been modified or changed by the Gospel accounts. Today such argument is a commonplace of biblical scholarship, universally debated and widely accepted; the nineteenth-century quest of the historical Jesus was its signal expression. In the days of Chubb, however, the argument was no less than revolutionary. In crude yet distinctly discernible fashion, Chubb anticipated the assertion of contemporary New Testament scholarship that the proclamation of the early church—Chubb would have said "private opinions" about Jesus—shaped the content of the New Testament, that the New Testament is a result of the church—and not vice versa. Interestingly enough, the scriptural references cited by Joseph Hallett in his *The Consistent Christian* against Chubb's contention that Christ's death and resurrection were not part of Christ's gospel —such as Col. 1:14; 1 John 1:7; Gal. 2:21; Rom. 4:25; 1 Pet. 1:3; 1 Cor. 15:17, etc.—did not fulfill Chubb's methodological requirements to come directly from Jesus—and thus Chubb could comfort himself at least that his point still stood. Of course, Chubb posited the existence of what he called an independent tradition of Jesus' *vox ipsissima,* which he placed alongside the "private opinions," and such postulate constituted a methodological hiatus in his argument. Yet Thomas Chubb bypassed the entire nineteenth-century quest for the so-called "historical Jesus" by being relatively unconcerned about the authentic reconstruction of Jesus' life so as to obtain the proper basis for his teaching. Chubb did not pursue the question of what is evidently historical in the Gospel record of Jesus, and what is not, considering such effort beyond fruitful realization, particularly with respect to miracles. Instead he ventured to distinguish between "layers" of the Gospel with respect to Jesus' teaching.

Thomas Chubb's concentration on the *vox ipsissima* of Jesus as the only legitimate source for the Christian faith constituted an intriguingly refreshing insight: this was his solution to the problem of the mixture of "true gospel" and "perversion" in the biblical record. Yet it entailed certain problems. Chubb assumed that the writers of the New Testament—writing some time after the events—did, on the one hand, adequately transmit Jesus' words, while, on the other, he argued that they added interpretations, views, perspectives, which were not a proper expression of the "true gospel." Chubb does not speak of perversion or intentional fraud here, but merely of the "personal opinions" of the New Testament writers—which may be true, false, or indifferent, but they are, at any rate, beside the point. This methodological distinction is not impossible to make, though it is difficult to see how the gospels were so accurate in one respect and so careless in others. In a way, Chubb's opponents argued their case on this ground, though by no means as incisively or succinctly as may have been desirable: thus, Horler's tediously voluminous *Vindication* insisted that "all the Testimonies of the Writers of the Gospel of Jesus Christ, must be allow'd to be of equal Weight and Validity, and every Particular, which they relate, must be allow'd to be the Gospel of Jesus Christ."[43] Thus Chubb concedes at one place that the biblical records must be supposed to be "originally true history and to have sustained no injury thro' its conveyance to us."

Chubb, in company with the other Deists, set out to reconstruct the "true Gospel." He was not so radical as some of his colleagues, who ventured to remove everything that smacked of supranaturalism from the Gospel accounts. Chubb acknowledged the problem created by the presence of supranatural elements in the Gospels, but he argued that the real issue was not to decide a question of metaphysics, but rather if the historical verification of certain "metaphysical" claims is possible.

Thus Chubb raised what we might call the historical question, though in a restricted sense: the Gospels contain two levels of historical material, a "supranatural" level of the miracles, including Jesus' virgin birth, his resurrection and ascension, and also a "natural" level, comprising the more ordinary aspects of Jesus' life—that he was born, that he lived, and that he died. Chubb commented on both aspects by insisting that at best their "probability" could be suggested, especially in case of the former; in case of the latter, Chubb was willing to subsume such probability under the statement that "in the main" Jesus lived as the Gospels recorded.

The theology of Chubb's day and age was confronted with two major problems—one old, the other new: the "metaphysical" and the "historical" question. The contested issues—such as the authenticity of revelation and miracles—involved not only a general metaphysical consideration as to their possibility, but the concrete consideration of the specific claims made in the New Testament.

On the level of metaphysical concerns the controversy ended in a draw; the notion of revelation and miracles could be well argued on both sides. Thomas Chubb neatly avoided taking a side by leaving the question open. Yet he forcefully shifted the emphasis onto the historical question: not the possibility of revelation as such was to be examined, but the specific claims made in the biblical record. Chubb argued that it was impossible to decide definitively on the latter question—and this made all the difference with respect to the former.

Then there is something else. When Thomas Chubb died, in 1747, the Evangelical Revival had been in progress for a decade; its phenomenal consequences attest that there is in religion an aspect that cannot easily be included in abstract theological discussion. As long as there is religion, the heart will demand its homage: when John Wesley stated that his heart was "strangely warmed" he testified to this aspect. Thomas Chubb had little understanding of the emotional realities of religious life and he, even as his fellow Deists, was swept away by the wave of the Evangelical Revival.

Thomas Chubb was a self-made theologian, we said at the beginning; yet, in the strict sense of the word, one may doubt if he was a theologian at all, since he lacked all the mandatory and necessary scholarly paraphernalia—the acquaintance with the theological tradition or with the biblical languages. To us this may appear as formidable vice—to Thomas Chubb it was pure virtue. There is a touching phrase in his *Farewell* that applies to his own literary effort as to the religious quest of his peers: "But, says the ploughman, the thresher, the illiterate tradesman, what shall we do? We have neither learning, nor reading, nor anything to qualify us for making such trial; nor have we any standard to try man's pretences by."

Docta ignorantia! But: "Surely the case is not so desperate," Chubb added. And he himself is a telling example! If nothing else, Thomas Chubb constitutes a splendid example of what is surely the Protestant principle: "Take and read."

If Müntzer, Franck, and Fox in one way or another propounded a religious radicality oriented by personal involvement, the radicalism of Thomas Chubb was that of a private scholar. He was no less impressive, for his questions are still very much our own.

5. The Agnostic Infidel:

David Friedrich Strauss

> Investigations of this kind may inflict a wound on the faith of some individuals.
>
> —David Friedrich Strauss, *The Life of Jesus*

First Academic Beginnings

The story of David Friedrich Strauss serves as a vivid reminder that all radicals perform a tightrope act, and that, to use biblical language, only he who endures to the end shall be saved. This is to say that the radical's repudiation of the religious status quo entails the danger of rejecting the faith completely. Of this danger, David Friedrich Strauss is a telling illustration: he started out as a radical and ended as an agnostic. After wavering most of his life as to whether he belonged to the Christian community, two years before his death he dramatically cut all ties in his last publication—although he leaves us wondering whether he did not even here want to propound the "true" understanding of the Christian religion.

David Friedrich Strauss is one of the most famous, if not infamous, figures of nineteenth-century church history. Though in his own day he was well-nigh unanimously repudiated by the Christian community, there can be little doubt that biblical scholarship, as well as theology, has not been the same since—for someone who, in the end, renounced the Christian faith, a rather remarkable feat.

David Friedrich Strauss was born January 27, 1808, in Ludwigsburg, a picturesque baroque town in Württemberg in southwestern Germany, about twenty miles from Stuttgart, and less than one hundred miles from the Swiss border. Württemberg was then, as it is in some measure even now, a citadel of Pietism; that the radical Strauss should come from there is one of the many ironies of his life. His father was a merchant who had failed to discern the signs of a changing time when, after the end of the Napoleonic spectacle, English goods flooded the Continent. When young David was born his father's days of economic success were long past, though a measure of middle-class respectability and solvency was still present. The infant was baptized with the name of his grandfather David Friedrich. He himself later on used both first names, though his family always called him "Fritz"; his enemies referred to him as "David"—surely to underscore the difference between the Old Testament man of God and the nineteenth-century agnostic.

Early the decision must have been made—undoubtedly it was a paternal decision—to have young David Friedrich study theology. In those days this was not an unusual decision; it offered excellent vocational possibilities and an economical way to obtain the necessary preparatory education in one of the *Seminare,* the state-supported boarding high schools in Württemberg. A. Hausrath, Strauss's first biographer, who saw in him "essentially a pathological phenomenon," felt that this vocational choice was "fundamentally an error" since Strauss possessed no religious sensitivity.[1] We must not be too harsh here. To be sure, Strauss's decision must have been influenced more by his father or by early nineteenth-century middle-class mores than by genuine religious commitment. Nonetheless, there is good reason to assume that young David Friedrich possessed at least an affinity to things religious that made theology not an improper vocational choice. He recalled warmly, toward the end of his life, the sermons of Schleiermacher which he had heard during his first stay in Berlin.[2]

In the fall of 1821 David Friedrich entered the *Seminar* at Blaubeuren, where some forty carefully selected pupils received four years' rigorous preparation for university work. David Friedrich distinguished himself at once as a superior student. His graduating diploma lauded his "very good comprehension and judgment," though it lamented his "easy-going attitude."[3]

In 1825 David Friedrich matriculated at the University of Tübingen. The customary course of theological study in those days covered five years, two devoted to philosophy and languages and three to theology. Again Strauss's academic record was distinguished. In 1828 he was runner-up for a prize awarded by the Catholic faculty of theology at Tübingen for an essay on the resurrection of the dead.

The evaluation of the judges observed that the exegetical and critical consideration of the scriptural texts was well handled, whereas the philosophical discussion left something to be desired. Strauss himself commented, in later years, that "after I had made the final period, I realized that there was nothing to it," but this was undoubtedly an *ex post facto* verdict caused by a desire to appear consistent from cradle to grave.

First in his class, Strauss passed his theological examination in 1830. He himself would have much preferred to return to the *Seminar* at Blaubeuren as teacher, but he was sent for a year as vicar to a small village. Yet the assignment must have been a tolerable one. Strauss noted happily in one of his letters that there were "no Pietists nor sects" in the congregation and that his responsibilities were far from taxing. Aside from conducting religious instruction for the schoolchildren and preaching an occasional sermon, he had no tasks and was able therefore to spend considerable time in reading—shades of the learned divine of yesteryear![4] A sermon which Strauss preached on what might be called Thanksgiving shows his religious attitude of that time.[5] He commented, somewhat gratuitously, on the King's benevolence in easing the recent famine, explained the spiritual blessings of schools and spoke on the proclamation of God's greatness as expressed in his works, and finally stressed God's love in Christ Jesus to all believers. Strauss's was not a particularly striking sermon —not for our time and surely also not for his. But there was, particularly toward the end, a solid theological emphasis and thus more than banal chatter.

The tranquillity of Strauss's pastoral bliss soon ended. His academic achievements suggested a scholarly career in the preparation of which the doctorate was essential. Having passed the theological examination with high distinction, receiving the degree was a matter of formality—even then German universities were delightfully nonchalant about procedure. The aspirant for the degree had to submit a short written work, whereupon the faculty of philosophy, without further examination, awarded the degree. Strauss had such a short paper—the essay on the resurrection of the dead which he had submitted to the Catholic faculty of theology two years earlier. But, for some reason or other, this essay could nowhere be found in the files, and Strauss's effort seemed temporarily thwarted. During his vicarate Strauss had written an essay on the "eternal return of all things" which he promptly submitted. The faculty members were divided in their opinion, not so much because of a lack of scholarly qualities, but because of the unmistakably Hegelian conclusion—and Hegel's philosophy was not very popular in Tübingen. In the end the complications were resolved and in November, 1831, Strauss received his degree. He subsequently moved to Berlin to study under the two men whose writings he had read so eagerly during his year in the village—Schleiermacher and Hegel. Much to his disappointment, a few days after his arrival Hegel died.

Strauss learned this unexpected news while paying a visit to Schleiermacher, who asked him, as Strauss wrote in a letter, "if the cholera epidemic had not kept me from coming to Berlin. I replied that the news had been more encouraging lately and the epidemic seemed to have run its course. Yes, he said, but it demanded a great victim. Professor Hegel died last night." In his first dismay Strauss burst out "and I came here for his sake," which came from his heart, but was neither proper etiquette nor good diplomacy.[6] The shock of Hegel's death probably influenced Strauss's initially negative opinion of Schleiermacher. "Thus far he has not especially attracted me," he wrote after a few weeks, in a letter.[7] His opinion became more positive later on, but when he studied Schleiermacher's Christology three decades later, he observed that Schleiermacher's religious position was, in general, idiosyncrasy, even though he deceived himself and others often with superficial insight in particulars.

Strauss stayed in Berlin for two semesters and would have remained longer, had not his funds run out. Together with Wilhelm Vatke, a young instructor in Old Testament at the university, he planned to publish what was to be called *Journal for Scientific Theology* in the hope that this literary venture would provide the needed income as well as serve as a mouthpiece for a Hegelian-oriented theology. The problem was—the scholar today will remark *tempora non mutantur*—to find a publisher, and here the two enterprising scholars, or scholarly entrepreneurs, were unsuccessful. They found one to be sure—but he was equally enterprising, demanding that he assume risk and profits. Since the financial side was as important as theology in the proposed venture, the two friends declined the offer.

And so economic necessity forced Strauss, in the late spring of 1832, to return southward. In May he became tutor at the so-called *Stift*, the theological college, at Tübingen. His responsibilities were to tutor entering students in philosophy and hold a colloquium in theology for more advanced students. For the next year he lectured on logic, the history of philosophy since Kant, on Plato's *Symposium* as well as the history of moral philosophy, and gave also a survey of the history of philosophy. He must have been an exciting and stimulating lecturer, for he soon became the *cause célèbre* of an academic controversy. Some of the senior members of the faculty argued that courses offered by tutors could not count as fulfillment of the regular requirements of philosophy—a general principle made primarily against the popular Strauss. The Ministry of Education, which made the final decision, agreed with the faculty members, but added that tutors who had demonstrated their teaching ability should be exempt from this ruling.[8]

Strauss, not unaware of such academic politicking, felt it best to terminate his work in philosophy and to return to theology, the field in which he was more properly qualified. His decision to pursue a career in theology meant that he had to select a field of specialization in theology and thereby he was led back to a project which he had pondered for over a year—a "life" of Jesus. In February, 1832, he had written to a friend that "most of all I am interested in a lecture on the life of Jesus, albeit presently only in my mind since I have no time to work on it. Probably you are surprised at this selection, but you will agree that this would be the best preliminary effort for a greater theological work."[9]

The Life of Jesus

Strauss selected a topic that was very much in the air in those days. Late in 1833 he began to read and to collect notes, and in an amazingly short time, in October of 1834, the manuscript was completed. When the work was published, in two volumes, in June and November, 1835, it was a weighty opus of 1,500 pages. Surely, this was a remarkable feat for a young author. Conversant with the scholarly literature of the day, *The Life of Jesus* was a learned book, too learned, perhaps, considering the widespread and violent controversy it evoked. As in the case of some other writings that have made history, one is surprised that such a sophisticated book could prove to be so sensational. Strauss himself called his work "an inspired book," and observed that "its author had assimilated the mightiest development of theology at that time which produced the book. Much was lacking; after all, he was too young, twenty-six years of age, when he began the work on the life of Jesus; much was lacking to make him a truly erudite theologian. Nonetheless, with the instinct of men who are destined to advance mankind, his youthful survey of scholarship had noticed precisely the point which then was crucial."[10]

Strauss's self-assessment may sound exuberant; but it was to the point. He *did* discern the Achilles heel of theology of his time and, in youthful vehemence, ventured to offer a solution. On the occasion of the twenty-fifth anniversary of the publication of the work, Strauss reflected melancholically that the book "excluded me from an academic career to which I aspired and for which I, perhaps, possessed some talent. It tore me loose from my natural way of life and forced me into an unnatural one; it made my life lonely." But to this note of disappointment Strauss added the self-confident assertion that "for the past twenty-five years not a single line of any significance has been written which would not show its influence." Again he was right. His *Life* showed that the right books, to be appreciated, must be written at the right time.

With the exception of a brief introduction, *The Life of Jesus* consisted of two major parts—a critical section comprising most of the book and a constructive conclusion, some sixty pages in length, which presented the lasting significance of Jesus. The critical section of the book dealt with the birth and childhood, public life, and arrest, death, and resurrection of Jesus. The approach was, again and again, the same. First the Gospel account was related, with all of its difficulties; then the "supranaturalist" and the "naturalist" interpretations were considered and dismissed as unsatisfactory, showing that neither the one nor the other interpretation was possible. By the time the reader is halfway through the book he is aware of the direction of things: the incidents pertaining to Jesus' life did not happen as they are described in the Gospels.

If *The Life of Jesus* is so readable, then it is because the book builds up its theme with an exciting crescendo, beginning dramatically, but proceeding to increasingly important issues: the most exciting sections—those dealing with Jesus' death, resurrection, and ascension—come at the end of the book. Moreover, David Friedrich Strauss was a master of style. Despite a somewhat stereotyped organization and tedious repetition of argument, this well-written book captivated the reader. Occasionally there was a lapse into sarcasm, as, for example, when in commenting on Matthew 21:1 ff., where it is reported that Jesus desired both an ass and a colt for his entry into Jerusalem, Strauss stated that the colt, yet unbroken, could not have been kept in order by human equestrian art but only "by divine omnipotence." Obviously, the ass "was only walking along in the head of the writer of the first Gospel."

Strauss's concern was to present a new approach to the life of Jesus. He stated the problem succinctly in the preface: "It appeared to the author of the work, the first half of which is herewith submitted to the public, that it was time to substitute a new mode of considering the life of Jesus, in the place of the antiquated systems of supranaturalism and naturalism." And a few lines later the history of the interpretation of the Gospels is summarized as follows:

> The exegesis of the ancient church set out from the double presupposition: first, that the gospels contained a history, and secondly, that this history was a supernatural one. Rationalism rejected the latter of these presuppositions, but only to cling the more tenaciously to the former, maintaining that these books present unadulterated, though only natural, history. Science cannot rest satisfied with this half-measure: the other presupposition also must be relinquished, and the inquiry must first be made whether in fact, and to what extent, the ground on which we stand in the gospels is historical. This is the natural course of things, and thus far the appearance of a work like the present is not only justifiable, but even necessary.

Strauss argued that the record of the events in the Gospels does not correspond to the actual happening. The character of this record allows neither a "natural" nor a supernatural interpretation, as is obviously intended by the writer. The criterion to analyze the Gospel record is what Strauss called the "law of nature." Whenever an account "is incompatible with the known and universally valid laws of events" its historicity must be questioned. Three such laws are mentioned: the law of "causality" makes it impossible that theophanies, miracles, appearances of angels and devils can be taken as historical. The law of "succession," in turn, insists that "even in the most forceful epochs and most rapid changes everything takes place in a certain order and sequence, in gradual growth and decline." Finally, the "psychological" laws argue that it is "improbable that a human being is to have felt, thought, and acted against human ways." Strauss suggested positively that the nature of the Gospel account is "mythical" —the stories and incidents related in the Gospels are, in varying ways, unhistorical legends, with little if any relationship to facts. Strauss neither invented the term "myth" nor was he the first one to apply it to Scripture. He must receive credit, however, for his utilization of the term for the understanding of the Gospels. He distinguished two types of "myth": "philosophical" myths which "clothe in the garb of historical narrative a simple thought, a precept, or an idea of the time," and "historical" myths which are the legendary ornamentation of simple historical happenings.

By characterizing the Gospel stories as myth, Strauss faced the crucial question as to how a simple historical event—the life of Jesus, who spent most of his life in Nazareth, then traveled through the land as a teacher, and finally died an early death—came to be surrounded by sundry unhistorical ornamentation. Not many lives in history have been thus dramatized or "mythologized." Even the agnostic—and Strauss was certainly not an agnostic at that time—must admit that perhaps this simple life was not so simple after all or that the scheming disciples ornamented the simple life. Hegelianism refuted the great individuals in history in favor of the "idea." Strauss found this "idea" in rudimentary fashion in Old Testament materials, in extracanonical Jewish messianic anticipation, and in parallels to non-Jewish religious history: these were the factors that put the complex mythological frosting on the simple historical cake.

Yet, despite their achievement, Strauss's two volumes were not without weaknesses. For one, Strauss failed to pay attention to certain formal questions pertaining to the nature of the Gospel accounts. He ignored a critical assessment of the sources, which must stand at the beginning of any scholarly venture. In a way, we are judging here with the insight of hindsight—criticizing Strauss for a lack of knowledge which his day and age did not possess. But he bluntly denied that any of the Gospels could be eyewitness accounts, and quickly bypassed the questions of origin, authorship, and interrelationship of the various accounts. He adopted a somewhat easygoing attitude which enabled him to play out one part of Scripture against the other, the Gospel according to John against the Synoptics, and vice versa.

A second point was even more significant. As the title of his book stated, Strauss sought to give a critique of the life of Jesus, and accordingly he was little concerned with presenting a positive reconstruction of this life. The reader who faithfully endured Strauss's book to the end encountered a host of critical insights into the erroneous understanding of the accounts of Jesus' life, also knew what caused the emergence of the Jesus "myth," but was hardly able to find a positive portrayal of Jesus of Nazareth—what man he really was, what message he really proclaimed, or what was his real purpose. All of this goes begging.

The final chapter dealt with the "dogmatic significance of the life of Jesus"—an indication that Strauss was cognizant of the problem. His first paragraph seemed indeed to offer much: "The results of the inquiry which we have now brought to a close," he wrote, "have apparently annihilated the greatest and most valuable part of that which the Christian has been wont to believe concerning his Saviour Jesus. . . . Thus at the conclusion of the criticism of the history of Jesus, there presents itself this problem: to re-establish dogmatically that which has been destroyed critically." But the pages that followed made it obvious that Strauss promised more than he delivered. There was virtually no positive statement, and thus the reader was left wondering.

Among the writings in the eventful course of the Christian church that have made history, Strauss's *Life of Jesus* certainly must be included. Like some others, its fame was unexpected, and in some measure due to the discussion it evoked. In the case of Strauss's book, the controversy was almost as spectacular as the book itself. Strauss himself was not unaware of the thin ice on which he was stepping by writing the *Life*. The letter in which he told of his plans to write a "life of Jesus" raised the question, "Do you not think that you will be locked out of the University?" and provided its own answer: "Yes, this is possible. I often regret that all the work I plan to do in theology is self-destructive."[11]

The Reaction

Strauss's premonition proved to be painfully accurate. Less than two weeks after the publication of the first volume, the *Studienrat,* or "Superintendent of Education" at Stuttgart inquired of the theological faculty at Tübingen whether Strauss's public pronouncements were compatible with his position at the *Stift*. This query came with amazing speed, considering that, after all, a weighty work of 700 scholarly pages had to be assessed. The memorandum noted that obviously no truth-loving student would be led astray by the untenable notions of the book, though "some of the more ignorant, reticent, uncritical students" might accept these ideas and engage in their work as teachers with such hesitation that it would make it impossible to teach the content of the Gospels in stimulating and fruitful fashion.[12]

The response of the faculty sought to make haste slowly. In June, 1835, the faculty reported that Strauss's book was scholarly in character and moderate in tone, that it represented the culmination of a certain trend in Protestant theology, and that it could conceivably exert a negative influence upon the young students. But, for the time being, a definite verdict was avoided. The publication of the second volume should be awaited before a final assessment, particularly since this second volume would relate the critical findings of the book to the teaching of the church.

This word of caution found no echo. Early in July the *Studienrat* wrote Strauss directly. Referring to several reviews of his book, which had by then appeared, Strauss was asked "how the views presented in the first volume of your work concerning the accounts of

Jesus' life and deeds can be harmonized with the responsibilities of a Protestant teacher of religion who is called upon to base his instruction of youth upon the historical foundation of the Gospel?" Furthermore, the *Studienrat* wanted to know if Strauss found his own official relationship with ministerial candidates compatible with the views as expressed in his book.

Strauss responded quickly with a polite, but forceful, statement. The position of his book, so Strauss argued, reflected a major trend in current theology. It could not, therefore, be regarded as the work of a single man or of youthful exuberance. "If the basic orientation of my work is identical to an important theological movement of our time, then it would seem not inappropriate that this movement should be represented by someone at an institution of higher learning." Strauss added that he had carefully avoided speaking about his book in his lectures while he was writing it. The publication of the book had created a new situation inasmuch as his work could be freely obtained everywhere. The position of its author as a member of a theological faculty made little difference therefore.

Strauss then explained the nature of his efforts:

> I should like to call attention to the fact that in my book not everything in the Gospels has been questioned. A great difference is made between the deeds and incidents related concerning Jesus and his words. As regards the latter, those most important and effective in the instruction of people and youth have not at all been contested concerning their content. Only here and there questions have been raised regarding their context. But even concerning Jesus' deeds and destiny there is retained everything that is necessary to the acknowledgment of his superior character, namely, his immaculate walk of life, his noble and unselfish deeds and his final sacrifice.

Finally, Straus distinguished between the views held by a minister and those held by his congregation. What the minister finds acceptable and appropriate must not necessarily be shared with the congregation. The former will emphasize ideas, the latter history. More than a decade later, when campaigning for political office in 1848, Strauss reiterated this basic distinction. He remarked, in an election speech, that he had not wanted the man-on-the-street to read his book, even as he himself would not read a book written by a farmer for farmers. The man-on-the-street fortunately knows little of the doubts that beset many theologians. If the common people read works of intricate scholarship, they would encounter all sorts of doubts. Such books are not written for them, however, but for theologians. Not to create doubt, but to dispel it, was the purpose of his work.[13]

On July 20, eight days after Strauss's memorandum, the *Studienrat* informed the Ministry of Education that the preservation of public confidence in the *Stift* at Tübingen suggested Strauss's removal from his position. While Strauss did not discuss certain issues publicly, his theological position was common knowledge, and thus a detriment to the *Stift*. The *Studienrat* recommended that Strauss be transferred as teacher of classical languages to the high school in his home town, Ludwigsburg. Three days later the Ministry of Education decided accordingly. After the publication of the second volume in November, 1835, Strauss left Tübingen for Ludwigsburg. He also left—though he must not have realized it—his academic career. His life was not to be the same again.

Within two months of the appearance of the first volume of his work Strauss had become an academic *persona non grata*. What a sad turn of events, made all the more tragic by the fact that this condemnation had occurred before the scholarly world had assessed the work. Yet the scholarly verdict came both quickly and vehemently, making Strauss's work the most controversial and most widely repudiated theological book of decades.

One of the foremost religious journals of the day, the *Allgemeine Kirchenzeitung,* devoted more than twenty reviews, articles, and editorials to the book in 1836 alone, even though it had remarked, in February of that year, that Strauss's *Life of Jesus,* as a distinctly scholarly book, would hardly be noticed outside the scholarly world.[14] This proved to be an illusion and the journal's correspondent from Württemberg quickly disagreed. The book had excited, so he wrote, most of the congregations; believers and unbelievers, Christians by name and Christians by conviction were bitterly feuding with one another. Consequently, the columns of the *Kirchenzeitung* devoted more and more space to the *cause célèbre*, repeatedly charging Strauss with a lack of religious sensitivity. "The calm and cold-bloodedness with which he attacks the anointed of the Lord, unmoved by the sight of the millions who have kneeled and still kneel before the one who has manifested himself, praying fervently 'in Thee do I have righteousness and strength.' No tear of melancholy flows from his eyes, though such is shed by all who possess a sensitive heart." The verdict was clear: "A man who establishes reason over against the Word of God must be left alone. He is a spiritual monster, a man without heart."

The *Kirchenzeitung* spoke of Strauss's book as "one of the most gratifying publications among recent theological literature," adding that "this work is significant not because it offers something absolutely new, but because it is the consistent delineation and synthesis of elements which are already present in our time." But such praise of consistency was spoken with tongue in cheek, for it surely was a consistency that came from the devil. A quotation from Scripture closed the matter for the journal: "Jeremiah is the right prophet for our day for he exclaims with such pain as in all its bitterness can only be understood by him who says himself: 'Oh, that my head were water and mine eyes a fountain of tears that I might weep day and night for the slain of the daughter of my people. Oh, that I had in the wilderness a lodging place of wayfaring men that I might leave my people and go from them! For they be all adulterers and an assembly of treacherous men.' "

The *Christenbote,* a Pietist periodical, first took note of Strauss's book by printing the letter of an anonymous reader who wrote that Strauss had dissolved the historical foundation of Christianity into myth, leaving him with the uneasy feeling of living in a house whose foundation had been removed. The editor of the *Christenbote* comforted his readers by pointing out that the educational authorities had already taken steps in this matter and a satisfactory conclusion could soon be expected.

The first lengthy scholarly repudiation of Strauss in book form came from the pen of one C. A. Eschenmayer, professor of philosophy at Tübingen. The title of his work, *The Iscariotism of Our Days. A Contribution to the Work by Strauss: The Life of Jesus,* was at once indicative of its character. Eschenmayer argued that Strauss was part of a long historical line that began with Judas Iscariot. Strauss subsequently returned the compliment and called the work a cross between theological ignorance and religious intolerance. Other monographs followed. An eager *defensor fidei* in Switzerland sought to show the unreliability of Strauss's method by applying it to Zwingli's life—with interesting results.[15] Albert Schweitzer's *Quest of the Historical Jesus* lists some sixty books written against Strauss and, more recently, Johannes Zeller has offered an interesting interpretation of the various responses.[16] Even Strauss's name—"ostrich" in German—was used in the polemic, since the Old Testament prophet remarked about Babylon that "ostriches shall dwell there"—and this seemed an appropriate identification of Strauss with the wickedness of Babylon.[17]

When all was said, Strauss stood alone against the religious and scholarly onslaught. In a letter to a friend of August, 1836, he summarized, not without humor, the various attacks. There were, he wrote, first of all

> the cries of distress—simple expressions of surprise, of terror, of abhorrence, without speaking to detail, rather like a woman's cries upon hearing bullet shots. The character of these writings is fanatical. . . . Secondly, there is criticism of details, but not seen from the overall perspective, namely, the life of Jesus or the Gospels, but from my book. There is no attempt to do it better or to state how the happening took place or how a comprehensive view of the life of Jesus can be given if the mythical position is repudiated. Here are but objections to my work, since the difficulties which the mythical interpretation does not resolve are not contrasted with the other possibilities. The character of these writings is spiteful and arrogant. . . . Thirdly, as soon as the matter itself is considered and an attempt is made to understand the Gospel accounts comprehensively, after the mythical position has been propounded, there is frequently agreement with me, as there is also a more moderate tone.[18]

The Aftermath

In the midst of the turmoil Strauss moved to Ludwigsburg. He had kept silent in the controversy; only his statement to the Ministry of Education had been published, in March, 1836, in the *Darmstädter Allgemeine Kirchenzeitung*. Then, in April a second edition of *The Life of Jesus* became necessary. Though the publisher pushed him and time was short, Strauss insisted on making several important modifications in the text. While he did not respond directly to his critics, he showed clearly that he was not beyond improvement. The introduction of the book was reworked and lengthened, the nature of the "myth" was more clearly defined, and four prerequisites for describing an account as "unhistorical" were stated: it must be incompatible with known and otherwise valid laws of nature; its form must be poetical and the words of the participants longer and more enthusiastic than their background and the situation allow us to expect; and, finally, the content of an account must reflect ideas held at the time.

In September, 1836, Strauss submitted a petition to the King of Württemberg in which he inquired, prompted "by the strange turn of events regarding my position in the Lutheran church," whether he could ever hope to be appointed to an ecclesiastical position. His petition was forwarded to the proper ecclesiastical and educational authorities. It received a negative response from the former; the latter replied that a theological professorship was out of the question, although a professorship in philosophy was not impossible. The suggestion was made that Strauss spend the immediate future as a private scholar. The official response to Strauss followed this suggestion.

Strauss received this news in November. The following month he gave up his high school responsibilities, left Ludwigsburg, and moved to Stuttgart. A shadow had fallen over his life. His parents were grieved over their son's infamy. Denunciations of all sorts reached the home. Former friends turned into strangers; acquaintances avoided him like the plague.[19] A Pietist visited at his home—for the sole purpose of converting him. He was followed by another, but both were unsuccessful.[20]

In 1837 came Strauss's response to the attacks upon his book. Entitled *Polemic Tracts in the Defense of my Work The Life of Jesus,* the defense almost meant to present *A Characterization of Current Theology*. The book was full of insight, sarcasm, and wit. But before Strauss could finish his ambitious intention to answer all his critics—who were like sand on the sea—his attention was directed back to *The Life of Jesus*. A third edition had become necessary and once again he made some changes. The unanimous repudiation of his book by the scholarly world had left its impact upon Strauss, and substantial modifications were the result. Strauss placed greater weight on the Gospel according to John and spelled out the positive implications of Jesus quite lengthily. He denied that he had meant to change everything in the traditional understanding of the life of Jesus into myth; he had only wanted to distinguish the truly creative and significant elements from subsequent additions. "Jesus is for me, too, the greatest religious genius known in history."[21] Accordingly, Strauss omitted the last chapter and replaced it with a new discussion with the revealing title "Attempts at Mediation." He noted that even as great individuals are the apex of the great movements of history, so religion is the apex of those areas in which the creativity of the spirit is possible. Jesus founded the highest religion; he was, therefore, the apex of spiritual life. As of no one else we can say that God was revealed in him. Jesus united the human and the divine. He was the highest of all men.

An essay, *Transitory and Permanent Elements in the Christian Religion,* written at the same time, pursued this perspective yet further. Strauss declared that Jesus could not be superseded, for he personified a unique unity of human self-consciousness and God-consciousness—shades of Schleiermacher's Christology. "If this unity was real in Jesus, if he not merely spoke about it, but realized it in all affairs of his life, then the highest apex in the religious realm has been reached, beyond which one cannot go."

The reason for Strauss's change of mind is difficult to discern. Was it the persuasiveness of his opponents or was he tired of the controversy which had, as it must have dawned on him at that time, ruined his life? In retrospect he wrote that "terror struck me when I saw myself all alone,"[22] and on another occasion he reflected, "I am no longer the one whom the theologians are out to attack; I no longer have the temper with which I hurt them and which, would I still possess it, everything could be borne more easily. But I no longer possess it."[23] He told a friend that once the third edition of his *Life* was completed, he would "never again touch a theological pen."

At that time a development at Zürich seemed to offer him, despite all that had happened, another chance at academic respectability. In 1833 a university had been founded in Zürich and its affairs were guided by an exceedingly liberal government. In the summer of 1838 the professorial chair for church history and historical theology became vacant. A member of the theological faculty by the name of Hitzig, one of the few who were benevolently disposed to Strauss, proposed him. The majority of the faculty did not concur in this suggestion, but Hitzig submitted a minority report to the department of education at Zürich, which had the final decision in the matter. Hitzig argued that Strauss had made, during the past two years, several important modifications in his earlier position. In particular, in the most recent edition of his work Strauss had written nobly about the significance of Jesus. Indeed, "considering that under advisement is not the appointment of an ecclesiastical superintendent, but the appointment of a teacher of scholarly theology and considering furthermore that Strauss will perhaps overshadow, but never remove completely, the influence of the other faculty members upon the students so as to make his perspective the only one, I cannot avoid recommending the appointment of Dr. Strauss."[24]

The committee of the department of education, entrusted with the decision, was divided with respect to the recommendation until finally the vote of the Mayor, on January 26, 1839, brought a decision in Strauss's favor. At once the storm broke loose. The *Regierungs-Rat,* or "Governmental Council," had to confirm the appointment but before it could do so a session of the *Grosse Rat,* or "Large Council," was held on January 31. At this session the opponents of Strauss moved that the *Kirchenrat,* or "Ecclesiastical Council," should henceforth participate in the appointment of all professors of theology.

The *Kirchenrat* was solidly against Strauss and thus not a general principle was at stake but the specific repudiation of Strauss. When the votes were cast after a heated and lengthy debate, 98 voted against and 49 for the motion; two-thirds of the representatives had approved the appointment of Strauss. Accordingly, the *Regierungs-Rat* voted, two days later, to appoint Strauss as professor of church history and historical theology at Zürich.

The conservatives were unwilling to accept this decision. Under the leadership of Johann Jakob Hürlimann-Landis the protest movement against Strauss gained impetus. Hürlimann was a dubious character whose opposition to the cantonal government was not new. The restriction of child labor by the liberal Zürich government had made him hostile before Strauss had even been heard of in Zürich. The academic controversy over Strauss's appointment was sharp and prolific—perhaps the most prolific one in Swiss history. All in all, some seventy-two publications appeared; thirty-two of these supported Strauss, the remaining forty were against him.[25] Among the literary products of the controversy was the following poem; in its brevity, and quality as well, it must suffice as illustration:

> Our religion is being attacked!
> Even though our people for 300 years
> The Old Faith have backed
> It has become a matter of sneers.[26]

Events moved rapidly. On February 13, representatives of twenty-nine villages met to formulate plans "against the appointment of Strauss as professor of dogmatics in Zürich."[27] Seven days later the superintendent of the church in Zürich sent a pastoral letter to the clergy in the Canton of Zürich in which he asserted that "the appointment of Dr. Strauss as professor of theology at our University, as well as the movement which was thereby occasioned, is more than a fleeting event of the day; whatever developments will yet take place will become part of the church history of our land." Committees were formed in all congregations; representatives from these committees constituted a central committee which confronted the *Regierungs-Rat* with the demand that the appointment of Strauss be rescinded, that he never be appointed to any educational post in Zürich, and that the vacant professorship be filled by a man of unquestionable evangelical-reformed conviction. The *Regierungs-Rat* refused to accept the "rude and improper" memorandum, but realized, no doubt, that popular sentiment was overwhelmingly against Strauss. A petition circulated by the central committee had received, by March 10, 39,225 approvals and only 1,048 disapprovals.

Strauss had accepted the appointment in the middle of February, informing the department of education at that time that he considered it not the least of his new responsibilities "to calm the sentiments of those who see in me a man endeavoring to use his university position for the undermining of traditional religion."[28] He pledged that he would "honor the divine truths of the Christian religion" and "cleanse these truths ever more of human additions"—the "true" Strauss once again came to the surface. When the popular reaction reached its climax, Strauss wrote an open letter to his Zürich supporters which his supporters published to swing the tide. Doing away with literal interpretation of biblical accounts, Strauss wrote, removes as little of their true essence even as the value of a beautiful painting is not diminished by the removal of a note which states that it is a beautiful painting.

> What is it to us that Christ healed the sick by mere words or touch? He does no longer help us with special powers, as he helped the blind man at Jericho or the leper and lame man at Capernaum or the dead man at Naim and Bethany. Rather, he opens our eyes through his teaching to allow us the awareness that God's divine will is with us; he strengthens our paralyzed power through his admonitions and promises by challenging us to follow his example.

Early in March the Zürich authorities clearly faced a difficult situation. Strauss had been formally offered the professorship, had accepted it, but the *vox populi* was increasingly vocal in its repudiation of the "atheistic" professor. What should be done? The *Regierungs-Rat* found an answer—to retire Strauss before he even assumed his position. The department of education, when asked for its comment, reiterated its earlier recommendation that Strauss should be appointed. The *Regierungs-Rat* favored Strauss's retirement "since the present notorious developments appear to make a profitable exercise of his responsibilities at our University impossible." On March 18 the *Grosse Rat* decided accordingly. The vote was 149 to 38—clearly the sentiment of the representatives was not as one-sidedly against Strauss as that of the people. The next day the department of education recommended Strauss's retirement with an annual pension of 1,000 Swiss francs and the *Regierungs-Rat* promptly approved this recommendation. The following day the central committee dissolved itself; its mission was accomplished.

Strauss had failed. During the stormy controversy he was more than a mere bystander and the waves of excitement reached him even at Stuttgart. In a letter Strauss described the situation:

How assailed I was! How many letters I have received! . . . How many more did I refuse, since they lacked postage! Finally these fellows hit upon the strategy of sending a package with slanderous papers and tracts to an innocent baker for which he had to pay over a florin. Upon opening it, he found no letter, but a second envelope addressed to me. I did not accept it, but promised the man I would request the postal department that he be reimbursed for his damages. I succeeded in accomplishing this, but when I informed the baker this mad fellow had opened the second envelope; no one can help him now.[29]

On March 18, at the climax of the Zürich episode, Strauss's mother died. The next day Strauss mentioned in a letter that the Zürich turmoil had burdened her last days. "One of her last words to me was: 'If I now die, people will think that I died out of grief over you.' My Zürich affairs were always her first attention when the newspaper reached our house."

A lengthy *Memorial for My Good Mother,* written by Strauss many years later, shows that her death constituted a theological problem for him. "After her death I thought that if there is no immortality, it should be invented for her. She believed it very firmly. Of the facets of my unbelief, that pertaining to immortality was the one to which she most seriously objected." But even on this occasion, when emotions were so close to the surface, skepticism prevailed. "Actually her death did not strengthen any belief in immortality on my part. After all, if a spirit so close to me continues, then I cannot fathom why it cannot give me any sign of its continuing life."

A fourth edition of *The Life of Jesus* was to be published in 1839—and Strauss eliminated the changes and concessions of the third edition. He reiterated his earlier doubts concerning the Gospel according to John as well as his basic assertion that none of the Gospels contains the account of eyewitnesses. Upon reading the previous edition Strauss found, as he wrote in the new preface, that it "was far too irenical," and that there were "changes which evoked my bewilderment." He had "lost sight of the matter itself." The new edition of *The Life of Jesus* returned to the beginning; it was to show that none of the criticism had persuaded him.

The prospect of the appointment in Zürich had prompted him to undertake extensive studies in historical and systematic theology. He read the ancient tomes, garnered material, synthesized insights, little realizing that he would never stand before a class of students. Then came the Zürich fiasco, but since he had the collected material

Strauss decided to put it into book form. During the Zürish controversy, Strauss had asserted that his teaching would stress the lasting truths of the Christian religion. The two volumes, published in 1840 and 1841, breathed a different spirit. The tenor was sharp and sarcastic; the content, critical and destructive. The title of the book, *The Christian Faith in its Historical Development and Encounter with Modern Science,* indicated its scope, a historical survey of the development and formation of Christian dogma. It was not a history of Christian dogma, for the outline was topical rather than historical. It was a "systematic" theology, with the arguments for the assertions taken from history. The complexity of historical manifestations was to speak its own persuasive language. "The true critique of dogma is its history,"[30] Strauss wrote, and thereby posited his thesis. This could be done without presenting his own views, which in the case of his *Life of Jesus* had led to disaster, but by synthesizing other writers. His task was like that of an auditor in a business—"to balance the books." When he was done, he thought optimistically that he had "driven the final eschatological nail into the coffin of dogma."[31]

The guiding star in the venture was Ludwig Feuerbach, whose *Essence of Christianity* appeared at the time when the first volume of the *Christian Faith* was being printed. Thus we must look to Feuerbach's earlier writings, and here the influence is obvious. Strauss was persuaded that Feuerbach had demolished the Hegelian identity of theology and philosophy, identical in content though different in form. Philosophy cannot have the task of supporting the truth of theological assertions which have their origin in man. Feuerbach "repudiated the effort to find corresponding philosophical truth in the Christian dogma," Strauss wrote and added, "on this premise I wrote my *Christian Faith.*"[32]

Feuerbach's *Essence of Christianity* turned out to be a sensation; Strauss's two volumes failed to be noticed and the reason must be sought in Strauss himself. His *Life of Jesus* had raised fundamental questions concerning the proper understanding of the Gospels. Though the response was unanimously negative, scholarship had begun to address itself to the problems that had been raised by Strauss. A lively discussion had ensued; yet in the midst of the discussion Strauss moved on to another area—that of systematic theology. Obviously it was too much to expect scholarship to follow him a second time. Moreover, according to Strauss himself, the "patient historical process of dissolution of church dogma, such as my *Dogmatics* undertook, did not suit, on account of Feuerbach's radical method in his *Essence of Christianity,* the impetuous spirits of these days; the edition of 3000 copies sold only slowly."[33] His work and that of Feuerbach set out to do the same: Feuerbach's was more persuasive.

The End of a Theologian

The two volumes were Strauss's farewell to theology; the end of the road had been reached. The story of his life could well terminate at this point. What followed was a life lived off the stage of history. Exit David Friedrich Strauss, the theologian and radical; enter a litterateur and essayist, indeed a *bon homme*. If we take pains to follow this life to its end, it is because its very banality constituted an important sequel.

The repudiation of *The Life of Jesus* and the impossibility of participating in academic life in Württemberg or in Zürich, had removed Strauss from the world of theological scholarship. His *Christian Faith* had indicated that the issue was not merely a radical thesis regarding biblical studies; at stake was the author's personal orientation which the *Christian Faith* revealed to be philosophical—in the sense of Feuerbach—rather than theological. Strauss was hardly a theologian; he spent the remainder of his life as litterateur, as writer of semi-popular studies and essays on a variety of topics. Fortunately, his financial situation was such that the lack of a regular occupation did not entail any economic hardship. Moreover each new publication improved his financial status.[34]

The first of the more mundane aspects of Strauss's life to be related was an *affaire d'amour* which concluded, after some interesting preludes, in marriage. Strauss's first amorous involvement had been in 1837. A young girl had become infatuated with the author of the famous *Life of Jesus*—perhaps the nineteenth-century equivalent of a twentieth-century teenager's swooning over a movie star. The *affaire* was, as became the time, quite proper, though not without its interesting sidelights. On one visit Strauss "was taken to her room, where I felt like a Horatian lover who had to fear to be torn into pieces at any moment by an irate husband."[35] In December, 1837, Strauss wrote a friend about further developments:

> Returning last Tuesday from the library, where I had checked Polybius and Diodorus, I gave instructions to add to the fire because it was so cold. Suddenly, there was a knocking at my door, at first so softly so that I could not hear it well, but then once again. I would never have expected it to be the beautiful unknown girl of last spring. That is who it was, come to town for her Christmas shopping. At first, everything was somewhat formal, since I had lost interest. I sat down in a chair opposite

her and not beside her. But soon the ice melted and I could not avoid trying some of the kisses which had tasted so good in the spring. The following day she returned, having made some purchases in the house, and told me that a young civil service official had asked her to marry him. When she mentioned that he was of good repute, not mentioning the impression he had made on her, I told her, while caressing her in my arms, that she should agree to marry the man—a situation which seemed to me alternately humorous and sad, frivolous and innocent.[36]

More serious was Strauss's encounter with Agnes Schebest, a celebrated singer. He had first met her in 1837 and had fallen in love with her. At that time he was swept off his feet—he received, as he put it, "a profound impression of the distinctly classical style of her beauty and of the artistic form and movement. Her speech is also noble and witty."[37] In those days, singers were hardly acceptable matrimonial candidates for respectable middle-class citizens, but perhaps Strauss himself was hardly the apex of respectability. At any rate, he knew about the risky venture—the sketch of a dialogue in one of his letters shows how he himself thought about the matter:

SILCHER: Do you know who wrote the two enthusiastic reviews about Miss Schebest in the *German Courier?*
WACHTER: Köstlin?
SILCHER: No; Strauss.
SCHRADER: Ah!
WACHTER: Ho-ho.
BAHNMEYER: What Strauss?
SILCHER: Well, you know . . .
BAHNMEYER: How low this man has sunk! Together with his religious faith he must have lost all moral strength.

The wedding took place on August 26, 1842. A friend commented on the occasion, that Strauss's "faith" was an important contribution to the marriage, for his disbelief in immortality meant that all love had to be expressed on earth. Unfortunately, such a concentrated amorous venture lasted only the better part of four years—and then their ways separated forever. Strauss subsequently made an effort to turn this separation into an outright divorce, but the legal situation made this impossible.

It is not difficult to say what caused this marriage to break apart. Agnes Schebest, though of lowly background, had seen the world, had moved in fashionable circles, had been admired and celebrated; Strauss had grown up in a restricted and provincial atmosphere, far removed from the *haute monde*. Add to this the fact that Strauss was a man without work, that he had got married at the time when the last hope of vocational respectability had vanished, and we can well understand that whatever love the two may have possessed for one another was insufficient to make this a lasting arrangement. In later years Strauss blamed his marriage for his literary unproductivity. "During the four years of my marriage I wrote nothing, no book, no monograph, no essay. Pressed by the most terrifying questions of life, as was then the case, I had no concern for scholarly questions, rather like a shipwrecked person who has water to his very neck cares little for the affairs of his farm or land."[38] One fears that Strauss deceived himself here. The reasons surely went far deeper and there is evidence from Strauss's pen to verify this point. He was always despondent and all of his letters, no matter from what time, contain echoes of the earlier comment—discouragement, despair, disinclination as regards scholarly effort. What should become of him, he wrote in 1841, now that his vocational goals had not materialized? The following year he noted that scholarly, theoretical, and theological matters had become detestable. "My wife would have more respect for me," he wrote a friend, "if I had regular employment. I frequently show her some of my writings and tell her that I wrote it—but soon she will no longer believe me. . . . You have a vocation, but no wife; I have a wife, but no vocation. . . . Your vocation means that you are greatly ahead of me. . . . My wife always tells me that I am lazy."[39] The birth of a daughter in 1843 and of a son in 1845 only postponed the inevitable conclusion favored by Strauss but refused by his wife.

After the estrangement from his wife Strauss lived a migrant's life —Munich, Weimar, Cologne, Heilbronn, Heidelberg, Darmstadt, Berlin were temporary stations on his uncertain way. No matter how much he tried, he could not get firm ground under his feet. The same held true for his literary production, which failed to avoid an element of random and heterogeneous selection—despite the emphasis on biographical studies.

The political turmoil in Germany in 1848 moved Strauss for a short while back into the public limelight. Some of his friends in Ludwigsburg wanted him as representative to the Constitutional Assembly in Frankfurt, which followed the 1848 "Revolution," but the rural segment of the district elected a theologically unsuspect and thus more acceptable candidate. But Strauss had become interested in politics, became a candidate, and was elected to the Württemberg Diet. Though he was in theology the radical of radicals, in politics he was an arch-conservative—much to the dismay of his electorate. Such combination of liberalism and conservatism in one person is surely intriguing. It occurs often enough—William Jennings Bryan is a good illustration of a combination the other way around—to dispel the notion that a man be only one or the other. Strauss found himself aligned politically with men, such as a Catholic professor of theology of Tübingen by the name of Kuhn, whom he theologically detested. The feeling was mutual, of course, which did not improve the situation. When a liberal by the name of Robert Blum was executed in Vienna and the Württemberg Diet proposed to hold a memorial session, Strauss emphatically spoke against this plan. A widely signed petition against him was circulated in his district and Strauss decided that he had had enough of politics and resigned his seat in the Diet. Like everything else in his life, this venture had ended in failure.

We can quickly pass the next decades of his life. He wrote much—mainly biographical essays: the heroes are by and large little-known figures—Märklin, a personal friend of Strauss; Schubart, a Swabian poet; Firschlin, a seventeenth-century humanist; and Ulrich von Hutten, the sixteenth-century knight, nationalist, and humanist. His plan to write sketches of German writers from Klopstock to Schiller never materialized. Neither did a far more ambitious undertaking—a biography of Martin Luther. For several months he read and collected notes for such a work; Mathesius' sermons on Luther's life particularly impressed him. He was even impressed by certain features of Luther himself—he called Luther "the great liberator," admired his "manliness," his "courage of conviction," his "full, wholesome humanity."[40] To understand Luther better, Strauss read in the works of the Swiss reformer Zwingli. In the end, one was as detestable as the other. In November, 1857, Strauss wrote:

> I have begun to read for a book on Luther. . . . To understand Luther one must become aware of and enter into his doctrine of justification and the inner struggles which led him to it. The latter effort is not easy, at least not for me. First of all, I abhor such states of mind; the result, namely the doctrine of justification, appears as nonsense. But then I tell myself that this fact has transformed the world; even you and all that is dear to you, is based upon it. It cannot be nonsense; go underneath the surface and pursue its true meaning. Well, this is what I am doing, translating each temptation and its solution into my own language. But do I not pervert it thereby? Is it still Luther's condition? Luther's response? And yet there must be a conciliation by which Luther's law and gospel channel into Kant's categorical imperative and Schiller's aesthetic education of mankind.[41]

The specifically religious side of Luther was alien to Strauss, though the richness of Luther's thought deceived him for a while. Once he had realized this, he abandoned his plan; as he remarked on another occasion, he had to love his biographical objects. And Luther he did not love.

The Life of Jesus Again

In 1862, rather unexpectedly, Strauss turned in his literary endeavors once again to the subject with which he had started his career—the life of Jesus. After all of his biting and vehement attacks upon the Christian religion, after he had written, in 1858, that he was about to sell his theological books, for "I certainly won't read these any more," he returned to theology.[42]

Perhaps the reason for his new theological effort was far less complicated. Only fifteen copies of the fourth edition of the *Life* had remained unsold in 1860. The necessity to consider a new edition perhaps prompted Strauss to engage in this project. Furthermore, Ernest Renan had published a popular *Life of Jesus* in 1863 which had quickly become a best-seller—eight editions in three months. Strauss must have felt that he, too, could write a popular work. In preparation he studied the writings of Hermann Samuel Reimarus, whose *Schutzschrift für die vernünftigen Verehrer Gottes* he described in an essay. He succeeded admirably in summarizing the somewhat long-winded, tedious argument of the Hamburg orientalist—the manuscript of Reimarus' work ran to some 2,100 pages—and his essay remains the best introduction to the work of which Lessing published only excerpts in his *Wolfenbüttel Fragments*.

Strauss exhibited a great measure of self-confidence when he undertook his task of a new "Life" of Jesus. More than twenty years of lively scholarship had investigated—in part directly influenced by his own *primum opus*—complicated questions pertaining to the Gospel records. In the span of a few months Strauss had to catch up with such scholarship. He did so with energy, persuaded that he had not missed much, and indeed that he could dismiss most, if not all, of what had been written. The result of this attitude was fatal, for when his book was published in 1864 it was hardly a worthwhile venture. Outwardly it proved to be a reasonable success—though by no means comparable to the sensational reception of his first work. Once more scholars closed ranks and unanimously repudiated the book. And this time they did so with a great deal more justification than in 1835.

In a way, Strauss's second *Life of Jesus* attempted to do away with the weaknesses of the first. The outline was different: a lengthy introduction considered questions regarding the nature of the Gospel accounts; a second section on "The historical basis of the life of Jesus" presented a positive sketch of Jesus' life—"as it really happened." The third and major part was the "critical history" which had been so important in the *Life* of 1835. But these were changes rather than improvements. The first part did not accurately reflect the state of biblical scholarship but gave a rather one-sided interpretation of current views. The earlier *Life of Jesus* had been far more astute in this regard. Moreover, the positive picture of Jesus, presented in the second part, is so pale and undistinguished that it raises more questions than it answers. The problem was here not so much the measure of historicity that can be attributed to the Gospel accounts; nor was it even Strauss's preference for the Gospel according to Matthew over that of Mark. The real problem was simply that there was no "greatness" of any sort in Strauss's historical Jesus. No effort was made to discern, on whatever meager historical basis, the significance of this man and his life. Even if Strauss argued that the historical Jesus was not what the church subsequently had made him, the fact remains that this life must have been, in some sense or other, unusual. The life Strauss put before his readers was hardly more exciting than that of the next-door neighbor. Thus, despite its historical emphasis, the book lacked true historical understanding. The third part of the book was but a restatement of what Strauss had said before. A sarcastic, derogatory, and biting style characterized the book and undoubtedly added to its repudiation.

In his suggestive study of Strauss, Karl Barth asserted—and he has been often quoted on this point—that the reason for the insignificance of the new work lay in the fact that it withdrew the more radical assertions of the first—and, according to Barth, Strauss himself was not even aware of this! What Barth has in mind is Strauss's position with respect to the question of the authentically historical residue in the Gospel accounts of the life of Jesus. The 1835 *Life* had radically minimized this and the 1864 *Life* supposedly affirmed this. While one may doubt if Barth is correct, the point is that in 1864 Strauss did not say anything he had not already said in 1835. His major contention in the 1864 work that the Gospel record is mythical had been known for a generation. Not surprisingly, no one got excited.

For David Friedrich Strauss the new *Life of Jesus* marked his return to theology. The renewed interest was sporadic and thus unlike the earlier and emphatic preoccupation with religious questions. In 1866 Strauss wrote, "my theological interests are exhausted"[43] and we are not sure what prompted the turn of events. Perhaps the reason must be sought in externals, such as the long-awaited publication of Schleiermacher's lectures on the life of Jesus in 1864. Strauss wrote a critical essay which appeared early the following year under the title *The Christ of Faith and the Jesus of History,* charging that Schleiermacher oscillated between supranaturalism and rationalism.

In the fall of 1872 Strauss published his *Old and New Faith,* a subtitle of which stated that it was "A Confession." The title indicated its twofold orientation. The book meant to pass review of the old and draw the blueprint for the new. Strauss had been working, or at least reflecting, on such a book for some time. In January, 1869, he confided his extensive reading to a friend: "I am interested in several books, none of which are in theology, however"; other letters indicate that he was reading Schopenhauer, Darwin, Hartmann, and others. In December, 1871, he wrote that he was "working presently on a little work which is to be the finale of my literary efforts. It is to be a kind of confession of faith as regards religion, philosophy, politics, etc. Even a chapter on music is going to be included."

The Old Faith and the New dealt with four basic questions: Are we still Christians? Are we still religious? How do we comprehend the world? How do we order our lives? Two somewhat heterogeneous additions—"Our Great Poets," on Lessing, Goethe, and Schiller, and "Our Great Composers," on Gluck, Haydn, Mozart, and Beethoven—rounded out the book.

Strauss answered his first question negatively and his second one evasively—"according to the definition of religion." His third answer pointed to Darwin and Haeckel; and the fourth suggested that our lives are to be ordered according to certain principles which most of us will see as a hodgepodge of middle-class morality, with appropriate comments about divorce legislation, monarchism, socialism, and capital punishment thrown in for good measure. Yet the book quickly became popular, perhaps on account of the fact that the last section propounded the obvious with penetrating sensitivity. Here the German burgher who gathered around in the *Bierstube* found what he needed—patriotism, repudiation of socialism and general suffrage, and *gemütlichkeit.* Wrote Strauss:

> We strive to keep our minds open for all the higher interests of mankind. During the last few years we were intimately involved in the great patriotic war and the establishment of the German Empire. This unexpected as well as glorious turn in the fate of our greatly tried nation has exalted our inmost being. To strengthen the understanding of these things we study history, which is now made easy even for the non-specialist by several attractively and popularly written historic monographs. We

> endeavor to increase our understanding of nature which is also made easy through popular writings. Finally we find inspiration for mind and heart, phantasy and humor, in the writings of our great authors and the performance of the works of our great composers. Nothing will be left to desire.[44]

Such conglomeration of banality and triviality under the pretext of religion will not be unattractive to some. In Strauss's book one could ignore—or at least treat as "forbidden fruit"—the "radical" first part about the Christian religion and still enjoy the last part. The more astute observer must agree with Nietzsche that Strauss "founded the most pleasant of all religions whose founder is honored by being laughed at."[45]

We must not, however, chide Strauss unduly, for what appears as glaring weakness in his book serves at once at good illustration for a far more basic point. It was easier for him to repudiate than to provide a positive reconstruction. Of course, the task to replace 1,900 years of Christian ethical reflection is not easy.

There was, of course, the first part of the book—the repudiation of the traditional Christian faith undertaken along the lines of a repudiation of the Apostles' Creed. Not much need be said here, except that basic notions from Strauss's earlier works are reiterated, that a final and definitive No is said to Christianity, and that the impossibility of arriving at a knowledge of the "historical" Jesus is asserted. Jesus' historicity is not denied; but denied is the possibility of using the available sources for an adequate historical reconstruction. Radical historical agnosticism thus stood at the end of the road.

Within one year of its publication six editions were necessary, but if another quotation from Nietzsche's biting *First Untimely Consideration* can be offered, this fact alone did not indicate any value. Moreover, popularity went hand in hand with widespread repudiation. Part of the problem was that Strauss had undertaken to stand *contra mundum*—against theology, philosophy, the proletariat, and even middle-class values. Understandably, he fought a losing battle. Among the many discussants of the book was the British Prime Minister Gladstone, who admired, as he said, the "straightforward earnestness and the fairness with which, so far as I have seen, he pursues his ill-starred and hopeless enterprise." Gladstone concluded, however, "It is to be hoped that it will cause a shock and a reaction, and will compel many who may have too lightly valued the inheritance so dearly bought for them, and may have entered upon dangerous paths, to consider, while there is yet time, whither those paths will lead them."[46]

Strauss felt he had to respond to his critics. He did so with a *Prefatory Postscript,* a moderate and resigned treatise. He mentioned that he had been moved by the widespread approval of his biographies of Hutten and Voltaire, and of his two letters to Ernest Renan.[47] He added that "this new tenor of the press is not new to me. It is the very first greeting I received when I entered on my literary career with the *Life of Jesus.*" And, finally, came the conclusion: "The day will come, as it came for the *Life of Jesus,* when my book shall be understood—only this time I shall not live to see it."

Did Strauss write with a measure of premonition? He had worked on this pamphlet in December, 1872, after having moved, the previous month, back to Ludwigsburg, possibly prompted by a desire to be close to his son, who practiced medicine in nearby Stuttgart. In March, 1873, he wrote that his health was still good, but already the following month he admitted that "I anticipate an end of life troubled by severe physical pain."[48] An abdominal growth caused increasing pain, though he continued to correspond prolifically and comment on Plato and Schopenhauer, Nietzsche and Treitschke, to write poems and to follow the political development in Germany.

On February 8, 1874, David Friedrich Strauss died; three days later he was buried. He himself had insisted, several years earlier, that no church bells should ring and that no minister participate in the funeral. Two friends and a relative spoke words of commemoration at the open grave.

A life had come to its end, which in its religious orientation had been as radical in the beginning as it had been embarrassingly commonplace in its end. The place of David Friedrich Strauss in nineteenth-century church history is uncontested. But what was his significance?

Scholar, but Above All Agnostic

Strauss was the first one to raise the *historical* question concerning Christian origins. The *historical* trustworthiness of the Gospel accounts was made by him a matter of examination. And such had not been done before. To be sure, many an opponent of Christianity, during the early history of the church and then again in the eighteenth century, had called attention to seeming discrepancies in the Gospels and had based his opposition on these errors. None, however, had questioned the historicity of the events so described; Christian apologetes, in turn, saw their task in showing that the four Gospels could be harmonized. Strauss questioned the historical events, and his legacy to theology is that biblical investigation has been under the necessity ever since to scrutinize Gospels as to the historicity of the events described. The very foundation, and not merely the description, of Christian origins has become a matter of critical concern.

The scholarly atmosphere was truly dynamic when Strauss arrived on the scene and published his *Life of Jesus.* Undoubtedly, sooner or later someone else would have propounded the same thesis. But as matters stand, the credit must go to Strauss. Today the scholarly consensus shares his thesis that the Gospels are not primarily historical-biographical documents, though Strauss's term *myth* has been replaced by a new one—*kerygma.* Karl Barth, from whose pen we have the finest available study of David Friedrich Strauss—even though Barth called him earlier an "unsympathetic figure who only takes on some brilliance against the background of tragic errors of Pietism"[49] —found that Strauss's major contribution in the first edition of his *Life of Jesus* was the radical historical skepticism concerning the history of Jesus. Strauss insisted that the Gospels do not necessarily record historical facts. The problem was not, to note one example, how the rending of the veil in the temple should be understood—and both the rationalist and the supranaturalist interpretation assumed the essential historicity of the event, only differing in their interpretation —but the shocking contention that this incident may only be a "myth."

One could also say that Strauss introduced "extra-biblical" criticism to the study of Scripture. At stake was the notion that a scrutiny of the Scripture passages themselves, no matter how minute, did not lead to a satisfactory understanding of the text and that "external" considerations—in Strauss's case the notion of "myth"—had to be applied for such an understanding. This "extra-biblical" stance is at once that of the historian who approaches the texts critically from "outside" the circle of faith. Since David Friedrich Strauss, the battle for the Christian religion has to be fought in the historian's study, though the preoccupation with this "historical" orientation must not overlook that for Strauss "historical" was a synonym for "scholarly" or "scientific." His critique of the Gospels meant to be scholarly critique, arising out of the methodology and insight of modern science. Strauss's starting point was a "critical" assessment of the Gospels, which he approached like any other book. What was so revolutionary here was that the understanding of Sacred Writ became dependent neither upon the pronouncement of the church nor of the believer, but upon the insight of the scholar. The scholar assumed the "royal function of the judge."

Strauss was only the capstone of a long development. That the Bible needs some guide to be interpreted has been the cause underlying the quest for ecclesiastical authority through the centuries, in Protestantism no less than Catholicism. The instances are rare when the illegible writing of a heavenly book is deciphered, as in the case of Joseph Smith, by a properly provided pair of spectacles. Most folks have to depend on the more mundane means of knowing Hebrew and Greek. Which is but another way of saying that the simple folk in the pews have always depended, at least for this basic linguistic assistance, on the aid of others. Once Sacred Writ was in the vernacular, however, each man was king, ready to interpret it in whatever way he deemed advisable. The annals of church history offer abundant proof that the faithful have not been slow to avail themselves of this privilege.

The history of Christianity might well be called, as has indeed been suggested, the history of the interpretation of the Gospels. Strauss introduced the "scholarly" interpretation of the Gospels. He postulated an exceedingly complex record which required the competence of the scholar to ascertain whether or not a given passage was genuinely authentic. This is, as should be painfully obvious, a new situation in Christian history.

Ernst Wolf has suggested, in contrast, that by raising the historical questions Strauss once and for all eliminated the historical emphasis from the consideration of the biblical religion and thereby re-established the authentic meaning of faith. Thus Strauss made, indeed, a positive contribution to biblical theology. The argument of these pages is obviously different. Unless the study of Christian origins is reduced to metaphysical speculation and thus obtains a coherent and, in its own way, persuasive system no matter what the historical "facts," "the quest for the historical Jesus" makes a great deal of difference for the nature of the faith.

But Strauss is unusual in yet another way. After all was said and done, he stood outside the Christian tradition. The radical ended as an infidel, illustrating the risk involved in repudiating the religious status quo. The radical always plays with fire. There is no insurance that thinking oneself wiser than all those who have gone before will, in the end, fasten one all the more securely in the tradition. Sometimes, as in the case of Strauss, the cup runneth over.

David Friedrich Strauss stumbled into the great controversy of his life, unaware and even innocent. His book, no doubt, reflected a stroke of genius, no matter how much the notion of myth was already part of the scholarly discussion.

Strauss was not really a "professor"; he was unsure of himself, given to doubts, uncertainty, self-incrimination. His letters poured out such sentiment endlessly. In a way he had a good reason to be so disposed. His life was a failure—not merely his scholarly pursuit, but his marriage and his venture in politics and popular philosophy as well. David Friedrich Strauss accomplished nothing in his life—and the awareness of this fact must have weighed heavily upon him. In part his temperament may have predisposed him to such melancholy temper. His first biographer, Hausrath, thought to have found the clue to his personality in upbringing and childhood, but the argument is not fully persuasive. Strauss himself thought that if he had been able to pursue an academic career everything would have been different and, indeed, had he been able to claim at least this achievement, he might have turned out a different man. This was, by the way, Nietzsche's interpretation. He found that "there was a Strauss, a courageous, strong, and well-equipped scholar"—and then the brutal assault of the theologians changed him. Not yet thirty years of age, Strauss had achieved spectacular fame; but if his rise had been meteoric, so was his decline.

For the theologians of the time Strauss was the bad conscience; thus their vehement and virtually unanimous opposition. The rationalists and supranaturalists feuded with one another bitterly, but in Strauss they discovered a common foe. Their attack ruined Strauss's life—and yet his question was inevitable and had to be answered. Strauss may have been overly confident when he remarked toward the end of his life that his *Life of Jesus* had been an "inspired" book. But there was a kernel of truth in his statement. Accordingly, the universal repudiation of his book was tragic, and Strauss himself was a tragic figure, a victim, as it were, for the greater cause of biblical scholarship. One must feel sorry for him—and there is a difference between feeling sorry and having pity, as Karl Barth suggested. Strauss was the victim of the circumstances of his time. But more than that: if he was not even aware of the nature of his contribution to biblical scholarship—which allowed him to modify his position in the third and fourth editions of the *Life of Jesus*—then his irony is all the more profound. Yet, if any one book is cited for a fundamental reorientation of New Testament scholarship in the nineteenth century, it can only be Strauss's *Life of Jesus*.

The irony of the matter is that, despite the fact that Strauss did not become a great theologian, that his later writings are somewhat banal and listless, indeed, that he ended his days as an enemy of the Christian faith (as his opponents had long predicted)—despite all this, David Friedrich Strauss was an important part of nineteenth-century church history.

But if David Friedrich Strauss was a tragic figure, so were his theological opponents. The zeal for the Lord's house consumed them; though they may have possessed both faith and hope, they lacked love. The fate of Strauss then—bold, probing, angry, tragic David Friedrich Strauss—reminds us all—as do Thomas Müntzer, Sebastian Franck, George Fox, and Thomas Chubb—that it is never enough to speak the truth; the mandate is always to speak it in love. And since the past is but a prologue and our own present will be someone else's past, this reminder is Strauss's legacy to us all.

Epilogue

So, we have passed review on these radicals—paradigms of countless others—five human, all too human, religious, and perhaps even all too religious figures. Müntzer, the sword of Gideon, enlightening the Saxon ruler on the meaning of the second chapter of the Book of Daniel; Franck, the maker and seller of soap, reflecting on the nature of universal religion; Fox, the man in leather breeches, shouting woes unto the "bloody city" of Lichfeld; Chubb, the glovemaker, pondering about Jesus' true gospel; Strauss, the young professor, deciding to write a new life of Jesus. Each of them was unique in his own way, confronting his particular time and its issues, and supplying his answers.

Thomas Müntzer had experienced the storm and stress of the early years of the Reformation and, like so many others, had found religious deliverance in Luther's proclamation. But he had grown dissatisfied with this proclamation, one of the first to insist on a reformation of the Reformation. He was overwhelmed by the majesty of God and thus he shared Luther's repudiation of the Catholic understanding of man's redemption, which he took to be *sola gratia*. He saw that God had a purpose for man and history—and that man was called upon to take his place in the realization of this purpose. This place was marked by suffering, by the stringent demands of the divine law. Christ was not "honey-sweet," but bitter. The "freedom of the Christian man" was not joyful, but the serious and painful pursuit of God's purpose.

Sebastian Franck's was a different problem. He despaired neither of Luther nor even of Catholicism, but of the hopeless empirical confusion of competing claims for religious truth: Catholics, Lutherans, Zwinglians, Anabaptists, indeed even Mohammedans and the other religious traditions of man asserted their claims of truth. Rather than extol one at the expense of all the others, Franck chose to conclude that in their own way all of them were right. But this he could only say by insisting on the priority of the inward essence of religion over external appearance, for only if the empirical divergences were labeled unimportant could the essential meaning be the same. Franck's reinterpretation of the Christian faith to fit his scheme entailed an embarrassingly far-reaching repudiation of traditional Christian belief. It also meant the repudiation of the empirical reality of the Christian church in favor of an inward spirituality that was equally close to—or removed from—any institutional manifestation.

George Fox, though arriving on the scene a century later, shared Sebastian Franck's concern—the question of religious certainty. The bewildering religious spectrum of seventeenth-century England raised that question. Like Franck, Fox repudiated the church as well as the Bible as normative sources of authority, finding them contradictory and vague. He offered the postulate of the "inner light," which he took to be both Christocentric and divorced from the Word—a somewhat paradoxical combination of prerequisites, which did not raise any particular problems for Fox. The stress on the "inner light," or "light of Christ," gave him an assurance and intensity of conviction uncommon in his time. More so than either Müntzer or Franck, Fox's life and thought were shaped by a fundamental religious experience; the two others were far more ideational.

Thomas Chubb and David Friedrich Strauss, finally, were men of words rather than of deeds. Though their lives were by no means uneventful, the dramatic flair of Müntzer, Franck, and Fox was gone. The routine of bourgeois existence overshadowed the radical religious thoughts Chubb and Strauss harbored in their minds and committed to print. Chubb wanted to make the Christian religion respectable and to be in harmony with the temper of society. He was thus the first one of a long line of Christian theologians who, concerned about the schism between the Christian faith and the world-view of society, pondered about a *rapprochement* between the two.

David Friedrich Strauss frankly had no such concern. He simply followed a scholarly insight—though he, too, addressed himself to a burning question of his day. He wanted to contribute to the advance of scholarship, which in this instance happened to be biblical scholarship, but initially at least he had little concern for the delineation of a new and comprehensive view of the Christian faith. Then came the scholarly and ecclesiastical reaction to his *Life of Jesus*. It disturbed him profoundly, and the remainder of his life, both professional and private, formed but a meager appendix to his dramatic novitiate effort. If Strauss was a reformer, then it was more by default than intent. Yet his concern was to improve upon an inadequate understanding of the Christian faith and in the process he became an infidel.

Such, then, was the significance of these five men. More could be said about their qualities, for perhaps above all their lives deserve to be recalled—Müntzer fatefully becoming involved in the peasants' war, Franck seeking only to live a quiet life, Fox wandering from jail to jail, Chubb living quietly, and Strauss finding his professional life ruined as a result of his *magnum opus*.

Did these five men possess, despite their obvious differences, a common quality? In one sense the answer is easy. They were all reformers and sought to change the ecclesiastical status quo in line with their own insights. Even Sebastian Franck, who pretended to be coy with respect to the dissemination of his ideas, left little doubt as to his conviction that his own insight was quite superior to that of the "establishment." Moreover, these men were "radical" inasmuch as their reforming propensity took place in a hostile ecclesiastical environment. Thus tensions, if not controversy, characterized the relationship between the two sides. These five men were opposed to the religious status quo on substantive issues and they consequently labeled it inadequate. Each one did this in different fashion and in his own way, but they all did it. The vehemence of their repudiation seemed to obscure for them that it was this "establishment" which transmitted to them the Christian heritage. In a way they were biting the hand that fed them.

The tensions were real—for Müntzer, Franck, and even Fox a matter of life and death—though after the eighteenth century the conflict became more mundane. Chubb had to endure only verbal onslaughts, which he happily returned in kind. Strauss ruined his academic career and afterward lived a pathetically empty existence, which tells us that even without violence the struggle could still be real. Yet all five men felt, at one time or another, like Athanasius, *contra mundum*—standing against the entire world. None of them was particularly dismayed by this fact and none saw such empirical evidence as a reason to modify his position.

The nature of the tension between these five radicals and their "establishment" suggests an additional observation. They were men of determination, and certainly no shaky reeds in the wind. They knew what they stood for and resolutely set out to attain their goals. Never did they concede a point to their opponents or change their own minds. Expedience, compromise, tradition were words not found in their dictionaries. Nor did they show patience or the willingness to make haste slowly. Had they done so, the vehemence of their encounter with the ecclesiastical "establishment" might have been softened. The five radical reformers shared what might be called a "messianic complex," the unwavering conviction, in other words, that they possessed the true and authentic interpretation of the Christian faith. Each of them felt that he was, to use G. K. Chesterton's words about the heretic, "the center of the universe; it was 'round him that the stars swung."

And they boldly announced this fact. They could not be silent, but had to proclaim their insights, as if compelled by an inner urge. George Fox serves perhaps as the best illustration, for his *Journal* strikingly reveals that he was prompted to proclaim his message without being able to state a reason. Thomas Müntzer was not much different. Nor was Sebastian Franck, who endlessly ground out pamphlets and books to spread his message.

All five men strove for what to them was the more perfect way. They willingly accepted the consequences of their stand, stubbornly held to their convictions, and suffered for their faith. This they had in common, though they also parted company with one another at some other points—not only because each one possessed his own theological propensity, but also because each one resolved the clash between his understanding of the Christian faith and the religious "establishment" in his own way.

Thomas Müntzer was impatient and restless about the realization of his religious vision. Though his involvement in the Peasants' War was haphazard and, moreover, mistaken, there can be little doubt that in principle he was willing to usher in that more perfect way by force and by a revolutionary upheaval of the existing order. Sebastian Franck, on the other hand, no less convinced of his insight, decided to stay aloof from the turbulent ecclesiastical controversies of his day. He preferred to divorce himself from all empirical forms of Christianity and to find comfort in the fact that all ecclesiastical traditions were equally good—or bad. George Fox was neither impatient nor an individualist; he founded a religious tradition that was to embody his religious insights and thereby perpetuate them empirically. Thomas Chubb buried himself in his study in order to ponder the more perfect way. We do not know if he ever attended church, but it makes little difference. And finally, David Friedrich Strauss. He, too, was a scholar, and as such he made his most profound contribution. He earned his place in this volume—if earned be the appropriate word—because his discontent took him outside the Christian tradition. Above all, he was an infidel.

A fellowship of discontent: Müntzer, the revolutionary; Franck, the individualist; Fox, the founding father; Chubb, the scholar; and Strauss, the agnostic. What variety of approach, and yet what identity of intent!

Did these men make a large contribution? That they strove to proclaim what they considered the authentic Christian faith, no matter how divergent from the traditional perspective, should not be held against them. The Christian tradition was made not only more complex, but also richer thereby. Perhaps we can call them the "gadflies" of the religious "establishment" of their times. They raised questions which even their more traditionally minded contemporaries found fruitful to ponder.

Bibliography and Notes

1. The Impatient Revolutionary: THOMAS MÜNTZER

There is no comprehensive treatment of Thomas Müntzer. The following studies are to be noted, however: M. M. Smirin, *Die Volksreformation des Thomas Münzer und der grosse Bauernkrieg* (Berlin, 1952); Carl Hinrichs, *Luther und Müntzer; ihre Auseinandersetzung über Obrigkeit und Widerstandsrecht* (Berlin, 1952); Walter Elliger, *Thomas Müntzer* (Berlin, 1960); Thomas Nipperdey, "Theologie und Revolution bei Thomas Müntzer," *Archiv f. Reformationsgeschichte,* 54 (1963); George W. Forell, "Thomas Müntzer, Symbol and Reality," *Dialog,* 2 (1963); Hans J. Hillerbrand, *A Bibliography of Anabaptism 1520–1630* (Elkhart, Ind., 1962); Abraham Friesen, "Thomas Müntzer in Marxist Thought," *Church History,* 34 (1965); E. G. Rupp, "Thomas Müntzer: Prophet of Radical Christianity," *Bulletin of the John Rylands Library,* 48 (1966).

Of Müntzer's works the following are available in English: the Daniel sermon in George H. Williams, *Spiritual and Anabaptist Writers* (Philadelphia, 1957), and the *Truly Occasioned Defense* in "Thomas Müntzer's Last Treatise Against Luther," *Mennonite Quarterly Review,* 38 (1964).

Müntzer's "political" writings have been edited by Carl Hinrichs, *Thomas Müntzer, Politische Schriften mit Kommentar* (Halle, 1950). A collection of Müntzer's writings in modernized German is found in Otto Brandt, *Thomas Müntzer, Sein Leben und seine Schriften* (Jena, 1933). See also H. Böhmer und P. Kirn, *Thomas Müntzers Briefwechsel* (Leipzig, 1931).

1. *Historie Thomae Müntzer,* as quoted in O. Brandt, *op. cit.,* pp. 38 f.
2. H. Böhmer, *Gesammelte Aufsätze* (Gotha, 1927), pp. 216, 200.
3. K. Kleinschmidt, *Thomas Müntzer. Die Seele des deutschen Bauernkrieges von 1525* (Berlin, 1952), p. 132.
4. K. Seidemann, *Thomas Münzer* (Dresden, 1842), pp. 4 f.
5. C. Hinrichs, *Thomas Müntzer,* p. 97.
6. Müntzer's teaching can be culled from the charges of his opponents:

Christ must die within us and one must live according to the gospel, which teaches to turn the other cheek: *Böhmer-Kirn,* Nr. 13, pp. 12 f.

7. H. Kirchner, "Neue Müntzeriana," *Zeitschrift f. Kirchengeschichte,* 72 (1961), 113 ff.
8. K. Seidemann, *op. cit.,* Beilage, 5c.
9. The changes are minor; see G. Zschäbitz, *Zur Mitteldeutschen Wiedertäuferbewegung nach dem grossen Bauernkrieg* (Berlin, 1958), p. 40.
10. A. Molnar, "Thomas Müntzer und Böhmen," *Communio Viatorum,* 1 (1958), 242–245.
11. A. Lohmann, *Zur geistigen Entwicklung Thomas Müntzers* (Leipzig-Berlin, 1931), pp. 18 f. Three versions of the *Manifesto* are extant—German, Latin, Czech. The two vernacular versions contain emphatic attacks upon the learned and educated, but this may be the result of an adulteration of the eighteenth-century Latin version.
12. A. Lohmann, *op. cit.,* p. 23, has suggested that Müntzer's break with Luther occurred then.
13. O. Schiff, "Thomas Müntzer als Prediger in Halle," *Archiv f. Reformationsgeschichte,* 23 (1926).
14. *Neues Urkundenbuch zur Geschichte d. evang. Kirchen-Reformation,* I (1842), 232.
15. M. Steinmetz, "Zur Entstehung der Müntzer-Legende," *Beiträge zum neuen Geschichtsbild* (Berlin, 1956), p. 59.
16. O. J. Mehl, "Thomas Müntzer als Liturgiker," *Theol. Lit. Ztg.,* 76 (1951).
17. *WA Br.,* 3:120.
18. O. Brandt, *op. cit.,* pp. 128 f., 127, 130, 135, 134, 65.
19. *Neues Urkundenbuch,* p. 231.
20. A. Lohmann, *op. cit.,* p. 50.
21. *Neues Urkundenbuch,* p. 234.
22. W. P. Fuchs, *Akten zur Geschichte des Bauernkrieges in Mitteldeutschland* (Jena, 1942), II, 30.
23. R. Friedmann, "Thomas Muentzer's Relation to Anabaptism," *Mennonite Quarterly Review,* 31 (1957), 75 ff., and Karl Holl, *op. cit.,* pp. 425 ff.
24. W. P. Fuchs, *op. cit.,* II, 29.
25. C. E. Förstemann, "Zur Geschichte des Bauernkriegs," *Neue Mitteilungen aus dem Gebiet hist.-antiquarischer Forschungen,* XII (1869), 157.
26. *Neue Mitteilungen,* pp. 167, 170.
27. G. H. Williams, *Spiritual and Anabaptist Writers* (Philadelphia, 1957), pp. 67, 64, 61, 69.
28. *Neue Mitteilungen,* p. 188.
29. *WA* 15: 203, 199 ff., 218 f.
30. *Neue Mitteilungen,* p. 180.

31. A transcript of the interrogation is found in *Neue Mitteilungen,* pp. 182–185; see also pp. 182, 154, 185.
32. *Ein nutzlicher Dialogus* (Wittenberg, 1525).
33. As quoted in C. Hinrichs, *Luther und Müntzer,* p. 77.
34. *Neue Mitteilungen,* pp. 186–187.
35. C. Hinrichs, *Thomas Müntzer,* p. 101.
36. O. Brandt, *op. cit.,* p. 72.
37. It is not certain if the letter was sent. See C. Hinrichs, *Luther und Müntzer,* p. 121.
38. O. Brandt, *op. cit.,* p. 85.
39. *WA* 15: 238 f.
40. F. Gess, *Briefe und Akten zur Kirchenpolitik Herzog Georgs v. Sachsen* (Leipzig, 1905), I, 749, prints a letter that emphasizes Müntzer's importance.
41. O. Brandt, *op. cit.,* pp. 92–93.
42. W. Metzger, *op. cit.,* p. 65.
43. *Ibid.,* p. 70.
44. C. Hinrichs, *Thomas Müntzer,* pp. 207 ff.
45. *WA* 10, III, 1.
46. C. Hinrichs, *Thomas Müntzer,* pp. 38, 43, 46.
47. *WA* 15, 210.
48. C. Hinrichs, *Thomas Müntzer,* p. 72.
49. G. Baring, "Hans Denck und Thomas Müntzer in Nürnberg, 1524," *Archiv f. Reformationsgeschichte,* 50 (1959), 154.
50. C. Hinrichs, *Thomas Müntzer,* p. 71.
51. E. Staehelin, *Briefe und Akten zum Leben Oekolampads* (Leipzig, 1927), I, 389 f.
52. G. Franz, *Der deutsche Bauernkrieg* (München-Berlin, 1933), pp. 176 ff.
53. O. Brandt, *op. cit.,* p. 94.
54. *Ibid.,* p. 95.
55. G. Franz, *op. cit.,* p. 424.
56. See Luther's comment, *WA Br.* 3:473.
57. K. Seidemann, *op. cit.,* p. 145.
58. Our description follows G. Franz, *op. cit.,* pp. 442 ff.
59. Chr. Meyer, "Zur Geschichte der Wiedertäufer in Oberschwaben," *Zeitschr. des Histor. Vereins f. Schwaben,* 1 (1874), 242.
60. W. P. Fuchs, *op. cit.,* II, 897.
61. O. Brandt, *op. cit.,* p. 45.
62. As quoted in G. Droysen, *Materialien z. neueren Geschichte* (Halle, 1881), Nr. 3, Anhang, p. 13.
63. See M. Steinmetz, *op. cit.,* pp. 43 ff., 50.
64. W. Falckenhaimer, *Philipp der Grossmütige im Bauernkriege* (Marburg, 1887), p. 67.
65. *WA Br.* 3, 510.

66. See O. Brandt, *op. cit.*, pp. 48–49, and the variant in *WA Br.* 4: 410 f.
67. O. Brandt, *op. cit.*, p. 50.
68. *WA TR* 1: 38.
69. *WA* 54: 174; *WA TR* 6: 195.
70. J. Beck, *Die Geschichtsbücher der Wiedertäufer in Oesterreich-Ungarn* (Wien, 1883), p. 12.

2. The Lonely Individualist: SEBASTIAN FRANCK

A competent though tediously verbose biography, with extensive excerpts from Franck's writings, is Will-Erich Peuckert, *Sebastian Franck: Ein deutscher Sucher* (München, 1943). Briefer, somewhat more scholarly, but equally confusing is Eberhard Teufel, *"Landräumig," Sebastian Franck, ein Wanderer an Donau, Rhein und Neckar* (Neustadt an der Aisch, 1954). The study by J. Lindeboom, *Een Franc-tireur der Reformatie, Sebastian Franck* (Arnhem, 1952) is the best brief introduction. See also the following studies: Alfred Hegler, *Geist und Schrift bei Sebastian Franck* (Tübingen, 1892); Alexandre Koyré, *Mystiques, Spirituels, Alchimistes: Schwenckfeld, Séb. Franck, Weigel, Paracelse* (Paris, 1955); Doris Rieber, "Sebastien Franck (1499–1542)," *Bibliothéque d'Humanisme et Renaissance* 21 (1959). There is a bibliographical survey by Eberhard Teufel, "Sebastian Franck im Lichte der neueren Forschung," *Theologische Rundschau,* 12 (1940).

The following works of Franck are available in recent editions: *Paradoxa.* Eingeleitet von W. Lehmann (Jena, 1909); *Kriegsbüchlein des Friedens* (Schwäbisch-Gmünd, 1929). Franck's *Letter to Campanus* is translated in George H. Williams, *Spiritual and Anabaptist Writers* (Philadelphia, 1957). See also Philip L. Kintner, "Sebastian Franck. An American Library Finding-List," *Archiv f. Reformationsgeschichte,* 55 (1964).

The following major works of Sebastian Franck are cited in our essay:

Vonn dem grewlichen laster der trunckenheit (Drunkenness). (n. p., 1528).
Chronica, zeytbuch und geschychtbibel (Chronicle). (Strassburg, 1531).
Weltbuch: spiegel und bildtnisz des gantzen erdbodens (World Book). (Tübingen, 1534).
Paradoxa ducenta octoginta (Paradoxes). (Ulm, 1534).
Germaniae chronicon (German Chronicle). (Augsburg, 1538).
Die guldin Arch (Golden Ark). (Augsburg, 1538).
Das verbuthschiert mit siben Sigeln verschlossen Buch (The Sealed Book). (n. p., 1539).
Handbüchlin *(Hand Book).* (Frankfurt, 1539).
Sprichwörter *(Proverbs).* (Frankfurt, 1541).

1. *WA,* 54: 172.

2. *Calvini Opera,* 9: 581.
3. *Chronicle,* p. 116.
4. *The Sealed Book,* p. 429.
5. A. Hegler, *Sebastian Francks lateinische Paraphrase der deutschen Theologie* (Tübingen, 1901), pp. 76 ff., cites the Dutch original of the three titles.
6. *Ibid.,* p. 29.
7. *Diallage,* 3.
8. *Zwinglis Werke,* III, 633.
9. A. Hegler, *Geist und Schrift,* p. 27.
10. The names are listed in K. Gödeke, *Grundriss zur Geschichte der deutschen Dichtung* (Dresden, 1886), II, 2, p. 11.
11. *Chronicle,* p. 119.
12. *Quellen zur Geschichte der Täufer, VII. Band Elsass, I. Teil.* (Gütersloh, 1959), pp. 359, 395, 543.
13. W.-E. Peuckert, *op. cit.,* p. 206.
14. *World Book,* Vorrede; 4.
15. As quoted in W.-E. Peuckert, *op. cit.,* p. 193.
16. P. Joachimsen, "Zur inneren Entwicklung Sebastian Francks," *Blätter f. deutsche Philosophie,* 2 (1928), 13.
17. As quoted in W.-E. Peuckert, *op. cit.,* p. 218.
18. *Paradoxes,* p. 1.
19. A. Hegler, *Beiträge zur Geschichte der Mystik in der Reformationszeit* (Berlin, 1906), pp. 199, 114, 115, 116 ff., 120.
20. J. Endriss, *Sebastian Francks Ulmer Kämpfe* (Ulm, 1935), pp. 36, 37.
21. A. Hegler, *Beiträge,* pp. 121, 122, 137 f., 140, 144, 184, 185, 186.
22. *Golden Ark,* p. 4.
23. A. Hegler, *Beiträge,* p. 195.
24. J. Endriss, *op. cit.,* p. 40.
25. A. Hegler, *Beiträge,* pp. 190, 192, 193, 194, 195, 197, 199 f., 205, 206.
26. *Ibid.,* pp. 215 f.; my chronology deviates from that of Hegler.
27. *Ibid.,* pp. 99 ff.
28. E. Teufel, *Landräumig,* p. 86.
29. *Corpus Reformatorum,* 3, 983 ff.
30. *Kriegsbüchlin,* 2 b.
31. *Proverbs,* Vorrede, 3 b.
32. W.-E. Peuckert, *op. cit.,* p. 549.
33. E. v. Gelder, *The Two Reformations in the 16th Century* (The Hague, 1961), pp. 13–108.
34. W. Dilthey, "Auffassung und Analyse des Menschen im 15. und 16. Jahrhundert," *Gesammelte Schriften II* (Leipzig-Berlin, 1921), pp. 85, 47 ff.
35. *Paradoxes,* p. 103.
36. *Ibid.,* p. 104.

37. *Paradoxes,* p. 307.
38. *Ibid.,* pp. 62; 137 ff.
39. *Golden Ark,* p. 154 a.
40. *Paradoxes,* pp. 125 ff.
41. *The Sealed Book,* p. 427.
42. *Paradoxes,* pp. 2, 141, 3, 271, 272.
43. *Paradoxes,* pp. 141, 165, 32, 161, 111.
44. A. Hegler, *Sebastian Francks lateinische Paraphrase,* pp. 62 f.
45. *Paradoxes,* pp. 46, 68, 26, 120, 52, 332, 315, 44.
46. *German Chronicle,* Vorrede aa 6, a 1.
47. *Chronicle,* Ketzerchronik, N iii b.
48. *Chronicle,* Vorrede.
49. *World Book,* 158 a, 147 b; see K. Räber, *Studien zur Geschichtsbibel Sebastian Francks* (Basel, 1952), p. 89.
50. *Chronicle,* Vorrede.
51. *World Book,* Vorrede.
52. G. H. Williams, *Spiritual and Anabaptist Writers,* pp. 160, 149, 150.
53. A. Hegler, *Beiträge,* p. 117.
54. R. Stadelmann, *Vom Geist des ausgehenden Mittelalters* (Halle, 1929).
55. *Paradoxes,* p. 39.

3. The Founding Father: George Fox

The following studies on Fox should be mentioned: W. C. Braithwaite, *The Beginnings of Quakerism* (London, 1912); P. Held, *Der Quäker George Fox: Sein Leben, Wirken, Kämpfen, Leiden, Siegen* (Basel, 1950); Vernon Noble, *The Life and Times of George Fox: The Man in Leather Breeches* (New York, 1953); Henry van Etten, *George Fox and the Quakers* (New York, 1959). See also the recent work by Hugh Barbour, *Quakers in Puritan England* (New Haven, 1964).

Fox's works were published in eight volumes under the title *The Works of George Fox* (Philadelphia, 1831). The most recent edition of George Fox's *Journal,* with an introduction by Geoffrey F. Nuttall and an epilogue by Henry J. Cadbury, was published in 1952. The parenthetical references in the text refer to this edition.

1. *Works* (London, 1896), I, 166.
2. Th. Macaulay, *The History of England from the Accession of James II* (London, 1913–1915), V, 1991.
3. Fox's work is entitled *A Battle-Door for Teachers and Professors to Learn Singular and Plural* (Glasgow, 1860), I, 17.
4. John Bunyan, *Works* (Glasgow, 1860), I, 17.
5. A. Neave Brayshaw, *The Personality of George Fox* (London, 1933), p. 115.

6. Richard Baxter, *The Practical Works of the Rev. Richard Baxter* (London, 1830), V, 559.
7. *Journal* (Cambridge, 1952), pp. 9, 274.
8. *The Works of George Fox,* III, 518.
9. *Journal* (London, 1891), I, 287.
10. *Journal* (Cambridge, 1952), p. 642. E. Grubb, *What is Quakerism?* (London, 1929), and H. G. Wood, *George Fox* (London, 1912), are two interpreters who identify Fox's "inner light" with conscience.
11. W. C. Braithwaite, *op. cit.,* p. xxxii.
12. J. W. Graham, *The Faith of a Quaker* (Cambridge, 1920).
13. See A. N. Brayshaw, *op. cit.,* p. 22, for a discussion of the sources on the origin of the name.
14. See the comments by Vernon Noble, *op. cit.,* p. 71.
15. *Journal* (Philadelphia, 1891), p. lxii.
16. *Journal* (Cambridge, 1911), I, 231.
17. W. C. Braithwaite, *op. cit.,* p. 105.
18. John Bunyan, *Works* (1862), II, 664.
19. E. E. Taylor, *Valiant Sixty* (London, 1951), p. 41.
20. *Journal* (Cambridge, 1952), p. lx.
21. *The First Publishers of Truth* (London, 1907), p. 243.
22. R. M. Jones, *George Fox, Seeker and Friend* (London, 1930), p. 105.
23. James Nayler, *A Collection of Sundry Books, Epistles and Papers* (London, 1716), p. 12.
24. E. Fogelklou, *James Nayler, The Rebel Saint 1618–1660* (London, 1931), pp. 184, 162.
25. *The Harleian Miscellany* (London, 1810), VI, 429.
26. R. Matthews, *English Messiahs* (London, 1936), p. 31.
27. E. Fogelklou, *op. cit.,* pp. 192, 198.
28. R. Matthews, *op. cit.,* p. 41.
29. G. F. Nuttall, *James Nayler: A Fresh Approach* (London, 1954).
30. R. Knight, *The Founder of Quakerism* (London, 1922).
31. *The Works of George Fox,* III, 246.
32. Cited in V. Noble, *op. cit.,* p. 166.
33. A. N. Brayshaw, *The Quakers: Their Story and Message* (London-New York, 1927), p. 131.
34. I. Ross, *Margaret Fell, Mother of Quakerism* (London-New York, 1949), p. 219.
35. A. N. Brayshaw, *op. cit.,* pp. 132, 139, 134, 218, 129.
36. *Journal* (Philadelphia, 1891), pp. 623 f.
37. *Journal* (Cambridge, 1911), II, 335.
38. *Ibid.,* p. 358.
39. H. G. Crosfield, *Margaret Fox of Swarthmoor Hall* (London, 1913), p. 188.
40. *Journal* (Philadelphia, 1891), p. 346.

4. The Private Scholar: Thomas Chubb

There is no monograph on Chubb; one must look for cursory comments in the *Biographia Britannica* (London, 1784), the *Dictionary of National Biography,* and Leslie Stephen, *English Thought in the Eighteenth Century* (London, 1881), as well as in Emmanuel Hirsch, *Geschichte der neuern Evangelischen Theologie,* Bd. I (Gütersloh, 1949).

1. *Posthumous Works,* I, 64.
2. *A Short and Faithful Account of the Life,* pp. 21 f.
3. *Memoirs of Thomas Chubb,* p. 76.
4. [P. Skelton], *Deism Revealed* (2nd ed.; London, 1751), II, 282.
5. J. Leland, *View of the Principal Deistical Writers* (London, 1798), I, 214.
6. *A Short and Faithful Account,* pp. 4; 15.
7. *Memoirs,* p. 23.
8. *Biographia Britannica,* III, 531, 530.
9. *A Short and Faithful Account,* pp. 6 f., 10 f.
10. *Memoirs,* p. 50.
11. *Posthumous Works,* II, 44; cf. also *The True Gospel,* p. viii.
12. *Biographia Britannica,* III, 532.
13. E. Law, *Considerations of the Theory of Religion* (6th ed.; Cambridge, 1774), pp. 304 f.
14. R. N. Stromberg, *Religious Liberalism in Eighteenth-Century England* (London, 1954), pp. 70 ff.
15. *Posthumous Works,* II, 370; II, 57; II, 246.
16. *The True Gospel,* p. viii.
17. *A Collection of Tracts,* Introduction.
18. *Posthumous Works,* I, 6, 7, 9; II, 124, 17, 259, 61, 74, 271, 77, 63.
19. *A Collection of Tracts,* I, 263 ff.
20. *The True Gospel,* p. viii.
21. *A Collection of Tracts,* I, 261, 262.
22. *The Sufficiency of Reason in Matters of Religion Farther Considered* (London, 1732), pp. 36, 58, 57.
23. *The True Gospel,* p. 190.
24. *The Sufficiency of Reason,* p. 58.
25. *Posthumous Works,* II, 42, 50, 57, 45.
26. *The True Gospel,* pp. 1, 30, 32, 103, 33, 113, 123, 125, 127, 18.
27. *Ibid.,* pp. 52, 20 f., 30, 25, 18 f.
28. *Posthumous Works,* II, 72 ff., 73.
29. *The True Gospel,* pp. 46, 47.
30. *Posthumous Works,* II, 181 f., 120, 192, 203, 210.
31. *The True Gospel,* pp. 43, 36.
32. *Posthumous Works,* II, 60; *The True Gospel,* p. 55.
33. *The True Gospel,* pp. 56, 55 f.

34. *Posthumous Works,* II, 253, 255; *The True Gospel,* p. 16; *Posthumous Works,* II, 45, 43.
35. *The True Gospel,* p. 232.
36. *Posthumous Works,* II, 178 ff.
37. *Discourse on Miracles,* pp. 70, 2, 92.
38. *Posthumous Works,* II, 211, 351, 355.
39. *Ibid.,* II, 368.
40. E. Law, *op. cit.,* p. 304.
41. Jonathan Edwards, *Freedom of the Will,* ed. Paul Ramsey (New Haven, 1957), pp. 66–81.
42. *Ibid.,* pp. 69, 70, 75.
43. *Posthumous Works,* II, 73, 129.

5. The Agnostic Infidel: DAVID FRIEDRICH STRAUSS

The best study on Strauss comes from the pen of Karl Barth, *Protestant Thought from Rousseau to Ritschl* (New York, 1959). Also to be noted is Ernst Wolf, "Die Verlegenheit der Theologie: David Friedrich Strauss und die Bibelkritik," *Libertas Christiana* (München, 1957). Günther Backhaus, *Kerygma und Mythos bei David Friedrich Strauss und Rudolf Bultmann* (Hamburg, 1956). See also the more recent study by H. Steussloff, "Die Religionskritik von David Friedrich Strauss," *Deutsche Zeitschr. f. Philosophie,* 10 (1962).

There is no recent biography. Of the older works we note Theobald Ziegler, *David Friedrich Strauss,* 2 vols. (Strassburg, 1908), a work especially valuable for its excerpts from otherwise unavailable primary sources. The only biography in English is a translation from German, Edward Zeller, *David Friedrich Strauss in His Life and Writings* (London, 1874). Strauss's works were, in part, published posthumously: *Gesammelte Schriften von David Friedrich Strauss,* 12 vols. (Bonn, 1876). A selection of letters has the title *Ausgewählte Briefe von David Friedrich Strauss, Herausg. und erläutert von Eduard Zeller* (Bonn, 1895). The *Briefwechsel zwischen Strauss und Vischer,* 2 vols. (Stuttgart, 1952–53), includes a full bibliography of Strauss's writings.

1. A. Hausrath, *David Friedrich Strauss, und die Theologie seiner Zeit* (Heidelberg, 1878).
2. *Gesammelte Schriften,* 7, 560; *Briefe,* p. 473.
3. Th. Ziegler, *David Friedrich Strauss,* pp. 32, 56.
4. *Briefe,* p. 2.
5. Th. Ziegler, *op. cit.,* pp. 63 ff.
6. *Briefe,* p. 8; Th. Ziegler, *op. cit.,* p. 94.
7. *Briefe,* pp. 10, 472.
8. Th. Ziegler, *op. cit.,* p. 121.
9. *Briefe,* p. 12.
10. *Gesammelte Schriften,* I, 4; VII, 561.

11. *Briefe,* p. 15.
12. Th. Ziegler, *op. cit.,* pp. 180, 183, 185, 186.
13. *Gesammelte Schriften,* I, 249.
14. *Allgemeine Kirchenzeitung* (1836), pp. 184, 557, 36.
15. See *Zwingliana,* 6 (1934/38), 235 ff.
16. See Albert Schweitzer, *Von Reimarus zu Wrede: Eine Geschichte der Leben-Jesu-Forschung* (Tübingen, 1921), pp. 643 ff. Johannes Zeller, *Stimmen der Deutschen Kirche über das Leben Jesu von Doctor Strauss* (Zürich, 1937).
17. A. Hausrath, *op. cit.,* I, 232.
18. Th. Ziegler, *op. cit.,* pp. 202, 228.
19. Additional comments are in *Gesammelte Schriften,* I, 102.
20. *Briefe,* p. 32.
21. As quoted in Th. Ziegler, *op. cit.,* pp. 273, 278.
22. *Gesammelte Schriften,* I, 13.
23. *Briefe,* pp. 48, 46.
24. Th. Ziegler, *op. cit.,* p. 292.
25. W. Hildebrandt, *Der "Straussenhandel" in Zürich (1839) im Spiegel der zeitgenössischen Literatur* (Zürich, 1939).
26. Th. Ziegler, *op. cit.,* p. 298.
27. W. Hildebrandt, *op. cit.,* pp. 6, 3.
28. Th. Ziegler, *op. cit.,* pp. 300, 304.
29. *Briefe,* pp. 82 f., 84, 85.
30. David Friedrich Strauss, *Die christliche Glaubenslehre,* pp. 75, viii.
31. *Briefe,* p. 99.
32. David Friedrich Strauss, *Die Halben und die Ganzen* (Berlin, 1865), p. 50.
33. *Gesammelte Schriften,* I, 14.
34. Th. Ziegler, *op. cit.,* p. 363.
35. *Ibid.,* p. 364; this section is omitted in the *Briefe.*
36. *Ibid.,* p. 367; this section is also omitted in the *Briefe.*
37. *Briefe,* pp. 42 f., 45, 130.
38. *Gesammelte Schriften,* I, 16.
39. *Briefe,* p. 143.
40. *Gesammelte Schriften,* I, 40.
41. *Briefe,* p. 373.
42. Th. Ziegler, *op. cit.,* p. 554.
43. *Briefe,* pp. 491, 506, 533.
44. David Friedrich Strauss, *Der alte und der neue Glaube,* p. 294.
45. Friedrich Nietzsche, *Gesammelte Werke* (München, 1922), p. 150.
46. *London Times,* December 23, 1872, p. 8.
47. *The Old Faith and the New* (New York, 1874), pp. viii, xxxiii.
48. *Briefe,* p. 548.
49. *Antwort. Karl Barth zum siebzigsten Geburtstag am 10. Mai 1956* (Zollikon-Zürich, 1956), p. 850.